I0605542

COCINA PUERTO RICO

COCINA PUERTO RICO

Recipes from My Abuela's Kitchen to Yours

MIA CASTRO

PHOTOGRAPHS BY JOHNNY MILLER

FOREWORD BY CHEF GIOVANNA HUYKE

Union Square & Co.
Hachette Book Group
1290 Avenue of the Americas,
New York, NY 10104
unionsquareandco.com
@unionsqandco

First Edition: February 2026

Union Square & Co. is an imprint of Grand Central Publishing, a division of Hachette Book Group, Inc. The Union Square & Co. name and logo are registered trademarks of Hachette Book Group, Inc.

The publisher is not responsible for websites (or their content) that are not owned by the publisher.

Union Square & Co. books may be purchased in bulk for business, educational, or promotional use. For information, please contact your local bookseller or the Hachette Book Group Special Markets Department at special.markets@hbgusa.com.

Editors: Caitlin Leffel and Amanda Englander
Food Stylist: Rebecca Jurkevich
Prop Stylist: Marina Bevilacqua
Designer: Ashley Tucker
Art Director: Renée Bollier
Production Manager: Kevin Iwano
Copy Editor: Ivy McFadden

Library of Congress Control Number:
2025941924

ISBN: 978-1-4549-5811-6 (hardcover)
ISBN: 978-1-4549-5812-3 (ebook)

Printed in China

1010

10 9 8 7 6 5 4 3 2 1

Additional image credits:
Shutterstock.com: Vero Rose: 54; Sonya illustration: 56

Por ti y para ti,
mi Abuelita Sara

CONTENTS

FOREWORD

PUERTO RICAN FOOD IS FULL OF COLOR AND FLAVOR and, in true spirit of the island, is to be shared with friends and family. For those who have parted, it is just that—the dishes, the flavors—that keep us close to our homes.

Chef Mia Castro was one of many young chefs who packed their bags and left the island to pursue her cooking career. A very successful one, I might add, having worked with some of the best chefs in Miami, Las Vegas and New York while fresh out of the Culinary Institute of America. Never shy from challenges, she beat Bobby Flay with her abuela's Arroz con Pollo (page 213). *That* is where her true passion for cooking grew: with her Abuela Sara, in her kitchen. Through the warmth of a good *guiso* (stew), this fearless chef became a voice for the diaspora and an ambassador of Puerto Rican flavors.

In her first book, *Cocina Puerto Rico*, you realize that no matter how much you learn, and how much you experience, you always return to the foods you grew up with. This foundation is especially relevant if you're Mia Castro. Whether she's competing or creating recipes, every dish carries the unmistakable flavor of Puerto Rico. Every dish in this cookbook tells the story of her close-knit family—and food is their language. That is what I most enjoyed about *Cocina Puerto Rico*. I could feel the excitement behind every ingredient, every instruction, every addition. Any two of her recipes side by side spark a feeling of celebration.

Through detailed charts, she introduces, standard ingredients found in Puerto Rican kitchens, like plantains and our indigenous root vegetables, making it completely accessible for anyone starting to learn about our cuisine. Food also evolves —Mia tweaks and adds her own twists on our beloved recipes, modernizing them for cooks today. And if you've never prepared concoctions and seasonings like our sofrito and adobos (pages 36–38), or used tools like a tostonera (see page 16), you'll surely become an expert after reading this cookbook.

True to any day in a cocina in Puerto Rico, she makes space for *el cafecito* (page 55)—a small but sacred tradition many of us still hold dear, adhere to, and would feel disheartened to lose. So much so, it's not uncommon to walk into some Puerto Rican homes and be greeted by the host asking, "*Cafecito*?" instead of saying "hello."

These are the type of recipes I'm certain will become part of your repertoire for get-togethers, celebrations, and holiday gatherings. This cookbook is an invitation to a Puerto Rican dinner you can easily re-create at home, starting with welcome drinks, culminating with dessert, and even our famous holiday coquito (page 79). If you're in the diaspora, nostalgic and longing to return, Mia welcomes you to savor and celebrate Puerto Rico through her cocina.

You'll get to see Puerto Rico through Mia's eyes and heart as she narrates her stories like a friend you haven't seen in a while. She opens her kitchen and invites us to cook with her, to listen to the waves at the beach, the afternoon traffic, and the harmonious song of the *coquíes* (frogs) in the evening. These aren't just recipes: *Cocina Puerto Rico* is a token of everything that defines Puerto Rican food—our ingredients, the aromas, and our flavor.

—Chef Giovanna Huyke

INTRODUCTION

I was born in San Juan, Puerto Rico, and grew up in the town of Cupey. I was partly raised by my *abuelos* (grandparents) in their vibrant house, surrounded by tropical vegetation and fresh ingredients. Abuelo and Abuela purchased their property in 1980 to fulfill their dream of retiring in *el campo* (the countryside) with enough land to cultivate their own food. They built their house from the ground up, and together, they planted seeds that grew into bushes of fresh herbs and pigeon peas and trees that bore tamarind, banana, passion fruit, avocado, and coconut, among many others. He harvested, and she cooked. They're a power couple of their generation. Their passion for food (and for each other) inspired me to learn how to cook at a young age, never imagining it would turn into my career and part of my identity. They instilled in me the importance of spending time around the dining table with loved ones.

My abuela Sara is a kind, energetic, and nurturing soul. She's petite, barely five feet tall, with soft, delicate skin and a radiant smile deceptive of her true age. Her hairstyle is short and chic, and her hair as shiny and white as the dainty pearls that perpetually stud her ears. She's funny and snappy, with a dark (and somewhat inappropriate) side to her humor. Abuela is a lot smarter than she lets on, so people (including other family members) often underestimate the extent of her knowledge. But she uses people's assumptions to her own advantage, a skill I learned from her that gets me through challenging times in my own life.

Abuela is from el campo in Arecibo, in the northwest of Puerto Rico. She learned how to cook from her mother. Their style is, as we say, *a ojo* (by eye), which refers to adding amounts that look and feel right—by instinct—instead of measuring. As a child, I'd kneel on an old wooden stool next to the stove so I could see what she was doing. Now that I'm taller than she is (which isn't saying much because I'm only 5 foot 1), I stand next to the stove and help her transfer hot liquids from one heavy pot to another, even when she refuses to accept help.

Watching her cook is fun. Not just because she's so tiny she could fit into one of her *calderos* (cauldrons), but because at ninety, she moves like lightning. One of the qualities I admire most about her is her humility, which is reflected in her desire to learn new ways to evolve herself and her food. She's very imaginative. She gets ideas about new dishes she wants to try or ways of revamping old classics—and she executes them. Her knowledge of food and instinctive nature allow her to elaborate her visions without using recipes. It's a skill I've adopted from her and implemented in my life as a professional chef, a career path I wouldn't have opted for if it weren't for another influential matriarch in my life: my mother.

Mama is a strong, loving, self-motivated, intelligent, career-driven woman, and one of my biggest inspirations. In my later high school years, as I was preparing college applications and beginning to consider a professional path, Mama noticed the passion I was developing for food and nurtured it. She encouraged me to pursue the culinary field and empowered me to seek the best education, both in Puerto Rico and beyond. She weighed out the challenges residents face in Puerto Rico (which is even more relevant now than it was then) and made many sacrifices to provide me with better opportunities, something I'll never take for granted. This meant leaving my island at eighteen years old, with a big push from her, to attend the Culinary Institute of America in 2006, and I've made my way in the culinary arts world since. Without her foundational support and constant nudging, I can't say I'd be where I am right now. For that, I'll be eternally grateful to her.

This cookbook summarizes my experience as a Puerto Rican living on the US mainland, and some of the challenges I've faced—times of joy, solitude, homesickness, loss, heartbreak, and love. These are the driving forces that inspire my creativity in *mi cocina* (my kitchen) and transport me back to Pe-Erre (PR). Most of the recipes in this cookbook began as staple meals at my beloved Abuela Sara's house, and I've adapted them to fit my lifestyle in New York City. That they're documented here, on paper, is a result of my incessant trailing of her as a child and my everlasting (and often irritating) FaceTime inquisitions as an adult.

Boricua

This cookbook celebrates the essence of my culture, rooted in resilience, community, creativity, adaptability, and evolution. Our cuisine, like *mi gente* (my people), is a vibrant fusion of cultures, races, and flavors. Puerto Rico was originally inhabited by the Taíno, the island's Indigenous people. They named our island Borikén (later Borinquen), meaning "Land of the Valiant and Noble Lord." Our Spanish colonizers changed the island's name to Puerto Rico (Rich Port) upon discovering gold in our rivers. Later, with a decreasing number of Taíno to work the land for sugarcane, coffee, and tobacco exporting, Spain brought African slaves.

If you've ever heard the word "Boricua," and didn't know what it meant, then learning Puerto Rico's original name should point to its meaning. A Boricua is anyone from Borinquen, *la isla del encanto* (the island of enchantment). You may have heard it in song lyrics—for older generations, in Noel Estrada's 1942 song "En mi viejo San Juan," and for younger generations, in interpretations by more current artists, like Marc Anthony's "Preciosa," and original songs such as Residente's "Hijos del cañaveral," and, more recently, Bad Bunny's "El apagón," "DtMF," and "Lo que le pasó a Hawaii." These songs manifest a collective sentiment of longing, heartbreak, and frustration for an island facing social and political hardships, natural disasters, and a general lack of equal opportunities. These injustices include the chronic instability and mismanagement of the island's power grid—now overseen by a private,

RAGUA
ARDAL

foreign-run company whose service has worsened conditions rather than improved them. They also include the displacement of local communities due to rising housing costs and gentrification, fueled in part by tax incentives that favor wealthy investors from the mainland United States, while offering little to no benefit to long-term Puerto Rican residents. These policies have deepened economic inequality and eroded local control over land, housing, and essential services, which make it nearly impossible for Boricuas on the island to stay or for those in the US diaspora to return. I'm one of the latter, and when I feel that aching nostalgia, I cook. These are the recipes that bring me back home.

Our *cocina criolla* (Creole cuisine) is an amalgamation of three cultures—Taíno, Spanish colonizers, and enslaved Africans—and the ingredients that represent them. The Taíno harvested yuca (cassava) and yautía (taro root), beans, ají peppers, achiote (annatto) seed, and recao (culantro). Spanish colonizers introduced pork, beef, rice, oil, herbs, and ingredients found in our *sofrito* and *adobos* (seasoning blends/rubs). Enslaved Africans contributed plantains, bananas, and possibly gandules (pigeon peas), just to name a few.

Throughout this cookbook, you'll find recipes that fuse all these ingredients and cultures. In a dedicated section, I provide a comprehensive guide to viandas, the root vegetables and starchy fruits considered the backbone our cuisine. I share how to make the perfect cup of *cafecito* (coffee) and the *panadería* (Spanish-style bakery) pastries we like to dunk in it. We take a road trip tour of Piñones in Loíza, one of the coastal towns distinguished for its rich African heritage and handmade *frituras* (fritters); I've included a guide to frying so you can perfect the art of making these at home. I share hearty, homey favorites from Abuela's repertoire, like her Carne Guisada (beef stew, page 251) and Arroz con Pollo (chicken rice, page 213)—the dish I made on *Beat Bobby Flay* (and beat him with). I describe the experience of dining at a local *restaurante criollo* (Creole restaurant) and share recipes for some of my favorite classic menu items. I end the book with a chapter on our traditional desserts with cheffy twists that have become hits among my friends, family, and clients—like infusing Puerto Rican coffee into my flan.

All these recipes use ingredients available in American grocery stores, so US home cooks and Puerto Ricans on the island can easily bring these flavors home. Use of modern, more efficient tools and equipment like a food processor, a high-speed blender, and an Instant Pot will make them a breeze to execute, so you won't need to bust out a box grater, a machete, or a *pilón* (wooden mortar and pestle), or wait hours for a cozy stew to develop depth of flavor.

This book is the culmination of my dream: to share with the world the comfort I've felt through re-creating Abuela's food, and to honor her for the devotion and the unconditional love she pours out for me and everyone she loves. For my US readers, I hope you fall in love with our sazón and feel empowered to celebrate our culture in your own cocinas. And for my Boricuas—I hope these recipes and flavors bring you back *a la isla*.

HANDY TOOLS AND EQUIPMENT

Caldero

Ubiquitous in many Hispanic households, a *caldero* (Spanish for "cauldron") is great for its durability and even heat distribution, which yields the best *pega'o*, the crispy, stuck-on rice crust that's a delicious by-product of rice preparation. If you don't have a caldero, you can use a heavy-bottomed pot like a Dutch oven or stainless-steel pot.

Greca

Also known as a percolator or moka pot, a greca is standard in most Puerto Rican households and we use it to brew espresso for our beloved cafecito. Puerto Rico's rich terrain yields some of the best coffee in the world, so it's no surprise that coffee comprises a big part of our culture. Grecas are inexpensive and easy to use, and make a bold cup without the need for a fancy, complicated espresso machine. More on this on page 55.

Handheld Mixer or Stand Mixer

Except for my Mallorcas (page 89), in any recipe that calls for a mixer, you can use a stand mixer or a handheld mixer interchangeably.

Tostonera

Tostoneras (tostones presses) are omnipresent in most Puerto Rican households, but they're not essential for making tostones. Often made of wood or plastic, they give you leverage when smashing plantains, but you can achieve the same result by using a heavy pot, plate, or even a spatula. You can purchase them at Latin grocery stores or online.

Instant-Read Thermometer

This inexpensive tool makes it easier to control cooking temperatures, especially when deep-frying, roasting meats, or making caramel for my Silkiest Meringue (page 309). Look for one at your grocery store or order one online.

Pressure Cooker or Instant Pot

While this is not essential, for many of my stews, a pressure cooker or multicooker like an Instant Pot will reduce the cooking time to a fraction of the alternative method (cooking in a pot). Nowadays, they're inexpensive (especially regular pressure cookers) and safe to use.

ESSENTIAL INGREDIENTS AND PANTRY MUST-HAVES

Achiote Seeds

Also known as annatto, these seeds grow in pods on the *Bixa orellana* shrub in tropical climates. Achiote (*ah-chee-oh-teh*) produces an intense natural red color, and was used by our Indigenous people, the Taíno, as body paint. It can also be used to dye clothes, for cosmetics, and as a food coloring. Many people in Puerto Rico use packets of store-bought sazón with artificial red and yellow food coloring to impart that reddish color to some dishes. But making Achiote Oil (page 37) is very easy and inexpensive, and a little goes a long way. You can find achiote seeds in most Latin grocery stores or order them online.

Ají Peppers

Ají (*ah-hee*) refers to both sweet and spicy small peppers. Ajíes dulces (sweet ajíes) resemble habaneros, but they're mild and come in different colors; we use them in sofrito. Ajíes picantes (spicy ajíes), like the ají caballero, are teeny-tiny and resemble Thai chiles. Beware: These are very hot. We use them in Pique (page 43), a vinegary hot sauce. If you can't source them, substitute sweet mini peppers or bell peppers for ajíes dulces and Thai chiles or habaneros for ajíes picantes.

Bouillon Cubes

In Puerto Rican cooking, when we say *cubitos*, we're talking about those little flavor-packed bouillon cubes. I use cubitos interchangeably with broth to add flavor and depth to soups, stews, rice dishes, and meats. Bouillon also comes in powder and paste forms; popular brands in Puerto Rico include Maggi and Knorr, and in the US, I often use Better Than Bouillon paste. One bouillon cube is roughly equivalent to 1 tablespoon bouillon powder or paste, and 1 packet of bouillon powder contains about 1½ teaspoons (½ tablespoon). You'll find different flavors like chicken, beef, vegetable, and ham, and I'll specify which to use in each recipe. For a quick guide to replacing broth with bouillon, see the box below.

Bouillon-to-Broth Equivalents

To substitute bouillon for broth, stir it into boiling water following this simple formula:

4 cups boiling water + 1 bouillon cube

OR

1 tablespoon bouillon paste or powder

OR

2 packets bouillon powder

Banana Leaves and Plantain Leaves

Banana leaves (*hoja de guineo, oh-ha deh ghee-neh-oh*) and plantain leaves (*hoja de plátano, oh-ha deh plah-tah-noh*) are bright green and sturdy. Caribbean, Hispanic, and Asian cultures use them for cooking, especially for steaming, where they impart an earthy flavor to different dishes. In Puerto Rico, we use them for Pasteles (page 267), to steam rice, and in casseroles like Pastelón (sweet plantain lasagna, page 255). I've also used them as serving mats and as a tablescape decoration. You can source them at Latin and Asian markets.

Coconut Milk

Coconut milk is produced by extracting coconut flesh from mature coconuts (the brown ones). In Puerto Rico, some people grate the coconut meat and steep it with coconut water or water, while others chop it up and blend it with coconut water or water. Then it's squeezed through a clean cloth to extract the slightly sweet, creamy liquid ever-present in Puerto Rican cocktails, desserts, fritters, and more. If you don't feel like making it, you can easily find it in grocery stores. For the recipes in this cookbook, use full-fat canned coconut milk, which is often sold in the Latin or Asian food sections. Also, don't confuse it for **coconut cream** (which has a higher fat content) or cream of coconut (see below).

Cream of coconut is a coconut milk derivative with added sugar and flavorings, resulting in an intensely flavored, sweetened coconut syrup. Coco López is a famous brand often used for piña coladas. Grocery stores stock it in their Latin foods section or near the premade cocktail mixers. Don't confuse or substitute it with coconut milk or coconut cream (see above). If you can't find cream of coconut, substitute sweetened condensed coconut milk.

Culantro

Also known as recao, culantro is in the same botanical family as cilantro, but its leaves are long, spiky, and tough, and I can best describe its flavor like cilantro on steroids. In Puerto Rico, we use it for our beloved sofrito. You can find it at Latin grocery stores, but in a pinch, you can substitute cilantro (including the stems, which are more intensely flavored than the leaves).

Garlic

Garlic (*ajo*) is ever-present throughout this cookbook. Please use fresh garlic, not prechopped or pureed garlic or garlic paste. There's a huge difference in flavor between fresh and preprocessed, and preprocessed garlic tends to burn faster. If you don't feel like peeling garlic, just purchase peeled garlic cloves and chop them or pulse them in a food processor.

Guava Paste

Guava paste, or *pasta de guayaba*, is made by cooking guava, sugar, and pectin down and letting it solidify into a sliceable paste. It has a chewy texture and provides sweetness and depth of flavor to many recipes. In Puerto Rico and many other Latin countries, it's often paired with fresh, mild queso del país (farmer's cheese) as a sweet-salty snack or dessert. You can find it in Latin grocery stores (labeled "guava paste" or "guava cake"), often shelved by the jams and jellies, and sometimes in the Latin section of regular grocery stores. You can also order it online.

Ham Steak

Also known as *jamón de cocinar* (cooking ham), ham imparts a meaty, smoky, savory flavor to different meals. It's used in many Puerto Rican dishes, like composed rices, soups, and stews. I like finding little chunks throughout my meals, so I purchase ham as bone-in steaks, cubes, or large chunks and cut them into smaller pieces. If you can't find larger cuts, you can certainly use thick-cut ham slices or even bacon. If you have leftover ham steak, you can portion it into smaller pieces, wrap tightly in plastic wrap, and freeze for up to 1 month to use in other recipes.

Passion Fruit Pulp

Known as *parcha* in Spanish, you can find this in the refrigerated produce section (often by where they have precut fruit) or in the freezer section by the frozen fruit (labeled "passion fruit puree"). Always check the label to make sure that the only ingredient is passion fruit. You can also make it yourself if you can find fresh ripe passion fruits (see page 65).

Pigeon Peas

Also known as gandules, pigeon peas are small brownish beans with a nutty flavor. They descend from Africa but are a staple throughout the Caribbean. (They were once used to feed pigeons in Barbados, hence the name.) In Puerto Rico, we use them in many dishes, the most popular being Arroz con Gandules (page 211), a holiday staple. I use canned gandules throughout this cookbook; they can be found in most grocery stores. If not, you can find them at any Latin market or easily source them online.

Plantain

Plantains (*plátanos* in Spanish) are afruit in the same family as banana that grows in tropical climates throughout the Caribbean and Latin America. Though it looks like a colossal banana, the two fruits are not the same, and they can't be used interchangeably. In Puerto Rico, we (mostly) use plantains at different stages of ripeness in savory applications (more on pages 25–26).

Puff Pastry

A type of laminated pastry made by layering dough and butter to achieve a flaky texture when baked. In Puerto Rico, we know it as *masa de hojaldre*. When it comes to making puff pastry dough, I simply don't. I wouldn't make you do that, either. You can find it in the frozen food section of most grocery stores (by the cakes and frozen pie shells). Do not substitute pie dough or phyllo dough—they are not the same. Keep it frozen until you're ready to use it to ensure the best, flakiest results.

Roasted Red Peppers

In Puerto Rican cuisine, we use *pimientos morrones* (preserved red bell peppers) to impart a sweet flavor and vibrant garnish to dishes like pasteles, rice, soups, and stews. Grocery stores stock them in cans or jars, which can be stored unopened in your pantry for months. If you can't find products specifically labeled "pimientos morrones," any canned or jarred roasted sweet red peppers will work as a substitute.

Rice

Medium-grain white rice is the default choice for most *arroz* (rice) dishes in Puerto Rico. The end result is tender and slightly sticky, making it ideal for classics like Arroz con Gandules (page 211) and Arroz con Pollo (page 213). In Puerto Rico, the most common brands are Arroz Rico and Sello Rojo, both known for their bright yellow labels. If you're in the US and can't find medium-grain white rice at your grocery store, head to a Latin market. Or swap in your preferred white rice—just make sure to adjust the rice-to-liquid ratio and the cooking time per the package directions. Lastly, the ever-lasting debate: to rinse or not to rinse. I don't rinse—I enjoy its sticky starchiness. But if you prefer a fluffier, looser grain, feel free to rinse your rice through a colander until the water runs clear, shaking off excess water before proceeding with the recipe.

Salt

My salt of choice for overall seasoning is finely ground **Himalayan pink salt**. It's minimally processed, with a natural pink color that comes from trace minerals, and the fine grains dissolve best and season food more evenly. You can use **fine sea salt**, **Celtic salt**, or **Diamond Crystal kosher salt** interchangeably in my recipes, as they have similar salinity levels. I **do not** recommend substituting iodized table salt. It has a sharper, more metallic taste and a much finer texture, which makes it behave differently in recipes and may throw off both the flavor and saltiness of the dish.

I like using **flaky sea salt** as a finishing salt for sweet and savory applications that need a cute little salty pop. The big crystals of salt often take the form of a pyramid, and the salt's irregular shape has a flaky appearance—hence the name. Flaky salt is delicate and brittle, which makes it easy to crush with your fingertips as you sprinkle it into food so it dissolves faster. You can find it in most grocery stores, or substitute freshly cracked salt (ground with a salt grinder) or coarse sea salt.

Sugar

When I refer to "sugar" in this cookbook, I mean cane sugar, but you can use it interchangeably with granulated white sugar unless I specify otherwise. Cane sugar is similar to white granulated sugar, but it's less processed and made solely from sugarcane. In Puerto Rico, we call it *azúcar morena*, which translates to "brown sugar" but is not the same as US brown sugar (refined white sugar with molasses added back in). Because cane sugar is less refined than regular white sugar, it has a slightly coarser texture and a light tan color instead of being pure white.

VIANDAS

Viandas (*vee-ahn-dahs*), also known as *verduras*, are a broad range of starchy fruits, tubers, root vegetables, and squash, often consumed in Puerto Rico as a main dish or combined with meats and proteins for a hearty meal. The Taíno cultivated some of these prior to colonization, including apio (celery root) and yuca (cassava), the flesh of which they turned into a type of flatbread called casabe. Spanish colonizers and slave traders brought enslaved Africans to the island, along with viandas that would later become essential staples of our gastronomy.

In the US, you can find most of these near the potatoes or near other "exotic" ingredients in the nonrefrigerated produce section of most large grocery stores. If you can't find them there, head to any Latin or Asian market. If you're in Puerto Rico, you can source them at any grocery store or *plaza del mercado* (farmers' market), and you may even spot *verduleros* (streetside vendors) displaying an array of fresh picks from their own *patios* (home gardens).

This chapter is a comprehensive guide to these nourishing ingredients, which you'll use throughout this cookbook. I encourage you to swap these in for potatoes, implementing the skills you learn here to transform them into delicious meals that become part of your repertoire.

Plantain

What they are: Plantain, or *plátano* (*plah-tah-noh*), is a starchy fruit in the same family as bananas, but much bigger.

How to select them: Plantains have three stages of ripeness: green, yellow, and ripe. The stage you select will depend on how you intend to cook it. The chart below explains how to pick and use them:

Ripeness	Verdes (Green)	Pintón (Green to Yellow)	Amarillo ó Maduro (Ripe)
Application	Starchy/savory	Savory/sweetish	Sweet/sweet
Visible	Green peel Creamy white flesh	Green to yellowish peel Yellowish flesh	Yellow peel, yellow peel with black freckles, or black peel Bright yellow flesh
Taste and Texture	Heavily starchy texture when cooked; absorbs savory flavors well; a hint of tropical sweetness	Soft, starchy texture when cooked and mild banana sweetness; may caramelize a bit from its natural sugars when cooked	Soft, creamy texture and sweet flavor; very sweet, like banana; will caramelize and possibly get syrupy from its natural sugars when cooked

How to prep and store plantains: Off the tree, plantains go from green to ripe very quickly. Keep unpeeled plantains in a cool, dry place until you're ready to use them or they've reached the desired ripeness level. To stop the ripening process, place them in the fridge; to accelerate it, place them in a brown paper bag at room temp. To peel a plantain, place it on a cutting board and use a sharp knife to cut off both ends (plantain can stain your skin, so wear gloves if you like). Using the tip of the knife, cut two or three long, shallow slits in the skin from end to end, rotating the plantain to space the cuts evenly. Holding the plantain under hot running water, slide the tip of your finger into one of the slits, under the skin, guiding it from one end to the other to release the skin. Repeat until you've peeled off all the skin. If there's any peel left behind, scrape it off with the back of a knife. If you don't plan on cooking it right away, submerge the peeled plantain in water until ready to use to keep it from browning.

Vianda vocab: *Mancha de plátano* ("plantain stain") is a term used to describe a birthmark, a reference to how plantain sap can stain your skin: *"Él lleva una mancha de plátano en el muslo."* ("He has a birthmark on his thigh.")

Green Bananas

What they are: Also known as *guineos verdes* (*ghee-neh-ohs ver-dehs*) or *guineítos* (*ghee-neh-ee-tohs*), these are underripe bananas. Their texture is firm and starchy, and they have an almost nutty flavor.

How to select them: Look for unripened mature bananas. Make sure they are completely green—don't substitute a ripe yellow banana for a green one. In a pinch, you can swap in green plantain.

How to prep and store green bananas: *See "How to Prep and Store Plantains" at left.*

Vianda vocab: *Estar pelao* ("being peeled") refers to being in a financial pinch. In Puerto Rico, we use the phrase *pela'o como un guineo* ("peeled like a banana") to state that we're strapped for money: *"No puedo salir a janguiar esta noche porque estoy pelá como un guineo."* ("I can't hang out tonight because I'm peeled like a banana.")

Breadfruit

What it is: Breadfruit, also known as *pana* (*pah-nah*) or *panapén* (*pah-nah-pen*), is a starchy fruit that grows on tall trees in tropical climates. When cooked, mature (but not ripe) breadfruit has a texture similar to potato and a subtle sweetness and breadlike flavor, hence the name.

How to select it: Look for breadfruit with yellowish, light green skin with a white, powdery latex drip from the stem down and brown lines between its polygonal sections. The surface should feel flat and firm.

How to prep and store breadfruit: Store whole breadfruit in a cool, dry place. If you don't plan on using it immediately, place it in the fridge to delay the ripening process for a day or two (don't worry if the skin gets brown).

To break down a breadfruit, cut it in half lengthwise with a large, sharp knife, then cut each half lengthwise into 4 wedges. Turn each wedge skin-side down and use a thin, sharp knife to cut out the porous core; for boiling, Abuela

Green Bananas

Breadfruit

Plantains

Breadfruit

Apio
Green Bananas
Chayote
Yautía
Calabaza
Malanga
Yuca
Breadfruit
Batata
Plantains

removes most of the core (about 2 inches); for tostones, she removes less (about 1 inch), which results in a starchy interior and crispier edges. Remove the skin with a vegetable peeler. If not using immediately, break it down into chunks, then store them submerged in water for up to 2 days to prevent browning, or freeze the chunks in zip-top bags for up to 3 months.

Vianda vocab: *Pana* is a slang term to refer to a close friend, pal, or buddy: "*¿Conoces a Pepe?*" "*Sí, él es mi pana.*" ("Do you know Pepe?" "Yes, he's my pal.")

Yuca

What it is: Yuca (*jooh-kah*), aka cassava, is a starchy root vegetable with a firm, slightly chewy texture that grows in tropical climates.

How to select it: The skin should look dark brown, waxy, and tough, but not cracked. It should feel heavy (not hollow) and firm throughout. The interior should look uniformly white and be odorless. To check this, tear off the tip or ask a grocer to cut a piece off for you.

How to prep and store yuca: Store whole yuca in a cool, dry place. If you don't plan on using it immediately, place it in the bottom drawer of your fridge for up to 1 week.

To break down yuca, place it horizontally on a cutting board. Using a large, sharp knife, cut it crosswise into manageable pieces (about 4 inches long). I wear gloves to protect my mani. Cut a shallow slit lengthwise through the skin, just until you reach the white flesh. Slide a butter knife between the white casing and the interior flesh, guiding it through from side to side to separate the casing from the flesh. Shave off any peel left behind with a sharp knife. If not using immediately, break it down into chunks, then store them submerged in water in the fridge for up to 2 days to prevent browning, or freeze the chunks in zip-top bags for up to 3 months.

Vianda vocab: *Yucas* is a slang term used to refer to feet: "*Tienes las yucas apestosas.*" ("Your feet stink.")

Yautía and Malanga

What they are: Yautía (*jow-tee-ah*), or taro root, and malanga (*mah-lahn-gah*), or cocoyam, are starchy tubers that we often use interchangeably in Puerto Rican dishes. They have a mild sweetness and nutty flavor. The chart below explains their key differences.

	Yautía (Taro Root)	Malanga (Cocoyam)
Shape	Smaller, with one bulby end and one tapered end	Bigger, wider, and more evenly cylindrical, with two bulby ends
Flesh	White, yellow, purple	White with purplish flecks/fibers scattered throughout; light purple/pinkish when cooked
Flavor	Neutral, nutty	Sweeter

How to select them: Yautía has hairy, rough, bumpy, ridged, dirty skin. Malanga is smoother-looking and less hairy, with larger ridges. In either case, make sure they feel firm throughout, not mushy, with no cracks in their skin that may expose their flesh.

How to prep and store yautía/malanga: Store whole yautía/malanga in a cool dry place for 1 to 2 weeks. Use a vegetable peeler to remove the skin, then rinse the yautía or malanga. If not using immediately, break it down into chunks, then store them submerged in water in the fridge for up to 2 days to prevent browning, or freeze the chunks in zip-top bags for up to 3 months.

Apio

What it is: Apio (*ah-pee-oh*), aka Creole celery root, *arracacha, apio criollo*, or Puerto Rican celery, is a starchy root. Although it's a type of celery root, it's not the same as celeriac, the kind of celery root you typically find in US grocery stores. This chart explains the key differences:

	Apio (Creole Celery Root)	Celeriac (Celery Root)
Shape	Ranges from curved, gnarled, and abstract to long and tapered	Round and bulby
Skin	Dirty, yellowish, and wrinkled	Dirty whitish to light green
Flesh	Pale to bright yellow	Creamy white
Aroma	Earthy, sweet, and pungent (like a parsnip)	Earthy and slightly sweet, but less pungent
Texture	Starchy and soft, like a potato	Lightly starchy and waxy, like a carrot
Taste	Sweet, nutty, earthy flavor	Mildly sweet, earthy flavor

How to select it: Apio should feel firm throughout, not mushy, and heavy, not hollow. The skin should not have cracks that may expose its flesh. In a pinch, you can substitute parsnips, which offer a closer flavor and a starchier texture than the waxier—though seemingly more logical—US celery root.

How to prep and store apio: Store whole apio in a cool, dry place for up to 1 week or in the fridge for 2 to 3 weeks. Remove the skin with a vegetable peeler to expose the yellow flesh. Shave off rough areas with a long, sharp knife, then rinse it thoroughly. If not using immediately, submerge it in water and store in the refrigerator for up to 1 day to prevent browning.

Calabaza

What it is: Calabaza (*cah-lah-bah-sah*), aka West Indian, Caribbean, or Puerto Rican pumpkin, is a type of winter squash. They're large, round, and stubby, with thick but smooth skin that can be tan, brown, and/or greenish in color. Calabaza flesh is bright orange, with a mildly sweet flavor and creamy, melt-in-your-mouth texture.

How to select it: Calabazas are so big, they're often sold precut into portions. Make sure the plastic is tightly wrapped and in direct contact with the flesh. The flesh should feel firm to the touch, not mushy, and should look vibrant (not dry or slimy), smooth, and bright orange, not pale. In a pinch, you can substitute butternut squash, or even kabocha squash, which is a bit starchier and takes longer to cook.

How to prep and store calabaza: Store whole calabaza in a cool, dark place for 1 to 2 months. Precut pieces should be kept tightly wrapped in plastic and stored in the bottom drawer of the fridge for up to 1 week from the date they were cut.

Use a large, sharp knife to cut the calabaza in half and scoop out the seeds with a spoon. Cut the halves into manageable portions you can hold in one hand. I like to shave off the peel with a sharp knife, but you can leave it on. If not using immediately, cover and store in the fridge for up to 3 days, or wrap tightly in plastic wrap (preferably in larger chunks) to prevent freezer burn and freeze it for up to 3 months.

SABOR Y SAZÓN

FLAVOR AND SEASONING

When I think of what it means to be Puerto Rican, two words come to mind: *sabor y sazón* (flavor and seasoning). In Puerto Rico, these words can also describe a person who has a bold, spunky, or sexy personality. You could say, "*Esa chica tiene sazón*" ("That girl has flavor/zest/seasoning/is full of color")—it's one of the best compliments. On the contrary, *soso* or *sosa* means bland and flavorless, and I'd take that as the ultimate insult. These same principles apply to our cocina, which makes this the most important chapter in this book.

One of the biggest components to our sazón is sofrito—a pureed blend of herbaceous vegetables and aromatics that becomes the flavor base for many dishes, including soups, stews, rice, and sauces.

Our *adobos* (dry seasoning blends/rubs) provide meat with that craveable, go-back-for-more quality. Sazón can be any ingredient that will add or enhance flavor. It's also the name for a reddish ready-made dry rub. That, and achiote oil add color and make our food as visually stunning as the red or yellow flowers on the *flamboyanes* (flame trees) that adorn our mountains and highways.

These recipes are simple, but essential, as they'll become ingredients you'll use throughout the book. Once you learn how to make sazón, you can use the rubs and blends daily and inventively to flavor up your own recipes.

THE IMPORTANCE OF SABOR Y SAZÓN

Whether I'm sitting down at a fine-dining restaurant or back home at Abuela's, when it comes to food and cooking, *sabor* (flavor) is everything (and precedes presentation). *Sazón* (seasoning) shouldn't be an afterthought in the form of salt sprinkled on at the end of a recipe. Sofrito, adobo, and sazón are the building blocks of sabor and are ubiquitous in my kitchen. They can turn an average dish into something unique and extraordinary. Perhaps you're unsure of what you're looking for when it comes to sazón. Here are a few rules of thumb I follow when conceptualizing meals:

1. **The objective of adding salt is to amplify the flavor of ingredients**, not to make food taste salty. I'd say sofrito is the MVP of our sazón. When I stir-fry it, I add a pinch of salt to enhance its flavors.

2. **Adding salt at many stages is imperative for developing flavor.** Many of my recipes call for adding salt at various steps. This allows you to season each component to boost their flavors individually.

3. **Flavor is a balancing act.** Sazón isn't just about enhancing flavor with salt, it's about balancing it. I use contrasting elements to add complexity. I contrast saltiness and acidity with sweetness, like adding a little sugar or honey to a tangy sauce. I balance richness with acidity, spice, or herbs, such as a squeeze of citrus, splash of vinegar, or a handful of fresh cilantro. These techniques can transform a bland, monotone dish into a well-rounded one.

4. **Tasting.** As a chef I often get asked the question: "How do I know if I've seasoned my meal properly?" For me, the answer is simple: You taste it! I learned to cook from Abuela, who solely relies on her senses and intuition for cooking. Getting into the habit of tasting your food as you prepare it will help you develop your palate, and eventually, you won't need to rely on recipes and measurements.

Adobo
Sofrito
Aceite de Achiote
Sazón con
Culantro
y Achiote
Adobo Mojado
Adobo
Aceite de Achiote

ADOBO

SAVORY DRY SEASONING

MAKES ABOUT 1 CUP

½ cup salt

¼ cup garlic powder

2 tablespoons dried oregano

1 teaspoon ground turmeric

In Puerto Rico, we use adobo interchangeably with salt, which gives our dishes umami and lip-smacky savoriness. If you head to our grocery stores, you'll find a whole section dedicated to adobos in the spice aisle. There's absolutely nothing wrong with buying prepared adobo—I have my whole life. But if you're unable to find it, here's my homemade version, which is a breeze to make and allows you to control the quality of the ingredients.

In a blender, combine the salt, garlic powder, oregano, and turmeric. Blend on high speed until the salt and spices are well combined and look powdery, 30 seconds to 1 minute. Allow the dust to settle before opening the lid. Transfer the adobo to a jar or shaker and store in a cool, dry place for up to 6 months.

ADOBO MOJADO

GARLICKY WET RUB

MAKES ABOUT ¾ CUP

½ cup peeled garlic cloves (from about 2 heads)

⅓ cup extra-virgin olive oil

¼ cup adobo, homemade (opposite) or store-bought

¼ cup fresh oregano leaves, or 1 tablespoon dried

3 tablespoons distilled white vinegar, rice vinegar, or apple cider vinegar

1½ teaspoons freshly ground black pepper

I called Papa for this recipe; while it seems very simple, it's very bold and assertive, like him. Papa uses this rub to marinate all the meats he's perfected over the years: *lechón de Noche Buena* (roast pork on Christmas Eve), *pavochón* (lechón-flavored turkey) on Thanksgiving, pork ribs at any given Friday cookout at Abuela's, and many other robust meat dishes that can stand up to the boisterous nature of Papa's personality—sorry, I mean his sazón.

In a blender or food processor, combine the garlic, olive oil, adobo, oregano, vinegar, and pepper. Blend on high speed until a smooth paste forms, 30 seconds to 1 minute. Use immediately or transfer to a jar and store in the fridge for up to 1 week.

ACEITE DE ACHIOTE

ACHIOTE OIL

MAKES ½ CUP

½ cup olive oil

2 tablespoons achiote seeds

The use of achiote (also known as annatto seed) in Puerto Rican cuisine dates back centuries in our cultural history to when the Taíno used it as body paint. Some believe this practice could be based in the West African tradition of coloring food with palm oil. Others think it started as an inexpensive alternative to saffron, an ingredient that came to our island by way of Spanish colonizers. Nowadays, we use it daily in our meals, and it's what imparts that characteristic reddish-orange hue to some of the dishes you'll find throughout this book. In a pinch, you can use prepackaged achiote oil, but making your own is easy, it stores well, and a little goes a long way.

In a small pot, combine the olive oil and achiote seeds and bring to a simmer over low heat. Simmer until the oil looks red, 5 to 10 minutes. Let cool completely, then strain the oil and discard the seeds. Transfer the oil to a small jar or bottle and seal. Store at room temperature for up to 1 month or in the fridge for up to 4 months.

SOFRITO

FLAVOR AND AROMATICS PASTE

MAKES ABOUT 4 CUPS

3 cups coarsely chopped onion (about 1 large)

2 cups coarsely chopped sweet ajíes or sweet mini peppers (about 20)

1 cup coarsely chopped cubanelle or green bell peppers (about 2)

¾ cup peeled garlic cloves (about 40)

3 cups coarsely chopped fresh cilantro (about 1 bunch)

20 culantro leaves, or an additional 3 cups coarsely chopped fresh cilantro

¼ cup extra-virgin olive oil

Sofrito (*soh-free-toh*) is a blend of aromatics that is used as the flavor base of many dishes in Puerto Rican cuisine. The word comes from the verb *sofreír*, meaning "pan-fry" or "sauté." Like mirepoix in French cuisine or curry paste in Thai cuisine, sofrito exudes most of its flavor when cooked in oil at the beginning of a dish. It's loud, bold, and in-your-face, just like us. Most households have their own *señora de sofrito* (sofrito lady) they source it from or their own family recipe. In my case, it's Abuela's. She uses a combination of different ajíes and culantro from her garden, which makes her sofrito magical. It can turn any mundane dish into something complex and extraordinary. Be ready to use it in throughout this book, and be creative with it in your own kitchen. I've used it in guacamole and pico de gallo, and to spruce up a soy dipping sauce for store-bought Chinese dumplings.

In a food processor, combine the onion, ajíes, cubanelle, garlic, cilantro, culantro, and olive oil and pulse on medium speed, stopping occasionally to scrape down the sides with a spatula, until the ingredients are broken down into a paste that resembles salsa. I prefer my sofrito a little chunky, so I stop pulsing right before it turns into a puree. (Alternatively, combine the ingredients in a blender and blend on low speed, simultaneously pushing the ingredients down with the tamper.) Transfer the sofrito to jars and store in the fridge for up to 1 week. Or divide the sofrito among four quart-size freezer bags, squeeze out the air, and seal, then freeze flat for up to 2 months. Break off chunks for cooking as needed.

SAZÓN CON CULANTRO Y ACHIOTE

COLOR AND SPICE DRY SEASONING

MAKES ABOUT ½ CUP

3 tablespoons salt

3 tablespoons achiote seeds, or 2 tablespoons ground achiote

2½ tablespoons garlic powder

1½ tablespoons ground turmeric

1½ tablespoons ground coriander

2 teaspoons ground cumin

In Puerto Rico, and many other Latin countries, sazón comes in a little foil packet and is sprinkled into pots of food to add flavor and bright red color. It contains some spices, but for the most part, it's MSG and artificial coloring. Like adobo (page 36), Puerto Rican grocery stores carry different brands and variations, and there's absolutely nothing wrong with buying premade sazón. But if you're unable to find it, or you prefer to cut out the fake stuff, here's my easy homemade version.

In a blender, combine the salt, achiote, garlic powder, turmeric, coriander, and cumin. Blend on high speed until the salt and spices are well combined and look powdery (if you're using whole achiote seeds, they'll stop banging around and sounding rocky), 30 seconds to 1 minute. Allow the dust to settle before opening the lid. Transfer the sazón to a jar or shaker and store in a cool, dry place for up to 6 months.

SALSITAS DE ABUELA

GRANDMOTHER SAUCES

Just as French cuisine is built on five classic mother sauces, Puerto Rican cocina has its own foundation of bold, unfussy, deeply flavorful staples. I call them "grandmother sauces"—a tongue-in-cheek nod to the French mother sauces I learned to perfect as a young cook at Chef Thomas Keller's Bouchon, reimagined through the lens of the island flavors I grew up with and learned from Abuela. These salsitas—fresh, humble, and full of sabor—are the building blocks of many recipes in this book.

Take *Mayo-Ketchup* (page 45), for instance: Found on nearly every table in Puerto Rico, it's as simple as it sounds, but every household has its own spin. At Abuela's, we add grated garlic for a punchy, pungent bite. Or Pique (page 43), the vinegary hot sauce that helped me win on *Beat Bobby Flay*—bright, fresh, and the perfect contrast to the richness of many Puerto Rican dishes. I reference these salsitas throughout the book, and unlike the French mother sauces, they are simple to make—but they don't skimp on sazón. They're versatile, flavor-packed, and meant to be used your way.

Pique
Chimichurri con Chorizo
Escabeche
Salsita
Criolla
Mayo-
Ketchup
Ajillo
Cebollitas
Encurtidas
Ájili-Mójili

PIQUE

SWEET AND TANGY HOT SAUCE

MAKES 1½ CUPS

1 cup white wine vinegar

½ cup sugar

1½ teaspoons salt

5 hot ajíes, or 3 Fresno peppers or jalapeños, thinly sliced

1 tablespoon stemmed whole ajíes caballeros, or 1 Thai bird chile, thinly sliced (optional, for an extra-spicy pique)

15 pearl onions, peeled and halved

1 tablespoon coriander seeds, lightly crushed

The word *pique* (*peeh-keh*) derives from *picante*, which means "spicy" (in the heat sense). We make ours with pickled hot ajíes (see page 19), spices, and aromatics. In Puerto Rico, you can purchase pique at grocery stores or from *verduleros* (streetside fruit-and-vegetable vendors), or make it yourself. Abuela Sara makes our family's pique à la minute by mashing fresh ajíes from her garden with vinegar. It adds a great kick and tangy contrast to many dishes, especially fried foods like Alcapurrias (page 168) and Pastelillos (page 165). Puerto Rican cooks often use recycled *canecas* (flask bottles) to bottle their pique. The condiment's long shelf life makes it a special, personal gift and great conversation topic.

In a medium pot, combine the vinegar, sugar, and salt and bring to a boil over high heat, stirring until the sugar and salt have dissolved. Remove from the heat and add the sliced ajíes, ajíes caballeros (if using), onions, and coriander. Cover and let cool to room temperature, about 1 hour. If you used ajíes caballeros, smash a few with the back of a spoon to release more of their spiciness. Transfer the pique to a bottle or jar, seal, and store in the fridge for up to 3 months.

MAKES 1½ CUPS

MAYO-KETCHUP

1 cup mayonnaise or Cashew Mayo (recipe follows)

⅓ cup ketchup

1 tablespoon grated or chopped garlic (from about 2 large cloves)

2 teaspoons sriracha (optional)

Mayo-ketchup, my condiment of choice, is a universal sauce used in many different applications in Puerto Rican cuisine. The basic recipe consists of just what the name says: mayonnaise and ketchup. Add-ins vary from home to home, including hot sauce, garlic, mustard, vinegar, spices, and herbs. Abuela always makes it for me to enjoy alongside her tostones (page 151), as shown here, and Sorullitos (page 157). I use it in place of straight ketchup for burgers, hot dogs, fries, etc. I'm also sharing my recipe for cashew mayo, a plant-based alternative that you can use in place of the mayo, if you prefer.

In a medium bowl, whisk or stir together the mayo, ketchup, garlic, and sriracha (if using) until homogeneous. Transfer to a jar, cover, and store in the fridge for up to 2 weeks.

CASHEW "MAYO"

MAKES 1 CUP

¾ cup raw cashews (see Note)

2 large garlic cloves, peeled

½ teaspoon salt

2 teaspoons apple cider vinegar

In a high-speed blender, combine the cashews, garlic, salt, vinegar, and ½ cup water. Blend on high speed until the sides of the blender are warm and the mixture looks creamy, 1 to 2 minutes. Transfer to a jar and store in the fridge for up to 5 days.

NOTE: *If you don't have a high-speed blender like a Vitamix, soak the cashews in water to cover in the fridge overnight. Drain before using.*

ÁJILI-MÓJILI

HOT AND SWEET CHILE CONDIMENT

MAKES ABOUT ¾ CUP

½ to 1 tablespoon sriracha, ½ to 1 red jalapeño, or 1 to 2 hot ajíes, seeded (see Note; optional)

1 cup coarsely chopped mini sweet red, yellow, or orange peppers or sweet ajíes (10 to 15; see Note)

5 large garlic cloves, peeled

3 tablespoons neutral oil, such as canola or sunflower oil

1½ tablespoons apple cider vinegar, distilled white vinegar, rice vinegar, or white wine vinegar

1 teaspoon honey

¾ teaspoon salt

¼ teaspoon freshly ground black pepper

Ájili-mójili (*ah-hee-lee-moh-hee-lee*) is as fun to say as it is to eat. It's mostly made up of sweet and spicy peppers, *tons* of garlic, and vinegar. The tanginess, sweetness, mild heat, and freshness from the peppers makes it a great contrasting flavor to almost any savory dish in this book. I like to make a big batch to last me a few weeks. You can use it to top my tostones (page 151), pasteles (page 267, any of the frituras from pages 146–169, fried red snapper (page 225), or even on eggs, like my Arepa Revoltillo con Jamón y Queso (page 109). Really . . . anything. I've even used it in my salad dressings or stirred up with some mayo or Cashew Mayo (page 45) to use as a sweet, creamy, peppery sandwich spread or dip for fries.

Place ½ teaspoon sriracha (or ½ jalapeño or ½ hot ají) in a food processor or blender. Add the mini peppers, garlic, oil, vinegar, honey, salt, and black pepper. Pulse 10 to 15 times, until the mixture starts looking saucy but still chunky. Taste and adjust with more sriracha (or jalapeño or hot ají), if you prefer. Transfer to a jar or airtight container and store in the fridge for up to 2 weeks.

NOTE: *It's difficult for me to find ajíes (see page 19) in New York, so I use a combination of mini peppers and sriracha for a comparable result that's just as punchy. If you're able to source ajíes, sweet and/or hot, even better. To control the heat, add ½ hot ají at a time, taste, and continue adding more until you achieve the level of heat you prefer. I like to keep it mild so I can use it on mostly anything and at any time of day.*

CHIMICHURRI (CON CHORIZO)

HERBY OLIVE OIL SAUCE (WITH CHORIZO)

MAKES 1½ TO 2 CUPS

¼ cup minced shallots (about 2 medium) or red onion

3 tablespoons grated or chopped garlic (from about 6 large cloves)

½ teaspoon red pepper flakes

1 teaspoon salt

4 ounces dry-cured chorizo, finely diced (optional)

2 tablespoons honey

2 tablespoons apple cider vinegar

¼ cup neutral oil, such as canola or sunflower oil

¼ cup extra-virgin olive oil

1 bunch cilantro, finely chopped

While chimichurri originated in Argentina, you may see it pop up in some Puerto Rican restaurant menus and at mi casa when Papa and his *primos* (cousins) are commanding the grill, cooking all kinds of meats. The fresh, herby, zesty sauce is a great contrast to any smoky, juicy meat, chicken, firm-fleshed steaky fish (like swordfish or mahi), eggs in the morning, or as a topping for tostones (page 151) or Buttery Plantain Mash (page 199). The chorizo adds smokiness and decadence, but it's optional, so leave it out if pork isn't your thing.

In a medium heatproof bowl, combine the shallots, garlic, red pepper flakes, and salt.

If using chorizo, place it in a small pan and cook over medium heat, stirring continuously, until the fat has rendered and the chorizo bits look crispy, 5 to 10 minutes. Remove from the heat and add the hot chorizo and its rendered fat to the bowl with the shallot mixture.

Add the honey, vinegar, neutral oil, and olive oil and stir well to incorporate. Add the cilantro and stir again. Cover and refrigerate for at least 2 hours or up to overnight to allow the flavors to come together before serving. Store in an airtight container in the fridge for up to 1 week.

NOTE: *For an easier, no-fuss approach, use a food processor: Cook the chorizo (if using) as directed and place it in a heatproof bowl. Coarsely chop the shallots, garlic, and cilantro and place them in a food processor. Add the red pepper flakes, salt, honey, vinegar, neutral oil, and olive oil. Pulse a few times for 2 or 3 seconds each time, stopping occasionally to scrape down the sides, until you achieve a fine paste (not quite a puree). Add the chimichurri to the chorizo (if using), stir to incorporate, and refrigerate as directed.*

SALSITA CRIOLLA

CREOLE PEPPER SAUCE

MAKES ABOUT 2 CUPS

½ cup extra-virgin olive oil

1 cup finely diced yellow bell pepper (about 1 pepper)

1 cup finely diced red bell pepper (about 1 pepper)

2 cups finely diced white or yellow onion (about 1 large)

½ teaspoon salt, plus more if needed

¼ cup grated or chopped garlic (from about 8 large cloves)

¼ cup tomato paste

2 tablespoons honey, plus more if needed

6 pitted green olives, minced, plus 1 tablespoon brine from the jar

1 cup light beer (such as Medalla), chicken broth, or vegetable broth

2 teaspoons apple cider vinegar

¼ cup chopped fresh cilantro

This sweet, savory, tangy condiment is great with proteins like shrimp, fish, lobster, pork, and chicken. Salsita criolla is also a great topping for Buttery Plantain Mash (page 199), tostones (page 151), and Pigeon Pea Hummus (page 137). I served it as a dipping sauce on *Hell's Kitchen*, desperate to share all my Puerto Rican sazón with Chef Gordon Ramsay. It was a big hit that made it onto my final menu in the season finale.

In a medium pot, heat the olive oil over medium heat for about 2 minutes. Add the bell peppers, onion, and salt and cook until they are soft and translucent, 10 to 15 minutes. Add the garlic and cook until the garlic is aromatic but has not taken on color, 1 to 2 minutes more. Add the tomato paste and honey and cook, stirring, until the tomato paste turns brickred in color and smells sweet, about 4 minutes. Add the olives, olive brine, beer, and vinegar. Reduce the heat to medium-low and cook, stirring occasionally, until the liquid has reduced by one-third and has a saucy consistency, 10 to 15 minutes. Taste for seasoning. It should be sweet from the peppers and tomatoes and have a slight saltiness from the olives. If needed, add more salt pinch by pinch, tasting after each addition. You can also add more honey 1 teaspoon at a time if needed to balance the bitterness from the beer and the acidity from the tomato paste.

If you plan to serve the salsita criolla immediately, stir in the cilantro. Otherwise, let it cool to room temperature, transfer to an airtight container, and store in the fridge for up to 3 days. Sprinkle the cilantro on top or stir it in when ready to serve.

ESCABECHE

VINEGARY ONION MARINADE

MAKES ABOUT 1½ CUPS

⅔ cup extra-virgin olive oil

2 cups thinly sliced white or yellow onion (about 1 medium)

½ teaspoon salt

1 teaspoon grated or chopped garlic (from about 1 large clove)

1 teaspoon whole black peppercorns

2 bay leaves

1 tablespoon sliced pimento-stuffed green olives (about 4), plus 1 tablespoon brine from the jar

¼ cup thinly sliced roasted red peppers (pimientos morrones)

⅓ cup distilled white vinegar or apple cider vinegar

1 tablespoon honey

Escabeche is a food preservation technique that we adapted from our Spanish ancestors. It's also used in other countries, like Mexico and Portugal, for seafood and vegetables. Recipes vary, but the main ingredients are oil and vinegar. In Puerto Rico, you'll likely see it used as a warm marinade poured over hot, boiled viandas (see pages 25–31), or to marinate seafood. You can even serve it as a sauce for steamed chicken or fish. Whether you use escabeche as a marinade or a condiment, its briny, vinegary flavor makes it a great complement to cold, cooked seafood dishes, especially in tropical weather and on hot summer days.

In a medium pot, heat the olive oil over medium-low heat for 1 to 2 minutes. Add the onion and salt and cook, stirring, until the onion is soft and translucent but has not taken on color, 4 to 6 minutes. Add the garlic, peppercorns, bay leaves, olives, olive brine, and roasted peppers. Cook, stirring, until the garlic is aromatic and looks soft but has not taken on color, 1 to 2 minutes. Add the vinegar and honey and bring to a simmer, stirring, then remove from the heat. If not using immediately, let cool to room temperature, then transfer to a jar or airtight container and store in the fridge for up to 2 weeks.

CEBOLLITAS ENCURTIDAS

PICKLED RED ONIONS

MAKES 1½ CUPS

⅓ cup apple cider vinegar

2½ tablespoons sugar

1 teaspoon salt

1 cup thinly sliced red onion (about 1 small, sliced into 1-inch-long pieces)

I love this recipe's versatility, visual appeal, and ease of preparation. From start to finish, it takes about 10 minutes to prepare. And a little goes a long way, especially since it keeps for up to 1 month in the fridge. Remember, it's a pickle! You can use white or red onions; I prefer red because after sitting in the vinegar for a few hours, they turn Barbie pink, and they make my dishes look as extra as the Puerto Rican contestant in a Miss Universe pageant. Use it to garnish any dish you think would benefit from a burst of bright, alliumy acidity and the most gorgeous pop of pink.

In a small pot, combine the vinegar, sugar, salt, and ⅓ cup water. Bring to a boil over high heat, stirring until the sugar and salt have dissolved, then remove from the heat and pour into a 1-pint jar. Add the onions and stir, pushing them down to fully submerge them in the liquid. Let cool to room temperature, about 1 hour, then refrigerate, uncovered, until cold to the touch, 2 to 3 hours. Seal the jar and store in the fridge for up to 1 month.

AJILLO

GARLICKY BUTTER

MAKES ABOUT 1 CUP

6 tablespoons (¾ stick) unsalted butter

¼ cup grated or chopped garlic (from about 8 large cloves)

2 tablespoons extra-virgin olive oil

½ teaspoon salt

Ajo means "garlic" in Spanish, so whenever Puerto Ricans refer to anything as *al ajillo*, we mean it's drenched with garlic butter. I like to cook the garlic slowly, which mellows out its pungent taste, so this is a good compromise for garlic newbies. You can use this as the base for a garlicky lobster or shrimp sauce (page 227) for an easy weeknight meal, or to level up tostones (page 151), Yuquitas Fritas (page 159), or Buttery Plantain Mash (page 199).

In a small pot, combine the butter, garlic, olive oil, and salt. Heat over medium heat until the butter melts and starts bubbling slowly, 1 to 2 minutes. Reduce the heat to medium-low so the mixture is gently bubbling and cook until the garlic is aromatic and sweet but not pungent, and is still pale in color, 10 to 12 minutes. Remove from the heat and use immediately, or transfer to a jar or airtight container and let cool to room temperature, then seal and store in the fridge for up to 1 week.

BEBIDAS

BEVERAGES

Beverages are essential to Puerto Rican gastronomy. Our day starts with *cafecito* (coffee, page 55, which comes in all shapes and sizes. To us, coffee isn't just a drink—it's a religion, with its own dedicated individual rituals. Our Quesitos (page 97), for example, are a beloved pastry that begs to be dunked in cafecito.

Then we have our *jugos naturales*, fresh juices prepared with local tropical fruits. You can find them at restaurants and food establishments all over the island, and here I've included my favorites of the ones Abuela makes with fruit she picks from her yard. They're refreshing, colorful, delicious, and even better with a glug of Puerto Rican rum splashed in . . . just like our people.

This brings me to booze—and rum, specifically. Puerto Rico is known as the rum capital of the world, so it's no surprise that most of our cocktails are centered around this spirit. Our *frituras* (fritters; see pages 146–169) scream for an icy rum with coconut water (see page 73) or a cold Medalla beer. From mojitos to sangría to our beloved coquito—a rich, creamy, coconutty icon that takes eggnog's place in our Navidades Boricuas (Puerto Rican Christmas)—these cocktails have all been baptized with the holy water of Puerto Rico.

PUERTO RICO Y EL CAFÉ (PUERTO RICO AND COFFEE)

Puerto Rico's rich terrain and elevation provide ideal growing conditions for coffee, which, in the late 1800s, made us one of the world's largest producers and exporters of the crop, mostly to Europe. A variety of factors led to the decline of the industry, including the rise of sugar production, repeated hurricane devastation, and a shrinking labor force unwilling or unable to take on the physically demanding work of coffee farming, particularly the hand-harvesting of beans on steep, mountainous terrain.

Despite this, to Puerto Ricans, coffee isn't just a beverage—it's a way of life, and provides a moment to slow down. We even have our own slang for it (see sidebar, page 56). At Abuela's house, we have it in the morning before breakfast, at *medio día* (midday) with a *merienda* (light snack), and sometimes in the evening after a big dinner, we may have a *pocillo* or *cortadito* (see sidebar, page 56).

Some family-owned haciendas (coffee plantations) remain in the mountainous central regions of Puerto Rico, so there is still a growing coffee scene, especially for those who value high-quality, single-estate coffee beans. I always stock up on local coffee when I go home to see my family. This means that upon returning to New York, I need to allow extra time for customs inspections at the airport (apparently a backpack full of coffee bags is *very* suspicious), but it's completely worth it when I hear the coffee sputtering out of my *greca* (percolator or moka pot; see page 16), followed by the rich, toasty aroma and that first glorious, creamy sip.

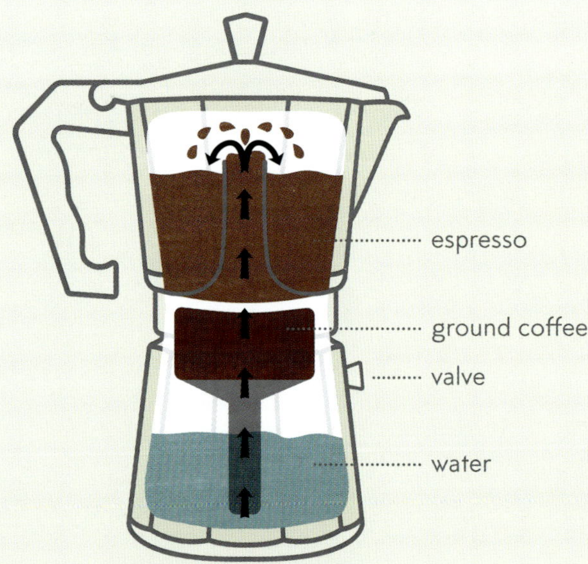

La Greca (The Percolator)

CAFECITO DE GRECA

PERCOLATOR ESPRESSO

YIELD VARIES

Ground coffee, as needed (depending on the size of your greca)

Milk or nondairy milk (see Note), for serving

NOTE: *To achieve the best foam, use whole or reduced-fat (2%) milk, or oat or soy milk if you're opting for dairy-free.*

When we refer to coffee, we mean espresso, not drip coffee, and when it comes to making coffee at home, I prefer to use a greca. When you purchase one (I got mine online), the label will list a "cup count." This refers to espresso-size portions, so if you're like me and prefer a large cup of coffee in the morning, keep in mind that a serving of espresso is 1½ ounces. My "6-cup" greca makes a single-serving extra-large cup of espresso for me. I also have a 9-cup greca that I use when I have guests, which makes about 2 large cups. Whether you make it with a greca or a fancy espresso machine, you can count on Puerto Rican coffee being bold and aromatic, with rich, chocolaty undertones. Abuela sometimes sprinkles mine with a little cinnamon, which just enhances those flavors.

Fill the bottom chamber of a greca with water until it reaches just below the side valve. Insert the basketlike middle chamber into the bottom section, fill it loosely with ground coffee, and lightly flatten the coffee with a spoon (without packing it in). Twist on the top chamber (with the spout and handle) and place on the stovetop. Heat over medium heat until you hear sputtering inside (which means the water has pushed through the coffee in the middle chamber and made its way to the top chamber), 5 to 10 minutes. Lift the lid to make sure it's full of brewed espresso, then remove from the heat and serve the coffee in any of the ways shown on page 56 (depending on your energy levels).

If you don't have a proper steamer, heat milk in a small pot over medium-low heat or microwave it in a mason jar in 30-second increments until it forms steam but doesn't boil or bubble. If you like it frothy, make sure your pot or mason jar is deep enough to froth the milk without spilling over, then use a hand frother or whisk it until it looks foamy. Pour or spoon the milk into your coffee and enjoy.

HOW TO ORDER COFFEE LIKE A BORICUA

All terms refer to espresso-style coffee, and either the size of the cup, quantity of milk, or both.

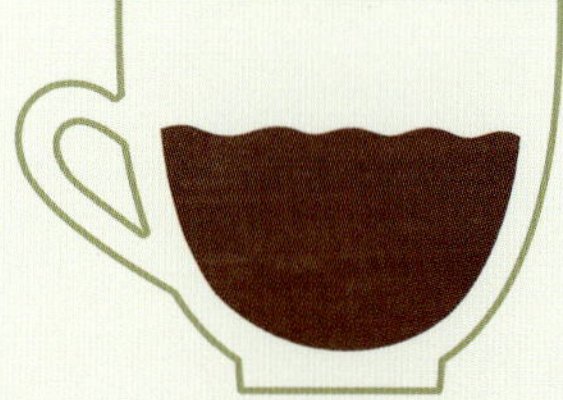

Pocillo:
a small cup
of espresso

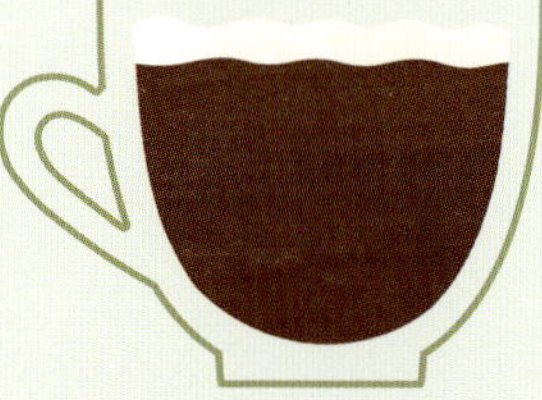

Cortado/cortadito (cut with):
a pocillo cut with
steamed milk froth

Término medio (halfway):
a pocillo with an equal
quantity of steamed milk

Bibi (baby bottle):
a large cup of
steamed milk with a
splash of espresso
(light caramel color)

Café con leche (coffee with milk):
a large cup of
equal parts espresso
and steamed milk,
like a latte

Cargado (charged) or oscuro (dark):
a large cup of
espresso with a splash
of steamed milk
(dark, but not black)

Cafequito (Coquito Coffee; see page 59):
a large cup of espresso
with a splash of coquito
topped with milk froth
and a sprinkle
of cinnamon

Negro (black):
no milk

Puya (sharp):
no milk or sugar

Agua'o or aguado (watered-down):
American-style drip coffee

Mela'o or melado (sugarcane syrup):
with a lot of sugar or very sweet

MAKES 2 LARGE MUGS

CAFEQUITO

COQUITO COFFEE

½ cup Coquito (page 79)

2 cups Cafecito de Greca (page 55)

½ cup milk, steamed and frothed (see page 55)

Ground cinnamon

Cafecito + coquito = cafequito. This is a coffee term of my own creation, which deserved to be included in the coffee slang list. I also call it *latte Navideño* (Christmas latte), since coquito is ubiquitous in Puerto Rican refrigerators throughout our (very long) Christmas season. The idea came about one morning when I was making my cafecito and realized I was low on milk. I decided to compensate with a little splash of coquito. After all, it has milk and sugar, so it's basically a boozy coffee creamer. If you're over twenty-one years old (or eighteen in PR) and want to up your coffee game over Christmas break, try this. And if you want to keep it PG, just set aside a portion of coquito without booze.

Shake the coquito well and divide it between two large mugs. Distribute the coffee between the mugs, then pour the frothy steamed milk over them. Dust each mug lightly with a tiny pinch of cinnamon. Stir well and enjoy.

CHOCOLATITO CALIENTE CON QUESO

CHEESY HOT CHOCOLATE

SERVES 1 OR 2

3 Chocolate Cortés hot chocolate tablets (see Note), or ⅓ cup semisweet chocolate chips

1¾ cups evaporated milk or whole milk

8 to 10 (1-inch) cubes queso de papa (mild cheddar cheese) or queso de bola (Edam cheese)

Tostadas (page 87) or Export soda crackers, for serving

In Puerto Rico, we start with coffee young. But before I was on the coffee train, Abuela got me onto *chocolatito caliente* (hot chocolate). She'd whip it up in a pot, pour it into a cup over a few cubes of cheese, serve it with her buttery tostadas (as shown here), and call it breakfast. I know the cheese sounds odd, but it just works—I don't make the rules. This is also a classic at wakes in Puerto Rico. It's sweet, salty, warm, and comforting. While you sip on the rich, milky hot chocolate, the cheese at the bottom melts and, rather than blending in, becomes a salty-sweet stringy fondue—perfect for dunking tostadas or Export soda crackers.

With your hands, break up the chocolate tablets into smaller chunks and place them in a small pot with ¾ cup water. Bring to a simmer over medium-high heat, whisking continuously to avoid lumps and to keep it from burning, 2 to 4 minutes. Add the milk and whisk until the mixture starts to steam and get frothy, 2 to 4 minutes. (If you have a hand frother, this would be a good time to bust it out.) Reduce the heat to maintain a low simmer and whisk vigorously (or buzz it up a few times with the frother) to create some *espumita* (foam) on top.

Place the cubes of cheese in a mug and pour the hot chocolate over them. Serve with buttery tostadas or a few soda crackers. Sip and dip away.

NOTE: *Look for hot chocolate tablets at Latin grocery stores (they may even have different brands) or order them online.*

BATIDA DE PAPAYA DE LA PLACITA

"LA PLACITA" PAPAYA MILKSHAKE

MAKES 4 MILKSHAKES

4 cups peeled ripe papaya chunks (from about 1 large)

2 cups ice

2 cups whole milk

¼ cup sugar, plus more if needed

2 teaspoons ground cinnamon, plus more for garnish

¼ teaspoon salt

This unassuming recipe is inspired by the iconic ones they prepare at La Placita de Santurce, a cultural landmark in San Juan where Boricuas gather and pick up the island's freshest produce from local vendors during the day and drown their sorrows at night. I've had this batida for breakfast, as a midday pick-me-up, as a post-beach cooler, for dessert, and even as a hangover elixir. This milkshake does it all for me.

Place four 12-ounce glasses in the freezer to chill.

In a blender, combine the papaya, ice, milk, sugar, cinnamon, and salt and blend on high speed until completely smooth, 1 to 2 minutes. Taste it with a spoon: It should be sweet, smooth, and creamy. If necessary, add more sugar 1 tablespoon at a time until you achieve the desired level of sweetness. Pour the milkshake into the chilled glasses, garnish each with a pinch of cinnamon, and serve.

Jugo/Refresco
de Parcha
Jugo/Refresco de
Tamarindo, page 66
Limonada
Espumosa,
page 68

JUGO/REFRESCO DE PARCHA

PASSION FRUIT JUICE

MAKES ABOUT 4 CUPS

10 to 15 passion fruits (see Note)

½ cup sugar, plus more if needed

NOTE: *Instead of using fresh passion fruit pulp, substitute 1 cup store-bought frozen passion fruit puree—just make sure that the only ingredient listed on the packaging is passion fruit. Thaw it at room temperature and combine with the sugar and water as directed.*

It's hard to keep up with the passion fruits at Abuela's house when they're in season. Her trees are as bountiful as her kitchen. Clever as she is, she's found a way to preserve them so they taste as fresh year-round as the day they fell off the tree: She freezes the pulp in my niece's recycled plastic juice bottles. They're the perfect size to thaw and use for a batch of fresh passion fruit juice, or for me to snag, pack in my cooler, and use as a mixer for cocktails at the beach. I love splashing some into my Yeti cup to liven up my Tito's vodka sodas.

Cut the passion fruits in half and scoop the pulp and seeds into a measuring cup; you'll need 1½ cups. Discard the scooped-out shells. Transfer the passion fruit pulp to a blender or food processor and blend on the lowest speed just until the seeds have separated from their soft outer membrane, about 1 minute. Set a fine-mesh sieve over a medium bowl. Pour in the pulp and seeds and press down with the back of a spoon to extract all the pulp; discard the seeds.

In a 1-quart pitcher, combine 1 cup of the passion fruit pulp, the sugar, and 3 cups water. (Freeze any unused pulp in freezer-safe airtight containers for up to 1 year; thaw before using.) Stir until the sugar has dissolved. Taste it. If you prefer it sweeter, add more sugar 1 to 2 tablespoons at a time, stirring and tasting after addition until you've achieved your desired level of sweetness. If it's too sour, add more water ¼ cup at a time until you achieve the acidity level you prefer. Refrigerate for 1 to 2 hours before serving. Serve cold, over ice.

JUGO/REFRESCO DE TAMARINDO

TAMARIND JUICE

MAKES ABOUT 4 CUPS

15 to 20 ripe tamarind pods (see Note)

½ cup sugar, plus more if needed

Abuelo and Abuela's house is surrounded by all kinds of tropical fruit-bearing trees, including tamarind. During my childhood, I'd think of their yard as a forest, where my sister and *primas* (cousins) and I would play adventure games while foraging for fruits like hidden treasures. I still love walking around and seeing what I can find. During one of those walks, my niece, Emma (a toddler at the time), followed me, wobbling and speaking gibberish. I pretended to understand her while distractedly scanning trees for inconspicuous ingredients. In the sweetest voice, she called out, "Titi!" ("Auntie!"), while tugging at my hand, then handed me something brown and dry, with a coarse, crackly texture. Upon closer inspection, I realized it was a pristine, ripe tamarind pod that had fallen off the tree above us. I'd been stomping over all the fruit Emma had found. We gathered all the good pods and brought them into the house. That day, Abuela made tamarind juice with our treasures.

Using your fingers, squeeze the tamarind pods until they crack open, revealing the sticky, pulp-covered seeds inside. Remove and discard the dry shell and the fibrous threads that run along the pods. Rinse the seeds and place them in a medium pot. Add enough water to cover the seeds and bring to a boil over medium-high heat, then reduce the heat to maintain a simmer. Cook until the water has evaporated to the same level as the seeds, 10 to 15 minutes. Transfer this mixture to a fine-mesh sieve set over a medium bowl and use a rubber spatula or spoon to push down on the seeds, extracting all the pulp. Return the seeds to the pot and repeat this process one or two more times, until there's no more pulp left on the seeds; discard the seeds. Let the puree cool to room temperature before using.

In a large (1-quart) pitcher, combine 1 cup of the tamarind puree, the sugar, and 4 cups water. (Freeze any unused puree in freezer-safe airtight containers for up to 1 year;

NOTE: *Instead of using fresh tamarind pods, substitute 1 cup store-bought frozen tamarind puree; just make sure the only ingredient listed on the packaging is tamarind. Thaw it at room temperature and combine with the sugar and water as directed.*

thaw before using.) Stir until the sugar has dissolved. Taste and add more sugar 1 tablespoon at a time, if you like, stirring and tasting after each addition until you've achieved your desired level of sweetness. Refrigerate for 1 to 2 hours before serving. Serve cold, over ice.

LIMONADA ESPUMOSA

FIZZY LIMEADE

MAKES ABOUT 6 CUPS

1⅓ cups fresh lime juice (from about 10 large limes)

1 cup sugar

1 (12-ounce) can Sprite, 7UP, or other lemon-lime soda (see Note)

The nature of fizzy drinks is that after some time, the bubbles will flatten, which is why this limeade sells fast at Abuela's. She makes it with fresh limes off her tree. It's tangy, sweet, and sparkly—the best thirst quencher for Puerto Rico's tropical heat.

In a 2-quart pitcher, combine the lime juice, sugar, and 4 cups water. Stir with a large spoon until all the sugar has dissolved. Refrigerate until just before serving, then add the soda and stir. Pour the limeade into glasses over ice and serve.

NOTE: *If you prefer less sweetness, substitute sparkling water or club soda.*

HORCHATA (REFRESCO DE AJONJOLÍ)

TOASTED SESAME HORCHATA

MAKES ABOUT 4 CUPS

1 cup sesame seeds

¼ cup sugar

½ teaspoon ground cinnamon (optional)

1 teaspoon pure vanilla extract (optional)

¼ teaspoon salt

Refresco de ajonjolí, also known as horchata in Puerto Rico, is a protein-rich, high-fiber beverage Abuela makes by blending toasted sesame seeds and water into a creamy, plant-based milk. Old wives' tales (and some doctors) associate it with aiding breastmilk production due to sesame's high levels of plant estrogen. Abuela used to make it for Mama when she was breastfeeding my sister and me. It's refreshing and nutritious, with a nutty, bittersweet flavor (like tahini). I enjoy it served chilled over ice, and I also use it as a "milk" base for banana smoothies.

In a medium skillet, toast the sesame seeds over medium-low heat, stirring continuously, until they're hot to the touch and start popping slightly in the pan, 5 minutes. They should be crunchy and slightly aromatic but with no color. Set aside on a plate to cool.

Transfer the cooled sesame seeds to a blender and blend on medium-high speed until they look powdery, 20 to 30 seconds. Add the sugar, cinnamon (if using), vanilla (if using), salt, and 4 cups water. Blend on high speed until the blender top feels warm and the mixture looks milky, about 1 minute.

Set a colander or fine-mesh sieve over a large pitcher or bowl and drape a piece of cheesecloth (or a nut-milk bag or clean kitchen towel) over it. Pour in the sesame mixture and twist to wring out the liquid; discard the solids. Refrigerate the horchata in an airtight pitcher or container for 2 to 4 hours before serving. Stir or shake it well and serve it chilled over ice, or use it in your favorite shakes or smoothies. The horchata will keep in the fridge for up to 5 days.

Titi's Sangría
Papa's Coco-Whisky, page 73
Tío's Mojitos, page 72

SERVES 25 TO 30

TITI'S SANGRÍA

1 (1.5L) bottle Ponte Vecckio Lambrusco, or 2 (750mL) bottles light-bodied red wine, such as pinot noir or merlot

1 (42-ounce) can pineapple juice

1½ cups vodka

1½ cups rum, preferably Don Q 151°

1 (12-ounce) package frozen orange juice concentrate, thawed

½ cup grenadine, plus more if needed

4 cups small-diced firm fruit (such as pineapple, strawberries, apples, grapes, and/or melon; optional)

Titi (Auntie) Cayita is Abuela's little sister—two true matriarchs. They look like twins. Both are petite, with shiny white hair and youthful spirits that always keep them smiling. They're like two pigeon peas in a pod. They bicker, banter, and cackle away with each other like only siblings can. I find them especially amusing after they've knocked back a couple of sangrías.

Titi's sangría is a staple at all our holiday family gatherings, like Noche Buena (Christmas Eve). Everyone in my family has as much love for Titi and her famous sangría as they do respect. It drinks like juice—but it's deceptively lethal, sneaking up on even the most well-seasoned drinkers. Growing up, my cousins (not me, I'm a saint) would conspire to sneak it behind our parents' backs, getting our own holiday buzz just in time for Santa Claus.

This is a great punch to throw together when hosting large parties. It's easy to drink and allows the host to relax with their guests without actively bartending. Be sure to warn them about its sneaky properties and to keep an eye on mischievous kids!

In a large pitcher or punch bowl, combine the wine, pineapple juice, vodka, rum, orange juice concentrate, and grenadine. Stir with a large spoon until well combined. Taste it; if necessary, add more grenadine ¼ cup at a time until you've reached the desired level of sweetness. If you're adding fruit, do so now and stir again to make sure the fruit is fully submerged. Cover and refrigerate for at least 2 hours (at least 6 hours if using fruit) before serving. Stir well before serving. Serve chilled, over ice. The sangría will keep, covered, in the fridge for up to 1 week.

TÍO'S MOJITOS

MAKES 6 TO 8 COCKTAILS

Juice of 6 limes

60 fresh mint leaves (about 10 per cocktail), plus mint sprigs for garnish

1½ cups agave syrup or simple syrup (see Note)

1½ to 2 cups white rum, preferably Don Q Cristal

1 liter club soda or sparkling water

NOTE: *To make simple syrup, stir together 1 cup sugar and 1 cup boiling water until the sugar has dissolved. Let cool to room temperature, then transfer to an airtight container and refrigerate until ready to use. It will keep for up to 3 months.*

This isn't a traditional mojito, but it's the only one I'll drink. One muggy, breezeless day, Abuela had just returned from her yard with fresh-picked limes and yerba buena leaves (a plant in the mint family) for my *tío* (uncle) to make a batch of mojitos. I was swinging on the hammock on Abuela's terrace when Tío came out to offer me one. I responded, "No, I don't like mojitos." He seemed puzzled, like it was impossible for anyone to dislike them. I explained that I enjoy their flavor, but the chunks of blackish muddled mint put me off. He said okay. Five minutes later, he handed me a tall, icy glass of a sparkly jade-green concoction. No chunks. I shrugged and tried it. It was lightly sweet, lime-y, with a cooling, minty aftertaste. He'd solved the problem by blending and straining his own cocktail mix—a mint syrup. It was the perfect day for a mojito. *Gracias por tu receta, Tío.*

Fill a medium bowl halfway with ice and water and place a small bowl on top in direct contact with the ice water. In a blender, combine the lime juice, mint leaves, and agave. Blend on medium-low speed until the mint is broken down and the mixture starts looking light green, about 30 seconds. Quickly strain the mixture through a fine-mesh sieve into the small bowl set over the ice bath. Stir the mixture until cold, about 2 minutes. (This will help preserve the bright green color from the mint.) If not using immediately, store the mint syrup in an airtight container in the fridge for up to 4 days.

Fill highball glasses with ice. To each glass, add 2 ounces of rum and 3 ounces of the mint syrup. Top with club soda, stir well, and garnish with a sprig of mint.

FOR A PASSION FRUIT MOJITO: Add 1 ounce passion fruit puree to each glass when you add the rum.

FOR A COCONUT MOJITO: Add 1 to 2 ounces full-fat coconut milk to each glass when you add the rum.

PAPA'S COCO-WHISKY

PAPA'S WHISKY AND COCONUT WATER

MAKES 1 COCKTAIL

1 large ice cube (see Notes)

2 ounces whisky or aged rum (see headnote)

2 ounces coconut water, chilled (see Notes)

This is Papa's go-to cocktail, and the "recipe" is as simple as it sounds: equal parts coconut water and whisky. But as a fine spirits enthusiast, I felt it was necessary to share why the combination just works. It starts with a hysterical performance that Papa and his brother, my tío, put on for us at Abuela's house every once in a while: Tweedle Dee knocks down coconuts from a palm tree using a rusty machete tied to a bamboo stick, while Tweedle Dum stands underneath the tree, ready to try to catch the coconuts if Tweedle Dee succeeds. If Tweedle Dum fails to catch it, he proceeds to chase after it down a hill. Their motivation is that they need their cocktail mixer: fresh coconut water. I'm not suggesting you should ever try this stunt. But coconut water makes the perfect mixer for a good-quality aged spirit. Its mild sweetness and delicate flavor dilute the alcohol just enough to make it easy to drink without masking its natural flavors.

Papa and Tío's spirit of choice is whisky. For beach days, Papa likes Johnnie Walker Black or Dewar's, served in his massive Yeti cup to keep it cold. For bougier evenings or celebrations, he prefers Johnnie Walker Blue or Macallan (also in his Yeti). I prefer Woodford Reserve bourbon for any occasion, or a nice aged rum—bonus points if it's Puerto Rican. My favorite is Ron del Barrilito.

Place the ice cube in a chilled lowball glass. Pour in the whisky and the coconut water. Swirl the glass and sip blissfully.

NOTES: *If you don't have a special tray for making large ice cubes, freeze some water in a small disposable cup instead.*

If using store-bought coconut water, make sure the only ingredient listed is 100% coconut water. If you can get your hands on a fresh young coconut, even better. Chill that MF up in the fridge, crack it open, drink some of the coconut water with a straw, and top off the rest with a healthy glug of your spirit of choice.

PIÑA COLADA

MAKES 4 TO 6 COCKTAILS

½ (15-ounce) can cream of coconut

4 cups pineapple chunks (from 1 large pineapple), frozen

4 cups ice

1½ cups (12 ounces) aged rum (I like Ron del Barrilito or Don Q añejo), preferably chilled in the freezer

½ teaspoon salt (see Note)

6 pineapple leaves, for garnish (optional)

6 Bing, Luxardo, or maraschino cherries, for garnish (optional)

Shaved fresh coconut, for garnish (optional)

Though its creator remains a subject for discussion, the piña colada is undisputably a luscious tropical vacation in a glass that originated in Puerto Rico. It's our national drink, after all, so it *had* to make an appearance in this book. We've all tasted a piña colada, and there's absolutely nothing to hate about it, especially on hot, summery days. I make it with frozen pineapple chunks instead of pineapple juice, resulting in an almost spoonable slushy consistency. If your blender is smaller, or if you don't plan to serve the drink at once, I recommend you prepare a half batch to start, then blend up the rest when glasses start looking empty.

Chill your glasses in the fridge or freezer before serving.

In a blender, combine the cream of coconut, pineapple, ice, rum, and salt. Blend on high speed until thick, smooth, and creamy, like a spoonable slushy, about 2 minutes. Use the blender tamper to get it evenly blended, if needed. Pour the piña colada into the chilled glasses and garnish each with a pineapple leaf, a cherry, and some shaved fresh coconut, if desired.

NOTE: *The salt keeps the drink icy longer and enhances all the flavors.*

LECHE DE COCO

COCONUT MILK

MAKES ABOUT 8 CUPS

8 cups diced fresh coconut meat (about 2 pounds, from about 8 ripe coconuts)

4 cups coconut water or water, plus more if needed

As delicate as she looks at ninety years old, Abuela is as hardheaded as a coconut. Her process for making coconut milk is as physically laborious, time-consuming, and tedious as it is rewarding in flavor. She goes out in the yard, gathers ripe coconuts she's spotted from her terrace, cracks them open with an axe, picks the meat out, and blends it with coconut water from the same coconuts. With her wrinkled hands, crooked from arthritis, she wrings the coconut pulp in a kitchen towel, extracting a lightly sweet, coconutty cream that's as white as the shiny hair on that hard head of hers.

I won't be cracking coconuts in my New York apartment, but with prepackaged fresh coconut meat and coconut water I purchase at the grocery store, I can achieve a very close result. When a recipe calls for only two ingredients, quality is crucial. Use this recipe in place of canned coconut milk for any of the recipes in this book.

In a blender, combine about one-quarter of the coconut chunks and about one-quarter of the coconut water. Blend on high speed until the mixture creates a vortex in the blender and looks like a thick, creamy milkshake, and the blender top feels warm to the touch, about 2 minutes. Add more water a tablespoon at a time, if necessary, to get things moving.

Place a fine-mesh sieve over a large bowl and drape a piece of cheesecloth (or a nut milk bag or clean kitchen towel) over it. Pour in the mixture from the blender and, using your hands and a lot of elbow grease, twist to extract as much liquid as possible, letting it fall through the sieve and into the bowl. Discard the coconut pulp. Repeat with the remaining coconut chunks and coconut water in three batches, then immediately transfer all the coconut milk to an airtight container and store in the fridge for up to 5 days.

Pistachio Coquito, page 80

Hazelnut Coquito, page 81

Nutella Coquito, page 80

Salty Vanilla Bean Coquito, page 80

COQUITO

Coquito (*coh-KEY-toh*) is a rum-and-coconut-based beverage enjoyed around the holidays in Puerto Rico. I refuse to call it "Puerto Rican eggnog," because it does not call for eggs, but it's a similar concept—a sweet, creamy, boozy holiday drink. Abuela makes large batches for holiday gatherings like Noche Buena (Christmas Eve). When I was a child, she'd always make a boozeless version and label it "*coquito de niños*" (kids' coquito). My *primas* (cousins) and I would dig through ice-packed Igloo coolers full of beers, Titi's Sangría (page 71), boozy coquito, and *pitorro* (Puerto Rican moonshine) for our special coquito like we were searching for a buried treasure. I think this is how the love for coquito starts for most Puerto Rican children.

Coquito isn't just a beverage—it's a sweet holiday tradition that allows for creativity, inspiring light-spirited competitions at holiday parties and on social media for who can make the best or most unique one. It's also great for gifting; I like to portion it into recycled glass bottles and embellish them with materials I have at home, like festive ribbons, ornaments, cinnamon sticks, tags, and holiday-themed adornments.

COQUITO PRO TIPS

CHOOSING YOUR VESSEL

Coquito should be shaken vigorously before serving, so anything with a tight-fitting cap or lid works. If coquito season is approaching, I wash out empty wine and spirit bottles (with their respective corks/caps) and hoard them. Mason jars also work. Abuela's batches are so big, she just recycles gallon-size plastic water jugs.

BOTTLING AND STORING

The spices and flavorings in coquito settle at the bottom after a few minutes, so if you're using multiple vessels for one batch, bottle it promptly after blending or whisking it to promote an even distribution of all the good stuff. Use a funnel to avoid spillage and leave a little room at the top to shake it. Chill your coquito for at least 6 hours or preferably overnight before serving. The longer it sits, the better it gets; it will also thicken. Store it at the back of the fridge for up to 1 month.

SERVING

Shake the coquito vigorously before serving each time to disperse the spices and flavorings that have settled at the bottom. I like serve it in dainty cordial glasses or shot glasses. I don't like serving coquito over ice, which dilutes it, so using small glasses ensures it remains chilled as you sip on it. I even keep one or two glasses in the freezer so they're cold and ready to go.

recipes continue

COQUITO DE VAINILLA SALAÍTO

SALTY VANILLA BEAN COQUITO

MAKES 8 CUPS (ABOUT 16 SERVINGS)

1 cup white rum, preferably Don Q Cristal, plus more if needed

¼ cup whisky or barrel-aged rum, preferably Ron del Barrilito, plus more if needed

1 (15-ounce) can cream of coconut

1 (14-ounce) can sweetened condensed milk

1 (13½-ounce) can full-fat coconut milk

1 (12-ounce) can evaporated milk

1½ tablespoons vanilla bean paste or pure vanilla extract

1 teaspoon ground cinnamon (or your favorite blend of ground spices)

½ teaspoon salt

2 or 3 cinnamon sticks, for bottling

In a blender, combine the white rum, whisky, cream of coconut, condensed milk, coconut milk, evaporated milk, vanilla, cinnamon, and salt. Blend on high speed until the mixture is well combined and there are no visible lumps from the coconut milk or cream of coconut, about 1 minute. (If your blender is too small for the volume of ingredients, work in batches, transferring the blended mixture to a 2-quart bowl or pitcher after each batch and whisking everything vigorously at the end until homogeneous.) Taste with a spoon, and if you're brave, add more white rum and whisky little by little as desired, blending and tasting after each addition.

When you're happy with the booziness, bottle the coquito immediately, adding 1 cinnamon stick to each bottle you use. Refrigerate for at least 6 hours or preferably overnight before serving. (See the Coquito Pro Tips on page 79 for more on bottling, chilling, and serving.) Store at the back of the fridge for up to 1 month.

FOR PISTACHIO COQUITO: Omit the evaporated milk and whisky. Reduce the condensed milk by half, the vanilla to 1 teaspoon, and the salt to ¼ teaspoon, and add 1 pint of your favorite pistachio ice cream (I like Van Leeuwen, Talenti, and Ben & Jerry's).

FOR NUTELLA COQUITO: Omit the sweetened condensed milk. Reduce the vanilla to 1 teaspoon and the salt to ¼ teaspoon, and add an entire 13-ounce jar of Nutella.

COQUITO DE AVELLANAS

HAZELNUT COQUITO

MAKES 8 CUPS
(ABOUT 16 SERVINGS)

SPICED HAZELNUT BROWN BUTTER

1 teaspoon ground cinnamon (or your favorite blend of ground spices)

2 tablespoons unsalted butter

½ cup hazelnuts, toasted and skinned

COQUITO

1 cup white rum, preferably Don Q, plus more if needed

½ cup Frangelico hazelnut liqueur

1 (15-ounce) can cream of coconut

1 (14-ounce) can sweetened condensed milk

1 (13½-ounce) can full-fat coconut milk

1 (12-ounce) can evaporated milk

1 teaspoon vanilla bean paste or pure vanilla extract

¼ teaspoon salt

2 or 3 cinnamon sticks, for bottling

Make the brown butter: Place the cinnamon in a heatproof small bowl. In a small saucepan, melt the butter over medium heat. Add the hazelnuts and cook, swirling the pan continuously, until the butter browns, becomes foamy, and has a toasty, nutty aroma, 1 to 2 minutes. Using a rubber spatula, immediately scrape the hot butter-hazelnut mixture into the bowl with cinnamon—don't leave any of those butter bits behind! (The heat from the butter will bloom the cinnamon, bringing out more of its flavor and aroma.)

Make the coquito: In a blender, combine the white rum, Frangelico, cream of coconut, condensed milk, coconut milk, evaporated milk, vanilla, and salt. Blend on high speed until the mixture is well combined and there are no visible lumps from the coconut milk or cream of coconut, about 1 minute. Scrape the hazelnut brown butter into the blender and blend on high until smooth, about 1 minute. Taste with a spoon, and if you're brave, add more white rum little by little as desired, blending and tasting after each addition.

When you're happy with the booziness, bottle the coquito immediately, adding 1 cinnamon stick to each bottle you use. Refrigerate for at least 6 hours or preferably overnight before serving. (See the Coquito Pro Tips on page 79 for more on bottling, chilling, and serving.) Store at the back of the fridge for up to 1 month.

CON EL CAFECITO

WITH COFFEE

This isn't a breakfast chapter per se, because Boricuas don't have much of a breakfast culture. Coffee, though—that's a different story, so it's no surprise that our breakfasts revolve around this beverage rather than the other way around.

I'm including my favorite recipes for Abuela's *cremitas* (porridges; pages 85–86), which are just as sweet as she is, and nostalgic for those who grew up eating them at home or ladled out of soup warmers from the school's cafeteria.

Other recipes, like the Mallorcas (page 89), quesitos (page 97), and mallorca sandwiches (page 95) are classics at panaderías, where they serve a range of sweet and savory pastries (like croquetas and pastelillos) all day long. Some of these these recipes could be served for breakfast or as a *merienda* (snack) with our ritual *café del mediodía* (midday coffee).

At the end of the chapter, I've included some recipes I've perfected over the years that fall into the category of "American-style breakfast with a Puerto Rican twist."

Cremita de Maíz,
page 86

CREMITAS

SWEET AND CREAMY PORRIDGES

Cremitas (which translates to "creamies") are heartwarming porridges made by abuelitas or sold in panaderías or cafeterias throughout Puerto Rico. This is the Boricua version of Goldilocks's porridge, and what I'd envision when Mama would narrate the fairy tale.

Even though the hot cereal packages always have directions, Abuela doesn't believe in following them. I'm sharing her tricks to achieve the creamiest porridges that are *juuuust* right, like lightly grinding her oats (for softness), simmering them in evaporated milk instead of water (for richness), and standing over the stovetop stirring continuously (to avoid lumps). The results are sweet, silky porridges that taste like warm pudding. Abuela serves cremitas plain, but when I feel like something heartier, I top them with fresh or dried fruits, nuts, granola, and a drizzle of honey or maple syrup.

CREMITA DE AVENA CON CANELA

CREAMY SPICED OATMEAL

SERVES 4 OR 5

2 cups rolled oats

4 cups evaporated milk or whole milk

½ cup sugar

1 tablespoon pure vanilla extract

½ teaspoon salt

½ teaspoon ground cinnamon, plus more for garnish

Place the oatmeal in a blender or food processor. Pulse quickly 5 or 6 times until it looks like coarse, slightly powdery breadcrumbs.

In a large pot, combine the evaporated milk, sugar, vanilla, salt, cinnamon, and 2 cups water. Bring to a gentle simmer over medium heat and cook until the liquid looks foamy and steamy, 3 to 5 minutes. While whisking continuously, slowly pour in the ground oats, then cook, still whisking, until you achieve a thick and creamy but pourable consistency, 4 to 6 minutes. If it's too thick, whisk in water 1 to 2 tablespoons at a time to thin it.

Serve immediately, in bowls, sprinkled with extra cinnamon, if desired.

recipes continue

CREMITA DE FARINA CON MANTEQUILLA

BUTTERY WHEAT PORRIDGE

SERVES 4 OR 5

4 cups evaporated milk or whole milk

½ cup sugar

1 tablespoon pure vanilla extract

½ teaspoon salt

¾ cup farina

4 tablespoons (½ stick) unsalted butter, cut into cubes

½ teaspoon ground cinnamon, for serving (optional)

In a large pot, combine the evaporated milk, sugar, vanilla, salt, and 2 cups water. Bring to a gentle simmer over medium heat and cook until the liquid bubbles slightly and begins to steam, about 5 minutes. While whisking continuously, slowly pour in the farina, then cook, still whisking, until you achieve a thick and creamy but pourable consistency, 2 to 3 minutes. If it's too thick, whisk in water 1 tablespoon at a time to thin it. Remove from the heat and whisk in the butter.

Serve immediately, in small bowls, sprinkled with the cinnamon, if desired.

CREMITA DE MAÍZ

SWEET CORN PORRIDGE

SERVES 4 OR 5

4 cups evaporated milk or whole milk

¾ cup stone-ground enriched cornmeal

¼ cup sugar, plus more if needed

1 teaspoon pure vanilla extract

1 cinnamon stick

½ teaspoon salt

½ teaspoon ground cinnamon for serving (optional)

In a large pot, combine the evaporated milk, cornmeal, sugar, vanilla, salt, cinnamon stick, and 2 cups water. Heat over medium heat, whisking continuously without stepping away, until the mixture comes to a simmer, about 5 minutes. Reduce the heat to low and cook, whisking, until thick bubbles rise to the surface and the porridge looks creamy but pourable, 5 to 10 minutes. If it's too thick, whisk in water 1 to 2 tablespoons at a time to thin it. Taste the porridge; it should be mildly sweet. If you prefer it sweeter, add more sugar 1 tablespoon at a time. It sets up quickly, so serve it immediately, in small bowls, sprinkled with the cinnamon, if desired.

TOSTADAS DE PANADERÍA CON MANTEQUILLA

BAKERY-STYLE BUTTERED TOAST

MAKES 1 TOSTADA

1 to 2 tablespoons salted butter, or 2 tablespoons unsalted plus ¼ teaspoon salt, at room temperature

1 (5- to 6-inch) piece pan de agua, or 1 hoagie, hero, or Portuguese roll, sliced in half lengthwise

Tostada in Puerto Rico refers to toasted bread. But not a sad, boring slice indolently thrown into the toaster. We mean fluffy *pan de agua* (water bread) or *pan criollo* (Creole bread) from a panadería. It comes as a two-foot-long loaf like a baguette, but softer and thicker. It's mild-flavored, which makes it a great vehicle for spreads and fillings. For our tostadas, we butter-slather the bread inside and out and grill it until golden—in essence, a butter panini. They're perfect for dunking into some cafecito foam (page 55) or scooping up molten cheese from a good cup of *chocolate caliente* (hot chocolate, page 61).

Preheat a sandwich press to medium or heat a skillet over medium heat. Slather the butter over the bread, covering the inside and outside surfaces completely. Put the bread halves back together and place in the sandwich press and cook until it's flat and toasty on both sides, 2 to 4 minutes. (If you're using a skillet, place the buttered bread in the pan and press down on it with a spatula as it cooks, then flip it and do the same on the second side, 1 to 2 minutes per side.) Slice it in half and serve hot.

MALLORCAS

SUGARY BUTTER BUNS

MAKES 12 BUNS

1 cup whole milk, lukewarm

1½ cups sugar

2½ teaspoons active dry yeast

6 large egg yolks

6 cups all-purpose flour, plus more for dusting

1½ teaspoons salt

½ cup (1 stick) unsalted butter, melted

¼ cup extra-virgin olive oil, plus more for greasing

1 large egg, beaten

½ cup powdered sugar, for dusting

Mallorcas (*mah-johr-kahs*) are highly underrated and deserving of attention. They're sweet, plush, buttery rolls we've adapted into Puerto Rican gastronomy from our Spanish ancestry. They originate from the island of Mallorca, Spain, where they are called ensaïmadas because they're made with *saïm* (Arabic for "lard"). In Puerto Rico, we mostly make them with butter. I also add olive oil, which keeps them soft and moist at room temperature. They require some time, so they're perfect for a lazy weekend baking project. You can turn them into the best breakfast sandwich you've ever had (page 95), or if they get stale, you can turn them into my guava bread pudding (page 297). If you visit Puerto Rico, be sure to stop by any panadería (Pepín is my local favorite) and order them with extra powdered sugar or as a breakfast sandwich with a cup of café con leche.

In the bowl of a stand mixer fitted with the dough hook (or in a large bowl), whisk together 1 cup lukewarm water, the milk, granulated sugar, and yeast until well combined. Let stand for 10 minutes, or until foamy on top. Whisk in the egg yolks. Using a spatula, gently incorporate the flour and salt into the milk mixture until there's no loose flour.

In a separate small bowl (or a measuring cup with a spout), whisk together half the melted butter and the olive oil.

With the mixer running on medium-low speed, pour in the butter-oil mixture in a slow, steady stream, about 1 tablespoon at a time, waiting for the dough to absorb each addition before adding the next. Scrape down the bowl as necessary. (If mixing by hand, add the butter-oil mixture to the dough in the large bowl 1 tablespoon at a time and work it in with your hands.) Increase the speed to high and mix until the dough is smooth and shiny, and starts pulling away from the sides of the bowl and climbing the dough hook, about 15 minutes. (Or knead the dough on the counter with your hands; it will be very sticky.)

recipe continues

Lightly grease a separate large bowl with olive oil. Turn the dough out onto a floured work surface and knead it, dusting it lightly with flour as necessary, until it forms a smooth ball that doesn't stick to the work surface or to your hands. When you poke the dough with your finger, it should spring back. Place it in the greased bowl and cover with a damp kitchen towel. Let rest in a warm, dark place until it has roughly doubled in size, at least 1 hour or up to 4 hours, then refrigerate for at least 6 hours or preferably overnight.

Line a 13 by 18-inch baking sheet with parchment paper. Transfer the dough to a lightly floured work surface and gently stretch it into a rough rectangle. Using a rolling pin, roll it out into an evenly thick 12 by 15-inch rectangle. Using a pizza cutter or long knife, cut the dough lengthwise into twelve 1-inch-wide strips. Working quickly, while the dough is cold, roll out one strip into a rope. Using a pastry brush or your fingers, gently smear the rope of dough with some of the remaining melted butter, coating it evenly from end to end. Form the rope into a coil, tucking the outside end underneath, and place it on the prepared baking sheet. Repeat with the remaining dough strips, spacing the coiled dough evenly on the baking sheet. Using a pastry brush, brush coils evenly on all sides and between the ridges with the beaten egg. Cover the baking sheet with plastic wrap and let rise in a warm, dark place for 30 to 40 minutes, until the buns look pillowy, plush, and bouncy and the dough springs back when gently poked with a finger. It's okay if they end up touching.

Meanwhile, place a rack in the middle of the oven and preheat to 350°F.

Remove the plastic wrap and bake the mallorcas for 20 to 30 minutes, until lightly golden and fluffy. Let cool for 10 to 15 minutes. Using a shaker or sifter, dust the mallorcas liberally with the powdered sugar. Enjoy warm or at room temperature, with a cup of freshly brewed cafecito (page 55).

SÁNDWICH DE MEDIANOCHE

PAPA'S LIFESAVING MIDNIGHT PORK SANDWICH

MAKES 1 BIG-GIRL SANDWICH

GARLIC BUTTER

½ teaspoon grated or chopped garlic (from about 1 small clove)

1 tablespoon unsalted butter, at room temperature

Pinch of salt

MUSTARD MAYO

1 tablespoon mayonnaise or Cashew Mayo (page 45)

1 tablespoon yellow mustard

SANDWICH

1 medianoche roll, sliced in half horizontally, or 2 (1-inch-thick) slices brioche, challah, or Hawaiian bread

2 to 4 slices Swiss cheese

5 or 6 dill pickle slices

½ cup leftover pulled pernil (see page 235), warmed

3 or 4 slices cooked ham

¼ cup potato sticks or hand-crushed potato chips (optional)

A medianoche is a Cuban sandwich on medianoche bread, a sweet, eggy, brioche-like roll shaped like a hoagie. It's considered late-night drunk food—hence the name, Spanish for "midnight." In Puerto Rico, we find them at panaderías, which basically makes them breakfast. They keep well for a few hours, so in my family, we'd pick them up on our way to the beach or before road trips. On one of those occasions, Papa and I were headed for a group zip-lining excursion along the Tanamá River in the northwest town of Arecibo. He wanted to treat everyone in our group to medianoches, so he packed five of the colossal sandwiches in his backpack. After going on one of those zip lines, he suffered a traumatic accident, breaking his back and ending up in the hospital. The doctors have no idea how he survived, but for all we know, the plush medianoche bread wrapped around approximately one ton of tender pork nestled in his backpack buffered the impact. The moral of the story here is: Make medianoches to stay safe.

Make the garlic butter: In a small bowl or ramekin, stir together the garlic, butter, and salt to combine.

Make the mustard mayo: In a small bowl or ramekin, stir together the mayo and mustard to combine.

Make the sandwich: Using the back of a spoon or butter knife, spread the garlic butter on the outside of the medianoche roll or slices of bread.

Heat a large pan over medium-low heat. Place the roll halves, buttered-side down, in the center of the pan and spread the mustard mayo over the tops. Place 1 or 2 slices of cheese on each half. Arrange the pickles on one half and the pernil on the other. Fold each slice of ham in half and place them directly on the pan around the bread. Cook the ham

recipe continues

NOTE: *If you have a panini or sandwich press like a George Foreman grill, feel free to assemble the entire sandwich without the potato sticks and press it until the cheese is melty on the inside and the roll is golden brown on both sides. Stuff the potato sticks between the slices after it's been pressed.*

until heated through, 20 to 30 seconds, flipping it over with tongs or a fork halfway through. Shingle the ham on the pickle half of the roll. Sprinkle the potato sticks (if using—and if you want a party in your mouth, you should be) onto the pernil half of the roll. Using a spatula, swiftly flip the pickle half onto the pernil half to sandwich everything together. Using the back of the spatula, press down lightly on the sandwich to compact it all together. Cook until the roll is an amber golden color on both sides, flipping the sandwich and pressing on it lightly as necessary to achieve this, 2 to 3 minutes more.

Transfer the sandwich to a cutting board and use a serrated knife to slice it in half. Devour immediately, or wrap it in foil and pack it up for a picnic, beach day, or road trip (but preferably not for zip-lining).

SÁNDWICH DE MALLORCA

CARAMELIZED MALLORCA BREAKFAST SANDWICH

MAKES 1 BIG-GIRL SANDWICH

2 tablespoons unsalted butter, at room temperature

1 Mallorca (page 89), sliced in half horizontally, or 2 (1-inch-thick) slices brioche, challah, or Hawaiian bread

1 or 2 slices cheddar cheese

3 or 4 slices ham

1 large egg

1 to 2 tablespoons powdered sugar

NOTE: *If you have a panini or sandwich press like a George Foreman grill, assemble the sandwich without the egg and press it. Cook the egg separately in a small pan and add it to the sandwich after it's been pressed.*

My sister and I aren't little rays of sunshine in the morning; our parents have compared waking us up for school with going to war. The announcement of this sandwich for breakfast was bribery, at best, but would get us out of bed immediately. It hits all the flavor and textural notes needed to make it addictive: sticky, chewy, sweet, salty, and drippy (from the runny egg yolk). Mama built the sandwiches and pressed them on our George Foreman grill—the *it* appliance at the time—which caramelized the sugary crust, forming a sticky brûléed shell. Counter space is prime real estate in my New York apartment, so I assemble this sandwich in a pan on the stovetop instead. If you're doing the same, make sure you have all your ingredients prepped and ready to go ahead of time so you don't burn your bread.

In a large nonstick pan, melt 1 tablespoon of the butter over medium-low heat, tilting the pan to coat the entire surface. Place the mallorca halves cut-side down on one half of the pan and toast until just golden on the bottom, 30 to 45 seconds. While they toast, crack the egg into an empty quarter of the pan. Place the ham in the last empty quarter of the pan and cook for 30 to 45 seconds. Flip the mallorca halves over and place the cheese slices on the bottom half. Using a spatula, shingle the ham on top of the cheese, pressing down on both mallorca halves to flatten them. Cook the egg until completely white around the yolk but still runny in the center, about 5 minutes, then place it on top of the ham.

Transfer the bottom half of the sandwich (with the cheese, ham, and egg) to a plate. Place the top half on top of the runny egg. Dust the top with the powdered sugar. Press down on it with your hands to pop the yolk, then use a serrated knife to slice it in half. Devour immediately, preferably with a freshly brewed cup of cafecito (page 55).

QUESITOS CON MIEL Y SAL DE MAR

SWEET CHEESE FLAKY PASTRIES WITH SALTED HONEY

MAKES 12 QUESITOS

1 (8-ounce) package full-fat cream cheese, at room temperature

½ cup honey

¼ cup powdered sugar

¼ teaspoon salt

1 large egg, beaten, for egg wash

1 (17.3-ounce) package frozen puff pastry sheets, thawed in the fridge

2 to 3 tablespoons all-purpose flour, if needed

12 (⅛-inch-thick, 3-inch-long) slices guava paste (see page 20; optional)

2 to 3 tablespoons sugar

1 tablespoon flaky sea salt

Quesitos are an iconic pastry you can find at any panadería or *repostería* (pastry shop). But when I think of these, only one place comes to mind: my alma mater, Cupeyville School in San Juan. Every day at 9 a.m., we were granted one fifteen-minute break between classes. It gave me just enough time to run down to the cafeteria and get myself a quesito, *the* best power snack (and my incentive to stay awake during morning classes). Quesitos are heavenly: a tangy cream cheese filling wrapped in buttery glazed pastry that glistens. The result is a chewy texture and sticky fingers perfect for cleaning up flyaway flakes. I've glammed up this icon by swapping the traditional syrup glaze for honey and adding a sprinkle of sea salt at the end to enhance its caramelly, floral notes.

In a medium bowl using a handheld mixer (or the bowl of a stand mixer fitted with the whisk attachment), beat the cream cheese, 2 tablespoons of the honey, the powdered sugar, and the salt on medium to medium-high speed until the mixture is smooth and there are no visible lumps, 2 to 4 minutes. (You can also do this by hand—use a rubber spatula to break up lumps first, then whisk to incorporate well.) Using a rubber spatula, transfer the cheese mixture to a piping bag or quart-size resealable plastic bag (the sandwich-size ones are too flimsy). Shake the bag lightly to force the mixture into the tip or corner of the bag, twist the top to seal it, and refrigerate while you work on the pastry. (This makes it easier and neater to fill the pastry, but you can omit this step, if you prefer—just place the bowl of filling in the fridge while you work on the pastry.)

Line two baking sheets with parchment paper.

Unfold one of the pastry sheets on a clean work surface. Using a rolling pin, gently roll it out lengthwise, then

recipe continues

NOTES: *Make sure you purchase a package that comes with two sheets of puff pastry (not phyllo dough—they're not the same). It's important that the puff pastry stays cold as you work with it, so work quickly and roll out one sheet at a time, keeping the other in the fridge. This will result in a layered, flaky quesito.*

If you're unable to get through all your baked quesitos on the first day, you can store them, covered, in the fridge for up to 1 week. Reheat in a toaster oven, air fryer, or oven at 400°F for 1 to 3 minutes, until they're hot to the touch and glistening.

crosswise. If necessary, dust it lightly with flour to keep it from sticking. Dust off any excess flour, flip the pastry sheet over, and repeat this step until you have a 10 by 15-inch rectangle. Try to avoid handling it too much—your hands are warm and will melt the butter in the pastry, so work quickly. Use a pizza cutter or sharp knife to cut the dough in half lengthwise, then in thirds crosswise, to yield 6 pieces. Repeat with the remaining pastry sheet.

If you're using guava paste, place one slice diagonally across each square of pastry. If you're piping the cheese filling, snip the tip of the bag to create an opening about ½ inch wide. Pipe or spoon half the cheese filling in a diagonal line over the guava paste (if using), leaving about 1 inch of space at both ends. Brush the beaten egg around the edges of each square.

To fold each quesito, start with the two side corners—the shorter ones—and fold them in toward the center. Then fold the third corner horizontally over the filling. Wrap the last corner over everything, tucking it underneath like you're swaddling a baby. Place the quesito on one of the prepared baking sheets. Repeat with the remaining pastry squares, placing no more than 6 quesitos on each pan and spacing them at least 3 inches apart. Refrigerate for at least 20 minutes or up to 1 day before baking.

Brush the tops and sides with the beaten egg and sprinkle generously with sugar. (At this point, the quesitos can be placed on a parchment-lined plate and frozen until solid, then transferred to an airtight container or zip-top bag and frozen for up to 2 months. Bake directly from frozen.)

Place a rack in the middle of the oven and preheat to 400°F.

Bake the quesitos one sheet at a time for 13 to 16 minutes (or 16 to 20 minutes if frozen), until puffed and golden brown. As soon as they come out of the oven, drizzle each quesito with about 1 teaspoon of the honey and brush it evenly over the surface. Crush a healthy pinch of flaky salt between your fingers and salt-bae those babies up. Repeat to bake the remaining quesitos. Let rest for 15 to 20 minutes before devouring, preferably with a freshly brewed cafecito (page 55).

ALE'S PAN DE GUINEO

ALE'S BROWN BUTTER BANANA BREAD

MAKES TWO 9 BY 5-INCH LOAVES

½ cup (1 stick) unsalted butter, cut into large chunks

2 cups mashed bananas (from 4 to 5 freckly overripe bananas)

2 large eggs

1⅓ cups sugar

1 teaspoon pure vanilla extract

2 cups pancake mix (see Notes, page 102)

Nonstick cooking spray

1 tablespoon Sugar In The Raw or cane sugar

Mantequilla de Parcha (recipe follows), for serving

This recipe started as a COVID lockdown hack. I was in Puerto Rico, flour was a hot commodity, and Abuela wouldn't stop giving me bananas from her yard. During lockdown, I'd often call my sister, Ale, to bitch about the slightest inconveniences, one of which was the lack-of-flour situation. Ale's a great home cook, and she enlightened me about how she'd been using pancake mix as a baking-flour substitute for years. This is Ale's recipe, with my own cheffy twist: the addition of browned butter. And if you don't have pancake mix, I've included a formula for a make-your-own mix using all-purpose flour. To bake this as a Bundt cake, see the Note on page 102.

Place a rack in the center of the oven and preheat to 350°F.

In a small saucepan, melt the butter over medium heat. Cook, swirling the pan continuously, until the butter browns slightly, gets foamy, and has a toasty, nutty aroma, 1 to 2 minutes. Using a rubber spatula, immediately scrape the butter into a large bowl. Don't leave any of those butter bits behind! Add the mashed bananas and whisk well to combine, then add the eggs, sugar, and vanilla and whisk until well combined. Using a spatula, fold in the pancake mix until just incorporated. Do not overmix.

Coat two 9 by 5-inch loaf pans lightly with nonstick spray, then line them with parchment paper, pressing it into the sides and bottom and leaving 2 to 3 inches overhanging the long sides. Coat the parchment and the exposed shorter sides of the pans generously with nonstick spray.

Distribute the batter evenly between the prepared pans. Smooth the top with the spatula, then sprinkle evenly with the Sugar In The Raw. Place the pans on a baking sheet and bake for 40 minutes to 1 hour, until a toothpick inserted into the center of each loaf comes out clean and the tops are golden brown. Let cool slightly, about 10 minutes, then use the overhanging parchment to remove the bread from the pans.

recipe continues

NOTES: *You can replace the pancake mix with 2 cups all-purpose flour, 1½ teaspoons salt, and 4 teaspoons baking powder; whisk to combine before using.*

To bake this in a Bundt pan, coat the pan liberally with nonstick spray, then scrape in the batter, smooth the top, and sprinkle evenly with Sugar In The Raw. Place on a baking sheet and bake as directed. Let cool slightly, then invert a large plate over the top of the pan and swiftly flip the pan and plate together to turn the bread out onto the plate.

Serve warm, with mantequilla de parcha. Store leftovers, covered, at room temperature for up to 1 day or in the fridge for up to 1 week. (I like to grill leftover slices in a buttered pan until lightly caramelized on both sides and top them with a scoop of vanilla ice cream.)

MANTEQUILLA DE PARCHA

PASSION FRUIT BUTTER

MAKES ABOUT 1 CUP

½ cup (1 stick) unsalted butter, at room temperature

6 tablespoons honey

6 tablespoons passion fruit pulp (see page 21)

½ teaspoon salt

Place the butter in a medium bowl. While whisking vigorously, slowly stream in the honey, then the passion fruit pulp, adding them little by little and whisking to incorporate thoroughly before adding more. Whisk in the salt until the mixture is smooth and homogeneous. Serve at room temperature or store in an airtight container in the fridge for up to 1 month.

PANCAKES DE QUESO Y GUAYABA CON SIROPE DE MIEL Y MANTEQUILLA

CHEESY GUAVA-STUDDED PANCAKES WITH HONEY BUTTER SYRUP

SERVES 4 OR 5

½ cup honey

2 teaspoons salt

½ cup (1 stick) unsalted butter, cut into 8 cubes

2 cups all-purpose flour

1½ teaspoons baking soda

1½ teaspoons baking powder

2½ cups buttermilk, or 1½ cups plain full-fat yogurt plus 1 cup whole milk

2 large eggs

1 teaspoon pure vanilla extract

¼ to ½ cup ghee (clarified butter), virgin coconut oil, or canola oil (see Note)

6 to 7 ounces guava paste (see page 20), cut into small dice

4 to 5 ounces fresh white cheese (such as queso del país, queso blanco, queso fresco, Halloumi, or paneer), cut into small dice

Pancakes are not Puerto Rican, but like the plane that brought me to New York in 2006, they became the vehicle to transport our sabor so it could shine. Guava and queso go together like Romeo and Juliet. As a kid, I never enjoyed this combination, but as a nostalgic Boricua and professional chef, I've realized it's genius: sweet, fruity, creamy, and salty. Studding pancakes with guava paste and cheese results in oozy pools of guava and melty cheese that crisps slightly at the edges.

Place the honey and 1 teaspoon of the salt in a medium bowl.

In a small pot, melt the butter over medium heat. Cook, swirling the pot, until foamy, slightly golden in color, and starting to smell nutty, 1 to 2 minutes. Remove from the heat. While whisking continuously, gently pour the melted butter into the bowl with the honey. Add 1 small ice cube and whisk until it melts and the mixture is well combined. Return the mixture to the pot and keep warm.

In a large bowl, whisk together the flour, baking soda, baking powder, and remaining 1 teaspoon salt to combine. In a separate medium bowl, whisk together the buttermilk, eggs, vanilla, and ⅓ cup of the warm honey butter to combine. Pour the wet ingredients into the dry ingredients and whisk until just combined. Avoid overmixing—the batter might look slightly lumpy, but that's okay.

recipe continues

NOTES: *All these fats have high smoke points, which will promote crispy edges on the pancakes. Ghee and coconut oil will impart their respective flavors, which can add depth to this dish, but I understand that they're pricey, so if you're on a budget, canola oil will do the same trick without imparting any flavor.*

If you have leftover pancakes, let them cool completely, then stack them with a small piece of parchment between each one to prevent sticking. Transfer the stack to a zip-top freezer bag and freeze for up to 2 months. Reheat in the microwave, toaster, toaster oven, or a warm skillet until heated through.

Heat a large nonstick skillet or griddle pan over medium-low heat. Add 2 to 3 tablespoons of the ghee to the pan. Working in batches of 2 or 3 at a time, scoop about ½ cup of the batter into the pan per pancake, then, working quickly, place about 10 pieces of the guava paste and about 10 pieces of the cheese on each pancake. Cook until you see bubbles on the surface of the pancakes, the edges look cooked, and the bottom is dry, cooked, and golden, 3 to 4 minutes, then quickly flip them and cook until they look puffy and golden and the cheese is slightly melted with some crispy edges peeking through, 1 to 2 minutes more. Transfer the pancakes to a baking sheet and cover with a clean kitchen towel. (To avoid deflating the pancakes, do not stack them until you're ready to serve them.) Carefully wipe out any caramelized guava or stuck-on cheese from the pan with a damp paper towel. Repeat with the remaining batter, adding more ghee between batches.

Serve immediately, with the remaining warm honey butter drizzled on top or served on the side.

GRILLED CHEESE DE GUAYABA

GUAVA GRILLED CHEESE

MAKES 1 SANDWICH

1 tablespoon unsalted butter

2 slices soft bread, such as white bread, brioche, or potato bread

2 to 4 slices mild-flavored, melty cheese, such as mild cheddar, mozzarella, muenster, Monterey Jack, or pepper Jack

4 or 5 (⅛-inch-thick) slices guava paste (see page 20)

I know, grilled cheese is an American classic. But like Puerto Ricans in the US diaspora, the guava made its way into it, and it works. The first time I made this for my niece, I immediately received her stamp of approval, along with a request for seconds. It's completely appropriate for adults as well, especially if you use pepper Jack cheese, which adds just another dimension of sazón and personality.

In a medium pan, melt the butter over medium-low heat. Add the bread and place 1 or 2 slices of cheese on each piece. Place the slices of guava paste side by side on top of the cheese on one piece of bread. Cook until the bread is lightly golden on the bottom, 1 to 2 minutes, then use a spatula to flip the cheese-only bread onto the slice with guava and press down lightly on the sandwich. Cook until the bread is deep golden on the bottom, then flip and cook until deep golden on the second side, 1 to 2 minutes on each side.

Transfer the grilled cheese to a cutting board and let rest for about 1 minute (the guava will be as hot as Puerto Rican sand on a summer day). Cut it in half and never go back to a basic-ass grilled cheese.

NOTE: *If you have a panini or sandwich press like a George Foreman grill, feel free to assemble the entire sandwich, spreading the butter on the outside, and press it until the cheese and guava are melty on the inside and the bread is golden brown.*

AREPA REVOLTILLO CON JAMÓN Y QUESO

CHEESY HAM SCRAMBLE FLATBREAD PUFFS

SERVES 1 TO 2

1 tablespoon unsalted butter

½ cup medium-diced ham steak, or 3 to 4 slices ham, cut into small dice

2 large eggs

¼ teaspoon salt

¼ cup shredded mild-flavored, melty cheese (like cheddar, mozzarella, Muenster, Swiss, Monterey Jack, or pepper Jack)

2 Arepas (page 163)

1 tablespoon thinly sliced scallion (optional)

¼ to ½ teaspoon freshly cracked black pepper (optional)

Papa always says, "*A falta de pan, galletas*" ("When there's no bread, eat crackers"). This recipe was born out of necessity when I ran out of bread but had two pieces of prerolled arepa dough on hand. I fried those babies up and topped them with cheesy soft-scrambled eggs and diced buttery ham chunks. It's naughty, a true breakfast of champs. You can take this idea and make it yours by cooking your favorite style of eggs or swapping the toppings. Just make sure to have all your ingredients prepped, ready, and close by, so you can serve the scramble on the hot, crispy arepas.

In a small nonstick pan, melt the butter over medium heat. When it sizzles, add the ham. Cook, stirring occasionally, until the ham is lightly golden and sizzling, 2 to 4 minutes. Meanwhile, in a medium bowl, combine the eggs and the salt and beat vigorously until they're foamy, about 30 seconds.

Using a spoon, transfer the ham to a paper towel–lined plate (leave the butter in the pan). Reduce the heat to low and gently pour the beaten eggs into the pan. Using a rubber spatula, immediately start stirring them in swift, circular motions until they look creamy but still a little wet and shiny, about 30 seconds. Turn off the heat, add the cheese, and stir until it melts, about 30 seconds. The eggs should still glisten and look creamy.

Spoon half the cheesy scramble onto each arepa and top with the ham. Garnish with the scallion and cracked pepper, if desired. Serve immediately and eat with your hands, like an open-faced sandwich.

ENSALADAS Y PLATOS REFRESCANTES

SALADS AND REFRESHING DISHES

For many Puerto Ricans, "salad" just means cold protein or mayo-dressed pasta or potatoes. Our diet is starch- and protein-heavy; greens and veggies are merely an afterthought. This is my favorite chapter, however, because I've focused on the salads Abuela often makes and the type of food I love to eat: fresh, light dishes with bright, zingy colors and flavors, showing a different side of Puerto Rican cuisine reminiscent of coastal beach towns.

GUINEÍTOS O YUCA EN ESCABECHE

GREEN BANANAS OR YUCA IN VINEGARY ONION MARINADE

SERVES 3 OR 4

Salt

2 to 3 pounds green bananas, peeled and cut into 1-inch-thick rounds; yuca, peeled and cut into 1 by 3-inch batons; or Yukon Gold potatoes, peeled and cut into 2-inch cubes

1 recipe Escabeche (page 49), warmed

Abuela and Abuelo's backyard is mostly taken over by a surplus of banana and plantain trees. Yuca, too. To mitigate waste, Abuela prepares her *guineítos* (green bananas) or yuca *en escabeche*, a vinegary marinade that extends their life by about one week. The result is a punchy, starchy tropical salad. Abuela prefers it warm (like a warm potato salad). But in my opinion, this dish is best served cold, the next day, when the guineítos or yuca have had a chance to soak up and get happy with the rich, sweet, tangy marinade.

In a medium pot, combine 2 quarts water, 2 tablespoons salt, and the green bananas. Bring to a boil over high heat, then reduce the heat to medium-high and cook at a gentle boil until the bananas are fork-tender (or translucent, if using yuca), about 20 minutes. Drain and transfer to a heatproof medium container with a lid. Pour the warm escabeche over them while they're hot.

If not serving immediately, let cool to room temperature, cover, and refrigerate for up to 1 week. Serve warm, at room temperature, or cold.

Tostones de Pana,
page 151

ENSALADA DE PULPO

TANGY OCTOPUS SALAD

SERVES 2 OR 3

½ cup Sofrito (page 38)

2 tablespoons salt, plus more if needed

1 pound fresh or frozen cooked octopus tentacles, sliced into ½-inch-thick coins (see Note)

½ cup minced cubanelle pepper (about 1)

½ cup minced red bell pepper (about 1 small)

¼ cup minced red onion (about ½ small)

1 tablespoon grated or chopped garlic (from about 2 large cloves)

7 pimento-stuffed Manzanilla olives, minced, plus 1 tablespoon brine from the jar

Zest and juice of 2 limes, plus more juice if needed

1 tablespoon apple cider vinegar, plus more if needed

¼ cup extra-virgin olive oil, plus more if needed

¼ cup chopped fresh cilantro

In Puerto Rico, this dish is considered a street food, and it's often sold in disposable cups at *kioskos* (food carts) along the coast. It's probably the only time you'll ever hear the word "salad"—leafy greens aren't what we're known for. It's often accompanied with crispy arepas, fried flatbreads that negate any possible greens-related health benefits. Nevertheless, it's refreshing and satisfying after a hot beach day. I learned to make this one day during COVID lockdown in New York City when I FaceTimed Abuela and my family during their lunch. They were having ensalada de pulpo with tostones, which immediately gave me an *antojo* (craving). With Abuela's guidance on the other line, I successfully re-created a huge batch to last me the rest of that week. Every quarantine day, I imagined watching a sunset over the Atlantic while I ate.

In a large pot, combine the sofrito, salt, and 2 quarts water. Bring to a boil over high heat. Add the octopus and cook until tender, about 5 minutes. Drain the octopus and transfer to a large bowl.

While the octopus is hot, add the cubanelle, bell pepper, onion, garlic, olives, olive brine, lime zest, lime juice, vinegar, olive oil, and cilantro. Toss everything well to combine. Cover with plastic wrap and marinate in the fridge for at least 6 hours or (even better) up to overnight, tossing every 1 to 2 hours.

Before serving, toss well and taste for seasoning. The octopus should be mild and sweet, with fruity hints of olive oil, a punchy flavor from the olives and vinegar, and floral notes from the cilantro. If necessary, adjust the flavor with more salt, vinegar or lime juice, and/or olive oil. Leftovers will keep, covered, in the fridge for up to 3 days.

NOTE: *Look for packaged precooked octopus tentacles in the fish section or the frozen food section of your grocery store. Sometimes it's sold presliced, which makes this dish even easier to execute.*

SERENATA DE BACALAO

SALTFISH SERENADE

SERVES 4

Serenata is a lunch staple at Abuela's. It's light, nutritious, delicious, and wallet-friendly. Serenata is slightly salty, but not fishy, and improves as it sits, so you can prepare it ahead of time. We serve it over hot, starchy vegetables to soak up all the fruity olive oil it's drenched in. To me, it's like the more laid-back, down-to-earth Latin cousin of a tuna Niçoise salad.

12 ounces bacalao (salt cod), desalted (see Note)

½ cup thinly sliced red onion

½ cup thinly sliced red or yellow bell pepper

1 teaspoon grated or chopped garlic (from about 1 large clove)

4 hard-boiled eggs, peeled and quartered

¼ cup chopped fresh cilantro

¼ cup extra-virgin olive oil, plus more if needed

Salt

1 cup large-diced avocado

1 large tomato, cut into large chunks

Boiled viandas (see pages 25–31)

Freshly ground black pepper (optional)

Place the onion in a small bowl or storage container and add water to cover. Cover and refrigerate for at least 1 hour or up to overnight (this will remove some of its pungency).

Bring a medium pot of water to a boil over medium-high heat. Drain and rinse the cod fillets. Place them in the boiling water and reduce the heat to medium-low. Simmer gently until the cod is flaky, 10 to 15 minutes.

Meanwhile, line a large bowl with paper towels. Drain the cod and rinse until cool enough to handle, then transfer to the paper towel–lined bowl to absorb excess moisture. Remove the paper towels. With clean hands, gently break up the cod into large flakes, discarding any pin bones you find.

Drain the onion and pat dry with paper towels. Add the onion, bell pepper, garlic, egg, cilantro, and olive oil to the cod. Gently toss with your hands until well combined. Cover and refrigerate for at least 2 hours or up to overnight.

Taste and season with more salt, if needed. Add the avocado and tomato and gently toss to combine. If desired, season with pepper and drizzle with more olive oil, then serve cold or at room temperature over your favorite warm viandas.

NOTE: *Bacalao is salt-cured and must be desalted before cooking. Rinse it under cold running water, rubbing off any excess salt. Place in a large container with cold water to cover by at least 2 inches. Cover and refrigerate for 8 to 48 hours, changing the water three times.*

CEVICHE DE CHILLO FRESQUESITO

FRESH SNAPPER CEVICHE

SERVES 3 OR 4 SERVINGS

1 pound skinless fresh (never frozen) wild-caught snapper fillets or other fresh wild-caught mild, flaky white fish, such as cod, mahi-mahi, or grouper

⅔ to ¾ cup fresh lime juice (from about 8 limes), chilled

¼ cup minced red onion

¼ cup minced red bell pepper

¼ cup minced yellow bell pepper

2 tablespoons chopped fresh cilantro

2 tablespoons extra-virgin olive oil, plus more if needed

¼ teaspoon salt, plus more if needed

1 to 2 teaspoons sugar, if needed

Ceviche is a Peruvian staple that's found in Puerto Rican and other Latin American countries with coastal cuisine, like Mexico and Colombia. It involves marinating raw fish in citrus juice, which cures the fish (see Note, page 120). I served this to chefs Gordon Ramsay and Richard Blais during one of my challenges on *Hell's Kitchen*; it earned me a perfect score and a win for that day.

If I'm serving this as individual appetizers, I like to spoon it over boiled sweet potato (room-temperature or cold) and top it with salty, crunchy corn for texture. If plating this as a family-style dish, I like dicing 1 cup of avocado into it for creaminess and serving it with thick corn tortilla, plantain, or yuca chips for scooping, or with hot fresh tostones (page 151) or arepas (see pages 163–164) on the side. If you purchased a whole fish, save the carcass for making Abuela's Caldo de Pescado (page 173).

Using a sharp knife, cut off any dark spots left on the fish from where the bloodline was. Using clean hands, feel for any pin bones and discard them. Cut the fish into ½-inch cubes (the size will determine the time it takes to marinate). Place the diced fish in a medium glass or ceramic bowl (not aluminum) and pour over enough lime juice to submerge it. Stir gently with a spoon so all the fish is in contact with the lime juice. Cover and refrigerate for 20 minutes. Uncover and stir; the pieces of fish should look opaque on all sides. If they're still translucent, return the bowl to the fridge and marinate in 5-minute increments for up to 45 minutes more until opaque. Drain the lime juice into a separate small bowl and set it aside.

To the bowl with the fish, add the onion, bell peppers, cilantro, olive oil, and salt. Stir gently and taste: If it's bland, add more salt a pinch at a time. If it's too acidic, add sugar about ½ teaspoon at a time. If you can't taste the fruitiness

recipe continues

NOTE: *While the acid in the citrus juice gives the fish a texture similar to cooked fish, it isn't "cooked" in the sense of being exposed to heat. The acid does kill some pathogens, but the fish is still essentially raw, so people who are pregnant or immunocompromised should avoid it. For this reason, quality and freshness are crucial—ideally, you want to use sushi-grade fish. Keeping it very cold if you're not serving it immediately is also essential.*

in the olive oil, add more oil 1 teaspoon at a time. If it needs more acid, add some of the reserved lime juice (this is called *leche de tigre*—"tiger's milk") 1 teaspoon at a time. You want to achieve a bite that's slightly tangy from the lime juice and fruity from the olive oil, with fresh notes of onion, pepper, and cilantro, while still feeling the soft texture of the fish.

Serve immediately or cover and refrigerate for up to 4 hours (but no longer than that or you'll risk "overcooking" the fish in the acid from the lime juice).

ENSALADA DE REPOLLO AL AJILLO

GARLICKY CABBAGE SALAD

SERVES 3 OR 4

½ head green cabbage (about 1½ pounds), cut into 4 wedges and cored

1 teaspoon salt

1 teaspoon grated or minced garlic (from about 1 large clove)

2 teaspoons apple cider vinegar

1½ teaspoons extra-virgin olive oil

For serving (optional)

1 large tomato, cut into large chunks

1 to 2 Hass avocados, or about ½ green-skinned avocado, peeled and cut into large dice

Flaky sea salt

This is the only "salad," in the green sense, I've ever had at Abuela's. She takes her time to slice the fresh cabbage almost impossibly thin, so it stands up like confetti. She gently tosses it with fresh garlic and a few more ingredients, creating a refreshing but hearty salad that balances the plethora of starches often present together on our table. You can also add other ingredients to spruce it up and make it your own.

Using a sharp knife or a mandoline, slice the cabbage into the thinnest shreds you can manage. Place the shredded cabbage in a large bowl, sprinkle with the salt and garlic, and drizzle with the vinegar and olive oil. Using clean hands, gently toss it from the bottom up until the garlic is well dispersed and the cabbage is evenly coated with the oil and vinegar. Serve immediately or cover and refrigerate for up to 1 day. If using tomatoes and/or avocados, arrange them on top just before serving and sprinkle lightly with flaky salt.

ENSALADA DE PEPINO Y AGUACATE

HERBY CUCUMBER AND AVOCADO SALAD

SERVES 3 OR 4

This refreshing salad is a great start to or accompaniment for a hearty Puerto Rican meal. Its tanginess and floral flavors brighten the palate, preparing it for other bold and hearty components. To make my life easier, I often make it with chimichurri left over from previous meals. This is also a great opportunity to use up random herbs you may have in the fridge from previous days' meals—win-win. I like serving this cold salad over warm boiled viandas—breadfruit is my favorite, but any of those from pages 25–31 will do. The bright, fresh flavor and juice from the herby cucumbers soaks into the starchy roots, which makes for an interesting combination of bright, fruity flavor and textures—and a hearty snack or wholesome plant-based meal.

2 large green cucumbers, peeled, halved lengthwise, seeded, and cut into ¼-inch-thick slices

½ cup Chimichurri (page 47, made without chorizo)

Zest and juice of 2 limes or 1 juicy lemon

¼ cup chopped fresh herbs (such as parsley, cilantro, chives, scallions, mint, tarragon, dill, or a mix; optional)

½ teaspoon salt, plus more if needed

1 ripe green-skinned avocado, or 2 ripe Hass avocados

In a medium bowl, combine the cucumbers, chimichurri, lime zest, lime juice, herbs (if using), and salt. Stir gently until well combined. Cover and refrigerate for at least 2 hours or up to 4 days.

When you're ready to serve, stir the salad well and taste for seasoning. It should be punchy and tangy from the lime, with hints of garlic, and bursting with fresh, floral flavors from the herbs. If needed, adjust the seasoning with more salt, adding it pinch by pinch and stirring/tasting after each addition.

Cut the avocado into medium dice and gently stir it in. Serve within 4 hours, before the avocado browns.

TROPICAL CAPRESE SALAD

SERVES 2 GENEROUSLY

2 tablespoons olive oil

1 (7-ounce) package queso del país, queso fresco, or any mild, fresh grilling cheese like Halloumi, cut into ¼-inch-thick slices

2 pounds any fresh, sweet, ripe, fleshy fruit (tomatoes, avocado, mango, papaya, star fruit, or peaches would all work), pitted or seeded (if necessary) cut into ¼-inch-thick slices

½ cup Chimichurri (page 47 made without chorizo), at room temperature

Flaky sea salt

I created this recipe during a time when the only thing certain for me was that I loved my family and needed to be close to them. I'd just arrived in Puerto Rico after one month of solo quarantine during covid in New York. While I completed my two week quarantine in Puerto Rico, my family sent me a welcome package with a year's worth of food and supplies. I had a surplus of tomatoes, a package of queso del país (our version of queso fresco), and some culantro from Abuela's yard. I turned that culantro into chimichurri, grilled up that cheese, and diced up those tomatoes. The result was reminiscent of an Italian caprese, but better. I had tomatoes that day, but any fleshy, sweet tropical fruit will do the trick.

In a large sauté pan, heat the olive oil over medium heat. Tilt the pan to coat with the oil, then place the cheese in the pan in a single layer, spacing the slices out. Cook, undisturbed, until golden brown on the bottom, 1 to 2 minutes. Using tongs or a spoon, flip the cheese and cook until golden brown on the second side, 1 to 2 minutes more. Transfer the cheese slices to a clean, dry plate.

Shingle the fruit over a large serving platter or two large individual plates. Arrange the warm grilled cheese slices between the fruit and evenly throughout the platter. Spoon over the chimichurri so every bit of fruit and cheese gets a drizzle. Sprinkle everything with flaky salt and serve.

DIPS Y ANTIPASTOS

DIPS AND SPREADS

It's no secret that Puerto Ricans like to party. Whether on the road or at a get-together, we always have an occasion to celebrate. When I think of these of fun times, I think of dips—they're versatile, and make hosting fuss-free. They're also portable, making them easy to transport when on the move, like for a weekend road trip, picnic, or beach day.

Some of these recipes, like Antipasto de Pollo o Atún (chicken or tuna salad, page 131), are inspired by *las mesas de entrememeses* (appetizer tables) at birthdays and *marquesina* (open garage) parties. Mezcla (page 129) is a classic spread we use for our famous *sandwichitos* (party sandwiches), but I also served it as a dip with buttery crackers. Humus de Gandules (page 137) is inspired by its Middle Eastern cousin, using Puerto Rican ingredients.

Whatever the occasion, these are all easy to make and *so much better* than any store-bought stuff. Next time you have a get-together, serve (or bring) a few of these along with an assortment of interesting chips or other "dippers."

Sandwichitos de Mezcla, page 130

Mezcla

MEZCLA

PARTY SANDWICH SPREAD

MAKES ABOUT 3 CUPS

1 (12-ounce) can Spam luncheon meat, cut into large chunks

1 (8-ounce) package mild cheddar cheese, cut into large chunks

1 (4-ounce) can or jar roasted red peppers (pimientos morrones), drained (liquid reserved)

½ cup mayonnaise or Cashew Mayo (page 45)

Crackers and crudités, for serving (optional)

No party in Puerto Rico is complete without a tray (or five) of *sandwichitos* (party sandwiches). These tea-size mini sandwiches are made with a creamy orange spread that, as a kid, I found as addictive as it was mysterious. In my mid-twenties, I finally solved the mystery: *Spam*, cheese, and roasted peppers are pureed together into a creamy spread sandwiched between soft white bread. Think of pimento cheese and pâté having a baby—that's mezcla. It sounds odd, and it's a guilty pleasure, for sure!

You can prepare this as a spread for my iconic sandwichitos de mezcla (see page 130) or use it as a dip for crackers or crudités.

In a food processor or blender, combine the Spam, cheddar, roasted peppers, and mayo. Process or blend on high speed until the mixture looks creamy, smooth, and spreadable, 1 to 2 minutes. To get the ingredients moving, if necessary, stream in the liquid from the roasted peppers while the food processor or blender is running. Use the blender tamper to help things along as well. Scrape down the sides and process or blend again until you achieve an even, homogeneous, spreadable mixture that resembles creamy peanut butter. If necessary, adjust the consistency with more of the reserved pepper liquid, adding it little by little. Transfer the mixture to a large (1-quart) airtight container, cover, and refrigerate for at least 4 hours before serving. It will keep in the fridge for up to 1 week. Use for sandwichitos or serve as a dip for crackers and crudités.

recipe continues

FOR SANDWICHITOS DE MEZCLA (PARTY SANDWICHES): Line two or three large serving trays or containers with lightly dampened paper towels. Form an assembly line in this order (from left to right): 2 pounds sliced white bread (about 2 loaves), the mezcla, a cutting board with a serrated knife, and the paper towel–lined trays. At this point, you may want to grab a couple of Medalla beers—you'll be here for a bit—blast some Bad Bunny, and summon a family member or friend to help you. One person can spread and sandwich the mezcla, the other can cut the sandwiches and arrange them on the tray. Using a butter knife, spread about 2 tablespoons of the mezcla onto each slice of bread, then place another slice on top. Place the sandwich on the cutting board and, using the serrated knife, cut off the crusts (save them for snacking on with your beer). Slice the sandwich into 4 small triangles (squares are for squares) and place them on the prepared trays. Repeat until you've used up all your mezcla or bread, whichever happens first. Cover the sandwiches with additional, slightly damp paper towels and cover the trays with lids or plastic wrap. Refrigerate the sandwichitos for at least 2 hours or up to overnight before serving. *Makes about 50 sandwichitos.*

ANTIPASTO DE POLLO O ATÚN

TANGY CHICKEN OR TUNA SALAD

MAKES ABOUT 4 CUPS

½ teaspoon salt, plus more as needed

12 ounces chicken breast (about 1 large), or 1 (12½-ounce) can chicken or tuna, drained

¼ cup extra-virgin olive oil

1 cup minced carrots (about 2 large)

1 cup minced onion (about 1 medium)

¼ cup Sofrito (page 38)

8 pimento-stuffed olives, minced, plus 1 tablespoon brine from the jar

2 teaspoons brined capers, drained and minced

1 cup ketchup

⅓ cup apple cider vinegar

2 to 4 tablespoons honey

Antipasto de pollo is one of the usual suspects on the *entremeses* (appetizer) table at Puerto Rican birthday parties and usually hangs around Ritz crackers (for topping) or is used as a filling for *barquillitas* (savory cones). It's sweet, savory, tangy, and often served cold—very refreshing for hot tropical days. The crunchy contrast from the cones makes it addictive and almost impossible to have just one. Pros like me will post up on a chair with a Medalla beer, some sandwichitos de mezcla (see oppoite), and this salad close at hand. You can shred the chicken yourself or use canned chicken or tuna, and you can make the salad up to 5 days in advance—it gets better as it sits. For a healthy, easy weekday snack or meal alternative, I use it to jazz up my green salads or serve it as a filling for lettuce wraps topped with slices of avocado.

If using chicken breast, in a medium pot, combine 4 cups water and 1 tablespoon salt. Cover and bring to a boil over high heat. Add the chicken breast, cover, and reduce the heat to medium-low to maintain a gentle simmer. Cook for 30 minutes, or until you can pull apart the chicken with two forks. Drain and let cool. Using clean hands, shred the chicken as thin as you can. Transfer to a medium bowl, cover, and refrigerate while you make the sauce.

In the same pot, heat the olive oil over medium heat for 1 to 2 minutes. Add the carrots and onion and cook, stirring, until the onion is soft and translucent, and the carrots are slightly softened, 3 to 5 minutes. Add the sofrito, olives, olive brine and capers and cook until the moisture has evaporated, 1 to 2 minutes more. Add the shredded chicken (or the drained canned chicken or tuna) and the salt. Cook, stirring, until the ingredients are evenly incorporated and the mixture has started sizzling, 2 to 3 minutes. Add the ketchup and vinegar and simmer until it looks saucy and homogeneous,

recipe continues

Antipasto de Pollo
Dip de Pollo y Cilantro, page 136

2 to 3 minutes more. Add water 1 to 2 tablespoons at a time as needed, until it's saucy.

Taste for seasoning; it should be slightly sweet from the ketchup and tangy from the vinegar, with savory notes from the olives and capers. If needed, add more salt pinch by pinch and/or lightly drizzle with honey to balance the acidity, tasting between additions. Transfer to a 1-quart storage container and let cool to room temperature, about 1 hour. Cover and refrigerate for at least 4 hours before serving. It will keep in the fridge for up to 5 days.

Three-Ingredient Guac (page 145)

Dip de Guayaba y Queso

Humus de Gandules (page 137) topped with Salsita Criolla (page 48)

DIP DE GUAYABA Y QUESO CON MIEL

CREAMY GUAVA AND HONEY DIP

MAKES ABOUT 2 CUPS

4 ounces guava paste (see page 20), cut into pea-size pieces

1 (8-ounce) package full-fat cream cheese, at room temperature

½ cup plain full-fat Greek yogurt or sour cream

2 tablespoons honey

½ teaspoon salt

Sweet, fruity, creamy, and salty, guava and cheese is a standard flavor combo throughout Latin America. This dip is a testament to that. Ready in less than 10 minutes, you simply whiz together all the ingredients in a blender or food processor. It's slightly sweet, creamy, and tangy with a stunning natural pink hue. I love serving it on an appetizer table alongside other dips—its sweet flavor adds a fun contrast to the usual savory spread. For dipping, I recommend María cookies, Ritz crackers, plain or cinnamon-sugar pita chips, or crostini.

In a food processor or blender, combine about three-quarters of the guava paste with ¼ cup hot water and process or blend until smooth. Add the cream cheese, yogurt, honey, and salt and process again until smooth, about 1 minute, scraping down the bowl halfway through. (Alternatively, combine the guava and hot water in a small pot and cook over medium heat, stirring continuously, until the guava dissolves into a spreadable consistency, about 5 minutes. Scrape it into a large bowl, add the cream cheese, and stir or whisk until smooth. Add the yogurt, honey, and salt and stir or whisk to combine.)

Scrape the dip into a small serving bowl and stud the top with the rest of the guava pieces. Serve immediately or cover and refrigerate for up to 1 week.

DIP DE POLLO Y CILANTRO CREMOSO

CREAMY CILANTRO CHICKEN DIP

MAKES ABOUT 3 CUPS

½ teaspoon salt, plus more as needed

12 ounces chicken breast (about 1 large), or 1 (12½-ounce) can chicken, drained

1 cup coarsely chopped fresh cilantro (about ½ bunch), plus more for serving

½ cup plain full-fat Greek yogurt or sour cream

¼ cup mayonnaise or Cashew Mayo (page 45)

1 teaspoon grated or chopped garlic (from about 1 large clove)

1 tablespoon fresh lemon juice

1 tablespoon extra-virgin olive oil, plus more for serving

1 tablespoon honey, plus more if needed

This recipe requires a few easy steps: Shred some cooked chicken; blend yogurt, cilantro, and a few other ingredients; pour them over the chicken; stir; and refrigerate for a couple of hours. Voilà. I like to serve this with *barquillitas* (savory cones), sturdy chips (like bagel or pita chips), toasted bread, hot tostones (page 151, or arepas (pages 163–164). When I have leftovers, I make myself a meal like a chicken salad sandwich or chicken lettuce wraps topped with avocado, pickled onions (page 50), and other fresh veggies.

If using chicken breast, in a medium pot, combine 4 cups water and 1 tablespoon salt. Bring to a boil over high heat. Add the chicken breast, cover, and reduce the heat to medium-low to maintain a gentle simmer. Cook for 30 minutes, or until you can pull apart the chicken with two forks. Drain and let cool. Using clean hands, shred the chicken as thin as possible. Transfer to a medium bowl, cover, and refrigerate while you make the sauce.

In a blender, combine the cilantro, yogurt, mayo, garlic, lemon juice, olive oil, honey, and salt. Blend on high speed until the mixture looks smooth and bright green, 30 to 45 seconds. (Don't overblend or the cilantro will darken.) Pour the mixture over the chicken and stir to combine.

Taste for seasoning. It should be lemony and slightly tangy from the yogurt, with grassy notes from the cilantro. If needed, add more salt pinch by pinch, and/or lightly drizzle with honey to balance the acidity, tasting after each addition. Transfer to a 1-quart storage container and let cool to room temperature, about 1 hour. Cover and refrigerate for at least 4 hours before serving; it will keep in the fridge for up to 3 days.

If you like, drizzle lightly with olive oil and garnish with more cilantro before serving.

HUMUS DE GANDULES

PIGEON PEA HUMMUS

MAKES ABOUT 2 CUPS

⅓ cup extra-virgin olive oil

¼ cup Sofrito (page 38)

2 tablespoons grated or chopped garlic (from about 4 large cloves)

1 teaspoon dried oregano, plus more if desired

½ teaspoon adobo, homemade (page 36) or store-bought

½ teaspoon ground cumin, plus more if desired

1 (15.5-ounce) can pigeon peas, drained (liquid reserved)

Salt

2 tablespoons chopped fresh cilantro

My pigeon pea hummus is inspired by its Middle Eastern counterpart, traditionally made with chickpeas. It comes together quickly and highlights pigeon peas—an iconic legume in Puerto Rico that grows wild at Abuela's house. If you want to get fancy, you can also top it with a few tablespoons of my Salsita Criolla (page 48) or chimichurri (page 47) for an added layer of sabor. I like serving this with thick plantain or yuca chips, warm pitas, bagel chips, or crostini.

In a small pot, heat ¼ cup of the olive oil over medium-low heat for about 2 minutes. Add the sofrito and stir-fry until it's aromatic and all the moisture has evaporated, about 2 minutes. Add the garlic, oregano, adobo, and cumin and cook, stirring, just until the garlic is aromatic, about 1 minute. Using a rubber spatula, scrape the mixture into a blender or food processor and add the pigeon peas. Pour in ½ cup of the reserved pigeon pea liquid. Blend on low speed, slowly increasing to high and scraping down the sides halfway through, until the mixture looks velvety smooth, about 1 minute. If needed, add more pigeon pea liquid 1 tablespoon at a time until you get a vortex going and the mixture has a creamy (but not runny) consistency, like hummus. Taste and add salt a pinch at a time until you can taste the sweet onions, garlic, spices, and nutty flavor of the pigeon peas.

Scrape the hummus into a serving bowl and spread it evenly with the back of a spoon, creating ridges to hold olive oil. Gently drizzle on the remaining olive oil, top with the cilantro, and sprinkle lightly with cumin and oregano, if desired, then serve.

DIP DE CAMARONES O LANGOSTA AL LIMÓN

ZESTY SHRIMP OR LOBSTER DIP

MAKES ABOUT 4 CUPS

1 tablespoon plus ½ teaspoon salt

1 pound peeled and deveined raw shrimp, or 1½ pounds uncooked lobster tails (see Note)

1 cup small-diced celery

½ cup coarsely chopped fresh cilantro, plus more for serving

½ cup full-fat coconut milk

¼ cup mayonnaise or Cashew Mayo (page 45)

Zest of 1 lime or lemon

2 tablespoons fresh lime or lemon juice (from about 1 lime or ½ lemon)

NOTE: *To save time, you can substitute 1 pound precooked shrimp or lobster meat (or a mix), finely chopped.*

This is one of my go-to recipes for hot summer days, road trips, or beachy weekend escapes. I make it a few hours ahead of time to allow the flavors to combine and chill. You can use your choice of lobster, shrimp, or both, and even purchase the meat precooked. I make a creamy, zingy citrus sauce to pour over the mildly sweet crustaceans. The result is bright, bouncy, and scoopable, versatile enough to use as a dip for sturdy chips (like pita chips), as a sandwich filling, in lettuce wraps (for a girl-dinner situation) or as a topping for hot tostones (page 151), Arepas (page 163), or Arepas de Coco (page 166), as shown here.

In a medium pot, combine 4 cups water and 1 tablespoon of the salt and bring to a boil over high heat. Fill a medium bowl with 2 cups ice and 2 cups water. Add the shrimp or lobster to the boiling water and reduce the heat to medium-low. Simmer until the shrimp are pink and opaque, 1 to 2 minutes, or the lobster tails are bright red, 4 to 5 minutes. Transfer the shrimp or lobster to the ice bath to stop the cooking, then drain and transfer them to a paper towel–lined plate to absorb most of the moisture. If using lobster tails, pick the meat out and discard the shells. Finely chop the shrimp or lobster meat and place it in a medium bowl with the celery.

In a blender or food processor, combine the cilantro, coconut milk, mayo, lime zest, lime juice, and remaining ½ teaspoon salt. Blend on medium speed or process until it looks smooth with tiny green cilantro flecks scattered throughout, 30 to 45 seconds. (Don't overblend or the cilantro will darken.) Pour the coconut milk mixture over the shrimp or lobster and celery and stir to combine. Cover and refrigerate for at least 4 hours or up to 1 day. Garnish with more cilantro, if desired, and serve.

CHILI DE CARNE

MAMA'S LIFE-SAVING CHILI

SERVES 3 OR 4

3 tablespoons olive oil

1 pound ground beef (90/10), ground chicken, or ground turkey

1 tablespoon adobo, homemade (page 36) or store-bought

1 tablespoon chili powder

1½ teaspoons ground cumin

½ teaspoon chipotle powder (optional)

¾ cup Sofrito (page 38)

1 tablespoon tomato paste

2 cups small-diced fresh tomatoes (about 1 large), or 1 (14.5-ounce) can stewed tomatoes

1 (15.5-ounce) can beans (such as pink, pinto, kidney, or black beans), undrained

1 cup light beer (like Medalla), chicken broth, beef broth, or vegetable broth

¼ cup chopped fresh cilantro or scallion, for serving

When I was in high school, one of my best friends invited our graduating class to her house for a farewell party. Everyone was assigned something to bring. I was famous for my *cielito lindo*—a layered, Tex-Mex-style dip—so I was in charge of that. The day of the party, Mama got off work late and couldn't make it to the grocery store in time to get the ingredients I needed. I knew that altering the appetizer table plan would set off a chain of comments from my friend, who was fiercely perfectionist and always wanted things done just so. I was so afraid of her wrath, I told Mama I wouldn't go to the party. In an effort to console me and remedy the situation, Mama made me a big batch of her chili (with mostly shelf-stable ingredients *did* have). She drove me to the party with that, along with a bag of shredded cheese and chips that we picked up at the gas station. She instructed me to serve it in batches that I was to reheat in the microwave and top with cheese. The chili didn't even sit on the table long enough to get cold. It was the first appetizer to be gone. Mama's chili was the star of the appetizer table, and on that day, I graduated from cielito lindo girl to chili girl.

You can serve this over white rice (page 205), a baked potato, or hot dogs, on loaded nachos, or with cornbread, or top it with cheddar cheese and serve it with thick tortilla chips on the side for scooping.

In a large pan, heat the olive oil over medium-high heat until the oil smokes. Add the ground beef and sprinkle with the adobo, chili powder, cumin, and chipotle powder (if using). Cook, breaking up the meat as it cooks, until all the spices are well incorporated and the meat looks loose (not clumpy), browned, and almost crispy, 5 to 8 minutes. Add the sofrito and cook, stirring, until the moisture has evaporated, 3 to 4 minutes. Add the tomato paste and cook, stirring to coat all the meat evenly, until the tomato paste looks brickred in color and smells sweet, 2 to 3 minutes. Stir in the diced tomatoes, the beans (with their liquid), and the beer. Bring to a boil, then reduce the heat to maintain a low simmer. Cook, uncovered, until the liquid has reduced by half and the chili looks thick and saucy, 15 to 20 minutes. Sprinkle with the cilantro and serve.

DIP DE HABICHUELAS

VELVETY BEAN DIP

MAKES 1 CUP

1½ cups leftover Habichuelitas Guisadas con Calabaza (page 193)

1 teaspoon apple cider vinegar

1 tablespoon extra-virgin olive oil, plus more to taste

½ teaspoon freshly ground black pepper, plus more to taste

This dip is a sazón-packed alternative to hummus. I first made it when a friend visited unexpectedly. She announced via text that she would drop by in 10 minutes. Immediately, I sprung up, changed into civilized clothing, and ran to my fridge. I had some leftover beans I'd made a few days prior, but no dippers. I reached for a frozen loaf of sourdough; drizzled that baby up with olive oil, salt, and cracked pepper; and threw it under the broiler. While it toasted, I whizzed the beans in the blender until they were velvety-smooth, then dressed them up with some leftover chimichurri (page 47) and pickled red onions (page 50). You can also sprinkle these with fresh herbs or spices like ground cumin or dried oregano, or crumble some queso fresco or feta on top. My friend arrived just as I pulled the warm, toasty bread out of the oven. My dip was our first conversation topic. She inquired about my inspiration for it. I explained that in Puerto Rico, we call this "De La Manga Productions," which means I pulled it out of my sleeve.

If you used ham in your beans, try to pick out all the pieces and set them aside. Using a large spoon, scoop the beans out of their stewy sauce and drop them into a blender or food processor. Add the vinegar, olive oil, and pepper. Blend or process on high speed until the mixture is silky smooth, about 1 minute. If the mixture seems too thick, blend in some of the stewy sauce from the beans. Taste; it should be savory and smoky from the ham or smoked paprika in the beans, with sweet notes from the squash and brightness from the vinegar. Adjust the seasoning with more salt and/or vinegar, if necessary, to bring out those flavors. Whiz it again until you get there. Scoop into a serving bowl or to-go container and garnish with the reserved ham (if you used it) and additional garnishes of choice (see headnote). This dip will keep in an airtight container in the fridge for up to 1 week from the date you cooked the beans.

Dip de Guayaba y Queso, page 135

GUACAMOLE

THREE-INGREDIENT GUAC

MAKES ABOUT 1 CUP

1 large ripe Hass avocado, cut into chunks

2 tablespoons Sofrito (page 38)

Zest and juice of 1 lime

Salt

While this recipe is not Puerto Rican, it's one of the many ways you can apply the power of sofrito and our sazón. It's a great trick to keep up your sleeve when you're short on time but want to prepare a delicious snack that does not fall short on flavor. Yes, making the guac seems effortless now, but don't forget, you already went through the trouble of making the sofrito—so pat yourself on the back. "You go, Glen Coco!"

Place the avocado, sofrito, and lime zest and juice in a medium bowl. Add a healthy pinch of salt and mash with a fork to your desired consistency (I prefer it on the chunky side). Taste: It should be slightly tangy from the lime with pungent hints of garlic, sweetness from the peppers, and grassiness from the cilantro in the sofrito. If needed, add more salt pinch by pinch, stirring and tasting after each addition. Serve immediately, or flatten with the back of a spoon and press a piece of plastic wrap directly on the surface of the guac (to prevent browning), cover, and store in the fridge for up to 1 day.

FRITURAS

FRITTERS

Frituras are endless throughout the island. They're such an obsession that locals visit certain towns just to nibble on them while sitting by the shore. I'm referring to the kioskos or *chinchorros* (food stalls) in Loíza and Luquillo, hubs to our African ancestors' culture. We even have a pastime called *chinchorrear*, a verb that refers driving in a caravan of cars throughout the island, hopping from chinchorro to chinchorro. Glass showcases display a variety of these crispy, handmade delicacies. It's so hard to pick just one that you don't. Pros like me will order one of each and share them with *el corillo* (the crew). I like to wash them down with a Medalla, our local beer, or coconut water from a freshly cracked coconut (if you're smart, you'll ask the vendor to top off your coconut with a splash of rum).

I start off this chapter with a guide to frying—an art that requires skill and craft. Abuela Sara has the magic touch, and she taught me all her expert tips and tricks. I'm including them here, along with some nerdy facts I learned in culinary school. The result will be visually stunning frituras that are perfectly cooked on the inside, crispy and *volaíta* (airy) on the outside, and, most important, packed with sabor.

This chapter embodies the essence of Puerto Ricans: fun, delicious, snappy, complex, and down to earth. These are merely a selection of my personal favorites.

A GUIDE TO FRYING

I know deep-frying may seem daunting. It can be dangerous, messy, and tricky. But there are some simple steps you can take to seamlessly achieve crispy, airy frituras like the ones you'd find at los kioskos.

EQUIPMENT

If you don't have a deep fryer (most of us don't), there's no need to panic. All you'll need is a heavy-bottomed pot like a caldero (see page 16), Dutch oven, or large stainless-steel pot—these vessels retain heat evenly, which allows you to keep the frying oil at the temperature necessary to achieve crispiness. I'd also suggest you use a kitchen thermometer, which will make it a lot easier to control your oil temperature.

AVOIDING MOISTURE

Believe it or not, frying is a dry cooking method, and moisture is the enemy of hot oil. To avoid painful splatters, always ensure that your cooking vessel and tools are dry before heating the oil, and make sure the food you're frying is free of excess moisture before you place it in the hot oil.

OILS

For frying, I prefer using neutral-flavored oils (like canola, sunflower, peanut, or vegetable oil), which have a high smoke point and don't impart flavor to my fritters. Make sure your oil is clean, clear, and fresh (not old or rancid). You can tell by the color (dirty oil turns darker and cloudy) and the aroma (it should be odorless).

CONTROLLING HEAT

Whether your stove is gas or electric can affect the speed at which it heats oil. The optimal oil temperature for crispiness when frying is 350°F; depending on the stovetop, the heat setting can range from medium to medium-low. For some recipes, your oil temperature may need to be lower—about 325°F; this setting can range from medium-low to low heat. In either case, and if you're a fritura rookie and don't have a deep fryer, use a kitchen thermometer to gauge your temperatures properly.

Always wait for your oil to come up to temperature before frying. This will prevent the food from absorbing excess oil, which will result in greasy fritters. To check your oil temperature, add a test fritter or portion of dough to the hot oil:

- No bubbles or movement means the oil isn't hot enough. This will result in soggy, greasy fritters. Wait for the oil to come up to temperature.

- Gentle, simmery bubbles without smoke is usually the sweet spot. Watch your fritter and the speed at which it colors. If it's perfectly cooked inside and out, keep the heat where it is and continue frying. If it's still raw in the center, you may need to reduce the heat. This will depend on the size and density of your fritters.
- Rapid, rolling bubbles with smoke often mean the oil is too hot. Reduce the heat and wait for it to cool down before proceeding.

You never want your frying oil to smoke. First, you'll end up burning your food's exterior without properly cooking the interior. Second, it can cause a fire. (If you ever start a grease fire, don't try to put it out with water. Depending on the size of the fire, turn off the heat, carefully cover it with a metal lid or baking sheet to smother it, and if needed, evacuate and call 911.)

OVERCROWDING

Crowding the pot or deep fryer will lower the temperature of your oil, thus raising the cooking time and the likelihood that the food will absorb oil. To avoid this, fry in smaller batches.

LANDING SURFACE

Before you start frying, make sure you've prepared a place to set the fritters as they come out of the oil. Line a plate or baking sheet with paper towels to absorb oil, or set a wire rack or colander over a baking sheet to let them drain.

REUSING FRYING OIL

Let it cool to room temperature, then strain it through a fine-mesh sieve to remove any bits of food left behind. I usually pour the oil back into its original container and store it at room temperature until I'm ready to use it again. Repeat this process every time you fry to prolong its use. You can recycle your oil for as long as it looks clean and translucent, and has no odor.

DISCARDING FRYING OIL

If the frying oil is no longer usable, let it cool to room temperature, then pour it into a disposable container (I use its original container). Seal it tightly to avoid leaking and discard it in the trash. Don't pour any oil, hot or cold, directly into the trash or down the drain.

TOSTONES

TWICE-FRIED GREEN PLANTAIN OR BREADFRUIT

MAKES 12 TO 14 TOSTONES

Salt

2 large green plantains, peeled and cut into 1½-inch-thick cylinders, or ½ large mature breadfruit, peeled, cored, and cut into golf ball–size chunks

2 quarts neutral oil, such as canola or sunflower oil

Tostones are ubiquitous at any Puerto Rican dinner table. These twice-fried smashed plantains (or breadfruit) are less a recipe than they are a technique. After years of trailing Abuela and learning the tricks to take them from yummy to legendary, I know it requires finesse. Growing up, I remember her shouting to my grandfather working in the yard downstairs, "Jose! Knock down some plantains!" Minutes later, he'd walk in with a whole freshly cut bunch, which Abuela would transform into golden-yellow discs with a crisp, *volaíto* (airy) exterior and plush interior. These pair perfectly with Mayo-Ketchup (page 45), but you can also top them with chimichurri (page 47), guac (page 145), or Ajillo (page 51) like the ones served at our famous Chino (Chinese) Boricua restaurants.

In a medium bowl, stir together 4 cups water and 1 tablespoon salt until the salt has dissolved. Submerge the plantains in the water for 10 minutes.

Cut two 8-inch squares of parchment paper. Pour the oil into a medium-large pot or a deep fryer and heat over medium-low heat to 325°F (check out my Guide to Frying on page 148 for tips). Using tongs, remove one piece of plantain at a time from the salt water, pat it dry with a paper towel, and place it in the hot oil, spacing each piece about ½ inch apart to avoid overcrowding. (Reserve the saltwater solution.) The oil should bubble gently when you add the plantain. Fry until they're bright yellow but not browned, soft on the inside, and can be pierced with a fork with no resistance, 7 to 10 minutes (flip them halfway through if they're not fully submerged in the oil). If you're unsure of the doneness, try smashing one (see below). When you're done frying all the plantains, increase the heat to medium and bring the oil to 350°F.

recipe continues

NOTE: *I know it seems odd to add moisture right before frying, but dipping the tostones in the saltwater solution does two things: it seasons the porous starch from within, and the steam from the water will cause the exterior of the tostón to separate from the soft, pillowy interior, creating an airy crust. Please wear an apron and be careful of oil splatters.*

Smash your tostones while the fried plantains are hot (this will prevent them from breaking). Place the two squares of parchment paper on either side of the fried plantain. Using a tostonera (see page 16), gently smash the plantain to a ¼-inch thickness. Peel off the parchment from either side, set the pressed tostón aside, and repeat with the remaining plantains.

Working in batches to avoid crowding, use tongs to quickly dip the each tostón in the saltwater solution for 1 to 2 seconds, dab it on a paper towel, and gently slide it into the oil (see Notes). The oil should bubble more rapidly now. Fry, carefully spooning oil over the tops of the tostones, until they look puffy and lightly golden, 1 to 2 minutes. Transfer to a paper towel–lined plate and sprinkle with salt while still sizzling and hot. Arrange them shingled on their sides—avoid stacking them, which will make them soggy. Repeat to fry the remaining tostones. Serve hot.

ARAÑITAS

LITTLE PLANTAIN SPIDERS

MAKES ABOUT 15 ARAÑITAS

2 quarts neutral oil, such as canola or sunflower oil

2 large green plantains, peeled

Salt

I love rainy days. They force us to slow down and, in some cases, stay home. At Abuela's it means she's making asopao (a rice-thickened soup; see pages 179–181), and if she's making asopao, then, by default, she's making arañitas. Logic. These crispy grated plantain fritters get their name from the loose, protruding bits of plantain that stick out of each fritter like spiky spider legs. Arañitas are a bit chewy in the center and light and crispy all around, which makes them the perfect dippable (or crushable) accompaniment to a thick, almost creamy soup. You can serve these with Mayo-Ketchup (page 45), chimichurri (page 47), or Ájili-Mójili (page 46).

Pour the oil into a medium-large pot or a deep fryer and heat over medium-low heat to 330°F (check out my Guide to Frying on page 148 for tips). Line a large plate with paper towels.

On the small holes of a box grater, grate the plantains directly onto a cutting board, allowing the shreds to land loosely on it (rather than getting compacted inside the grater). If needed, move the grater to different parts of the cutting board, leaving loose mounds of grated plantain behind. Sprinkle the grated plantain evenly with about 1 teaspoon salt and use two forks to toss lightly without compacting the plantain. This will ensure the arañitas will be light and airy.

Using one clean hand and the tips of your fingers, gently pinch some grated plantain into a loose, craggy bundle that's about the size of an uncracked walnut. Press it gently so it holds together in the center with loose, craggy sides. Don't try to compact it too much; bits of grated plantain sticking out are good—these are the "spider legs" and will create fun, crispy textures. Place it on a spoon and use a fork to gently slide it off the spoon into the hot oil. It should

recipe continues

sizzle immediately, but gently, and not smoke. If it doesn't sizzle, raise the heat a bit. If it smokes, reduce the heat and wait for the oil to cool down.

Working in batches to avoid overcrowding, continue adding arañitas to the oil, leaving at least an inch of space between them. Cook until the arañitas are bright yellow and feel crispy on both sides if you tap them with a spoon, about 5 minutes, flipping them halfway through to fry each side evenly if they aren't fully submerged. Transfer them to the paper towel–lined plate and sprinkle with salt while they're still hot and sizzling. Serve hot.

SORULLITOS

CREAMY CORN FRITTERS

MAKES ABOUT 30 SORULLITOS

Olive oil spray

1½ cups enriched fine yellow cornmeal

1 teaspoon salt

1 tablespoon unsalted butter

2 quarts canola or vegetable oil, for deep-frying (optional)

Sorullitos (*soh-roo-jeeh-tohs*) are sweet and savory cornmeal fritters, characterized by their long, finger-like shape with tapered edges. Their lightly crisp exterior gives way to a soft, creamy, corny mixture that melts in your mouth.

Abuela makes them for breakfast or as a midday snack with cafecito (page 55). She forms them by hand, one by one. If she's feeling adventurous, she'll cut batons of *queso de papa* (cheddar cheese) and form the sorullitos around the cheese, which melts as it cooks, creating an oozy interior. I've included Abuela's variation on page 158, but this is my lazy-girl version. Instead of forming them one by one, I compact the dough into a pan and let it cool before slicing it into batons. If you want the classic shape, and have the time, do you! Make sure you do it while the mixture is still slightly warm and malleable. I'm also giving you the option to bake or air-fry instead of deep-frying, which will make it easier if you're entertaining. Serve these hot, with Mayo-Ketchup (page 45) on the side for dipping.

Coat a 9-inch square baking pan with olive oil spray. Line it with parchment paper, leaving 5 inches overhanging two sides, then coat the parchment and the exposed sides of the pan with oil as well.

In a medium pot, combine the cornmeal, salt, butter, and 3 cups water. Cook over medium heat, stirring continuously with a rubber spatula, until the mixture starts to thicken and forms a smooth, clean dough that pulls away from the sides of the pot, 5 to 10 minutes. Transfer the dough to the prepared baking pan and, while it's still warm, flatten it with a spatula into an even layer over the bottom of the pan. Spray the top with olive oil and fold the overhanging parchment over the top to cover the dough. Refrigerate until completely firm, 30 minutes to 1 hour (or up to overnight).

Using the overhanging parchment as handles, remove the dough from the pan and place it on a cutting board. Slice into ½ by 3-inch rectangles that look like thick-cut fries.

recipe continues

To deep-fry: Pour the oil into a medium-large pot or a deep fryer and heat over medium-low heat to 330°F (check out my Guide to Frying on page 148 for tips). Line a large bowl or plate with paper towels. Working in batches of 8 to 10 to avoid overcrowding, add the sorullitos to the hot oil and fry until lightly golden and crispy, 3 to 5 minutes. Immediately transfer to the paper towel–lined plate to drain.

To bake: Preheat the oven to 450°F. Line a baking sheet with parchment paper and spray it liberally with olive oil. Arrange the dough batons on the prepared baking sheet, spacing them at least ½ inch apart. Spray the tops with olive oil. Bake for 20 minutes, flipping them halfway through, or until golden and crispy on all sides.

To air-fry: Preheat an air fryer to 375°F. Spray the dough batons generously with olive oil on both sides. Arrange them on the air fryer tray, spacing them at least ¼ inch apart. Air-fry for 5 to 10 minutes, until golden and crispy on all sides.

Serve hot.

FOR SORULLITOS DE QUESO (CHEESY SORULLITOS): Skip preparing the parchment-lined pan. Make the dough, then transfer it to a large bowl or storage container, cover, and let cool to room temperature. Cut an 8-ounce block of queso de papa (mild cheddar) or Monterey Jack cheese into 2-inch-long by ¼-inch-thick batons. With clean hands, take 3 tablespoons of the cooled dough and use it to encase the cheese batons. Roll it gently against a clean, flat surface to flatten the sides. With your fingers, taper the edges slightly, pushing down on them to make sure there's no exposed cheese. Deep-fry, bake, or air-fry as directed.

YUQUITAS FRITAS

CRISPY YUCA FRIES

SERVES 2 OR 3

1 pound yuca (see Note), peeled and cut into ½-inch-thick by 3-inch-long batons

Salt

2 quarts canola or vegetable oil (optional, for deep-frying)

Olive oil spray (optional, for baking or air-frying)

NOTE: *You can substitute 10 to 15 pieces leftover Yuca al Mojo (page 197) for the boiled yuca here. Using a fork, fish the yuca out of the mojo and scrape off the onions and garlic. Dab on clean paper towels to remove excess moisture, then deep-fry, bake, or air-fry as directed.*

Yuquitas fritas trump *papitas fritas* (french fries). There, I said it. The light, tempura-like exterior gives way to a fluffy, chewy, almost layered interior. Texture-wise, there's no comparable starch. I'm giving you the option to bake or air-fry instead of deep-frying. It takes a little longer, but baking or air-frying leaves your hands free to do something else while your yuquitas do their thing. These are delicious on their own, dipped in Mayo-Ketchup (page 45), with a drizzle of chimichurri (page 47), as a side, or topped like nachos—with Mama's Lifesaving Chili (page 141), cheese, and guac (page 145)—as a stand-alone meal.

In a medium pot, combine the yuca, 1 tablespoon salt, and 2 quarts water. Bring to a boil over high heat. Reduce the heat to medium-high and cook until the yuca is tender and translucent, 20 to 30 minutes. Drain.

To deep-fry: Heat the oil in a medium-large pot or a deep fryer over medium heat to 350°F (check out my Guide to Frying on page 148 for tips). Line a large bowl with paper towels. Working in batches of 8 to 10 to avoid overcrowding, add the yuca to the hot oil and fry until lightly golden and crispy, 3 to 5 minutes. Transfer to the prepared bowl to drain and immediately sprinkle with salt while they're hot.

To bake: Preheat the oven to 450°F. Line a baking sheet with parchment paper and spray it liberally with olive oil. Line a large plate with paper towels. Arrange the yuca batons on the prepared baking sheet in a single layer, spacing them about ½ inch apart. Sprinkle them with salt and coat liberally and evenly with olive oil spray. Bake for 25 to 30 minutes, flipping halfway through, until crispy and golden throughout. Transfer to the paper towel–lined plate to drain before serving.

To air-fry: Preheat an air-fryer to 375°F. Coat the yuca generously with olive oil spray on both sides. Arrange them on the air fryer tray, spacing them at least ¼ inch apart. Air-fry for 10 to 15 minutes, until golden and crispy on all sides.

Serve hot.

Bacalaítos, opposite

Pastelillos, page 165

Alcapurrias de Jueyes, page 168

Yuquitas Fritas, page 159

BACALAÍTOS

SALTFISH FRITTERS

MAKES ABOUT 30 MINI FRITTERS

12 ounces bacalao (salt cod), desalted (see Notes, page 117), drained, and patted dry

2 cups all-purpose flour

¼ cup chopped fresh cilantro or thinly sliced scallion

2 tablespoons grated or chopped garlic (from about 4 large cloves)

1½ tablespoons adobo, homemade (page 36) or store-bought

1 teaspoon dried oregano

2 quarts neutral oil, such as canola or sunflower oil, for frying

Bacalao, aka salt cod or saltfish, is cod that's dried and salted as a preservation method. Bacalaítos are a popular Puerto Rican fritura made from a savory bacalao-flecked batter. They're unmistakable and inviting as you drive past any beachside kiosko: flat, glistening, golden discs, often bigger than your head. The best ones have crispy edges with a slightly chewy center that holds pockets of salty cod. If you're on your way to or from the beach, it's almost sacrilegious not to get one with a cold Medalla. Abuela likes making these as a starter to pass around when she's entertaining. She makes cute mini ones (shown here) so everyone gets a little teaser taste without spoiling her guest's appetites. Bacalao is very affordable, and you can purchase it at most Latin grocery stores or order it online.

Using clean hands, flake the cod into small, pea-size pieces, discarding any pin bones you find. Transfer the fish to a large bowl. Add the flour, cilantro, garlic, adobo, oregano, and 2 cups cold water and stir until just combined. Cover and refrigerate for at least 3 hours or up to 3 days.

Fill a large, flat pan with 1 inch of oil and heat over medium-low heat to 320°F (check out my Guide to Frying on page 148 for tips). Line a large bowl with paper towels. Working in batches, carefully drop about ⅓ cup of the batter into the hot oil for each fritter (or about 3 tablespoons for mini bacalaítos), letting each addition spread into a thin, flat disc before scooping in the next. If the batter sits in a clump without spreading, it's too thick; stir in water 1 tablespoon at a time, until you achieve the right consistency. Fry until golden and completely crispy on both sides, 3 to 5 minutes per side. Stand them up in the paper towel–lined bowl to drain. Taste for seasoning—it should taste like salty cod and grassy cilantro. If needed, adjust the seasoning of the batter with more salt. Adjust your oil temperature, if necessary, and proceed with frying until you've used up all the batter. Serve immediately, while they're hot.

AREPAS

FLATBREAD PUFFS

MAKES ABOUT 6 AREPAS

8 ounces (about 1⅔ cups) all-purpose flour, plus more for dusting

½ teaspoon salt

¼ teaspoon baking powder

1 tablespoon unsalted butter, cut into pea-size pieces and chilled

¼ to ½ cup warm water

2 quarts neutral oil, such as canola or sunflower oil, for frying

Puerto Rican arepas are a type of fried flatbread made with wheat flour (different from Colombian or Venezuelan arepas, which are made of corn). In Puerto Rico, they're a street-side snack often sliced in half and filled with fresh conch or octopus salad (page 115) or served with Mayo-Ketchup (page 45) for dipping. Some restaurants serve them as a side with Chillo Frito (whole fried snapper, page 225) or asopao (thick rice soup; see pages 179–185). Papa's grandmother Abuelita Tina taught him how to make this dough, and he's mastered it throughout the years, earning him the honorary title Rey de Arepas (Arepa King) in my family. They're a breeze to make, because they require no special equipment and you most likely already have all the ingredients.

In a large bowl, whisk together the flour, salt, and baking powder until well combined. Add the butter and, using clean, dry hands, smush and scatter the pieces into the flour. Add ¼ cup of the warm water and mix with your hands until you achieve a semidry craggy dough that holds together and pulls away from the sides of the bowl, about 4 minutes. If it's still too dry, add more warm water 1 tablespoon at a time. If it's too wet and sticky, sprinkle in a little extra flour. Transfer the dough to a clean, dry, lightly floured work surface. Knead the dough, pushing it away from you with the heel of your hand and rotating it a quarter turn each time, until it's smooth, pliable, and springs back when pressed with your finger, about 4 minutes. Place it in a clean bowl, cover it with a lid or plastic wrap, and let rest for 30 minutes.

Cut six to eight 5-inch squares of parchment paper.

Test the dough by poking it with your finger; if it holds the indentation, it's ready to roll. Transfer it to a clean, dry, lightly floured work surface. Stretch it lightly, like pizza dough, then roll it out to about ⅙ inch thick, lightly flouring it and flipping it over as you roll to prevent it from sticking

recipe continues

to the counter. Using a 4- to 5-inch round cutter (or the rim of a bowl), cut the dough into rounds and place each round on a parchment square. You can gather the scraps and reroll them one time, but you'll need to reknead the dough and rest it again, covered, for 30 minutes. If not frying them right away, stack them with the parchment squares between them, slide them into a zip-top bag, and refrigerate for up to 2 days or freeze for up to 1 month.

Pour the oil into a medium-large pot or a deep fryer and heat over medium-low heat to 320°F (check out my Guide to Frying on page 148 for tips). Line a large bowl with paper towels. Working in batches of 2 or 3 to avoid overcrowding, carefully slide the arepas into the hot oil. They should sizzle, but not smoke, and puff immediately. Using a large dry spoon, carefully spoon oil over the arepas to start cooking the side that's not submerged, then cook until lightly tanned on the bottom, 3 to 4 minutes. Gently and carefully flip the arepas, and cook until lightly tanned on the second side, 1 to 2 minutes more. Transfer to the paper towel–lined bowl, standing them up to drain and immediately sprinkle lightly with salt while they're still hot and sizzling. They should be puffy, crispy, bready, and slightly chewy—if they're doughy, the oil was too cold; if they're snappy and dark, the oil was too hot. Adjust the oil temperature, if necessary, and repeat to fry the remaining arepas. Let cool slightly before serving.

PASTELILLOS

SAVORY HAND PIES

MAKES ABOUT 6 PASTELILLOS

1 recipe Arepa dough (page 163)

About 2 cups filling, such as Picadillo (page 260), Salmorejo de Jueyes (page 247), or Picadillo de Cerdo o Pollo (page 265), chilled

2 quarts neutral oil, such as canola or sunflower oil

These portable snacks are sold at kioskos throughout the island. They're stuffed with all sorts of tasty fillings like meat, shrimp, crab, octopus, even "pizza" (think tomato sauce, cheese, sometimes pepperoni). Though they resemble empanadas, in Puerto Rico they're called pastelillos. (Ask for an empanada here and you'll get a giant breaded and fried cutlet instead.) What to call them is still up for debate. Some Puerto Ricans would argue they're empanadillas (which, to me, are bigger—almost the size of a meal). Others call them pastelillos, like we do in mi casa. In a pinch, you can purchase premade dough from the freezer section of Latin grocery stores, but I really hope you'll try this recipe—the soft, puffy, buttery dough kicks store-bought's ass. I serve these with Pique (page 43), adding a drop or two on every bite. Or for a fresh kick, drizzle them with chimichurri (page 47) or Ájili-Mójili (page 46).

Cut eight to ten 6-inch squares of parchment paper. Place a small bowl of water close by. Roll out the dough to ⅛-inch thickness as directed on page 163 and cut it into 6-inch-wide rounds. Scoop about 3 tablespoons of the filling into the center of each round. Dip your finger in the water and run it around the outer ½ inch of the dough. Fold the dough over the filling to form a half-moon, then press the edges firmly to seal, working close to the filling to push out any air. Using a fork, crimp the edges (do not pierce the dough). This is optional, but I like to run a pizza cutter along the edge to make it look more even. Fry as you would arepas (see page 164) and serve hot.

AREPAS DE COCO

COCONUT FLATBREAD PUFFS

MAKES ABOUT 6 AREPAS

½ cup unsweetened shredded coconut

8 ounces (about 1⅔ cups) all-purpose flour, plus more for dusting

1½ tablespoons sugar

½ teaspoon baking powder

½ teaspoon salt

1 tablespoon virgin coconut oil

½ to ¾ cup well-shaken full-fat coconut milk, at room temperature

2 quarts neutral oil, such as canola or sunflower oil, for frying

These arepas are as easy to make as their plain counterpart (page 163). The only difference is the subtle, sweet, tropical flavor of the coconut, which, in my opinion, best complements seafood. I like to turn them into *arepas rellenas* (stuffed arepas) by slicing them open like a pita and filling them with Tangy Octopus Salad (page 115), Fresh Snapper Ceviche (page 119), Zesty Shrimp or Lobster Dip (page 139), or Salmorejo de Jueyes (crab stew, page 247). Alternatively, you can drizzle them with a little local honey and sprinkle them with flaky salt for a delicious sweet-salty snack.

Preheat the oven to 350°F. Cut six to eight 5-inch squares of parchment paper.

Spread the shredded coconut over a small baking pan and toast in the oven for 5 to 10 minutes, until the coconut is lightly golden brown and aromatic. Let cool completely, 5 to 10 minutes, then use clean, dry hands to gently crush the toasted coconut and break it up into smaller pieces. Transfer the coconut to a large bowl and add the flour, sugar, baking powder, and salt. Whisk until well combined. Add the coconut oil and use your hands to smush and scatter it into the flour. Add ⅓ cup of the coconut milk and mix with your hands until you achieve a semidry craggy dough that holds together and pulls away from the sides of the bowl, about 4 minutes. If it's still too dry, add more coconut milk 1 tablespoon at a time. If it's too wet and sticky, sprinkle in a little extra flour.

Transfer the dough to a clean, dry, lightly floured work surface. Knead the dough, pushing it away from you with the heel of your hand and rotating it a quarter turn each time, until it's smooth, pliable, and springs back when pressed with your finger, about 4 minutes. Place it in a clean bowl, cover it with a lid or plastic wrap, and let rest for 30 minutes.

Test the dough by poking it with your finger; if it holds the indentation, it's ready to roll. Transfer it to a clean, dry, lightly floured work surface. Stretch it lightly, like pizza dough, then roll it out to about ⅙ inch thick, lightly flouring it and flipping it over as you roll if necessary to prevent it from sticking to the counter. Using a 4- to 5-inch round cutter (or the rim of a bowl), cut the dough into rounds and place each round on a parchment square. You can gather the scraps and reroll them one time, but you'll need to reknead the dough and rest it again, covered, for 30 minutes after kneading. If not frying them right away, stack them with the parchment squares between them, slide them into a zip-top bag, and refrigerate for up to 2 days or freeze for up to 1 month.

Pour the oil into a medium-large pot or a deep fryer and heat over medium-low heat to 320°F (check out my Guide to Frying on page 148 for tips). Line a large bowl with paper towels. Working in batches of 2 or 3 to avoid overcrowding, carefully slide the arepas into the hot oil. They should sizzle, but not smoke, and puff immediately. Using a large dry spoon, carefully spoon oil over the arepas to start cooking the side that's not submerged, then cook until lightly tanned on the bottom, 3 to 4 minutes. Gently and carefully flip the arepas, and cook until lightly tanned on the second side, 1 to 2 minutes more. Transfer to the paper towel–lined bowl, standing them up to drain and immediately sprinkle lightly with salt while they're still hot and sizzling. They should be puffy, crispy, bready, and slightly chewy—if they're doughy, the oil was too cold; if they're snappy and dark, the oil was too hot. Adjust the oil temperature, if necessary, and repeat to fry the remaining arepas. Let cool slightly before serving.

ALCAPURRIAS

STUFFED MASA FRITTERS

MAKES 6 TO 8 FRITTERS

1 pound yuca, green bananas, or, in a pinch, green plantains, peeled and chopped into 1-inch chunks

8 ounces white yautía or malanga (or russet potato in a pinch), peeled and chopped into 1-inch chunks

1 tablespoon grated or chopped garlic (from about 2 large cloves)

3 tablespoons Achiote Oil (page 37)

1 teaspoon salt, plus more if needed

About 2 cups filling, such as Picadillo (page 260), Salmorejo de Jueyes (page 247), or Picadillo de Cerdo o Pollo (page 265), chilled

2 quarts neutral oil, such as canola or sunflower oil, for frying

Olive oil spray, for storing (optional)

Alcapurrias are handmade frituras found at the chinchorros or kioskos in Puerto Rico. The towns of Piñones in Loíza and Luquillo are considered hubs for the best frituras and have the widest selection of kioskos, but you can spot them all around the island. Alcapurrias have a crispy/chewy exterior made of a starchy root vegetable masa encasing a protein *relleno* (filling). Bonus points from me if the masa is made of yuca (rather than the usual green banana). For the relleno, I like using any not-too-saucy shredded, chopped, or ground meat or fish filling. In the US diaspora, these are harder to come by, so making them when I'm feeling homesick is healing. I like serving these simply with Pique (page 43) and a cold Medalla beer, nothing else needed.

In a blender or food processor, combine the yuca, yautía, garlic, 1 tablespoon of the achiote oil, and 1 teaspoon of the salt. Puree on high speed just until you achieve a smooth, creamy paste with a pale yellow tinge like corn, 2 to 4 minutes, stopping occasionally to scrape down the sides. Use the blender tamper to help things along as well, if needed, but don't add water or liquid. Do not overliquefy the mixture, which will make it too runny to work with later. Taste the masa: It should be slightly garlicky and salty. If not, adjust the seasoning by adding more salt pinch by pinch, tasting and adjusting after each addition, and adding more achiote oil, 1 teaspoon at a time, until you achieve a pale yellow color. Transfer to an airtight container and refrigerate for at least 4 hours or up to 2 days to thicken and firm up.

Pour the oil into a medium-large pot or a deep fryer and heat over medium-low heat to 320°F (check out my Guide to Frying on page 148 for tips). Line a large plate with paper towels. Scoop a tablespoon of the masa into the hot oil and fry until it firms up and looks golden and crispy, 1 to 2 minutes. Taste the fried masa—it should be slightly savory and garlicky. Season with more salt, if necessary, before forming the alcapurrias.

Dampen your clean hands with water. Scoop about ⅓ cup of the masa into the cupped palm of one hand. Using the back of a spoon, spread the masa into your hand, creating a bed for the filling. Scoop about ¼ cup of the filling into the middle of the masa and use the spoon to scoop masa from the sides over the filling. Top with more masa, if necessary, to completely enclose the filling. Transfer the alcapurria back and forth from one damp hand to the other until the filling is no longer visible and the alcapurria has a torpedo shape. Repeat to form the remaining alcapurrias. (At this point, you can cut 3-inch squares of parchment paper, spray with olive oil, and place each alcapurria on a sprayed parchment square in an airtight container. Refrigerate for up to 2 days or freeze for up to 2 months. Fry them directly from the fridge or freezer.)

Working in batches to avoid overcrowding, place the alcapurrias on a spatula one at a time and gently slide them into the hot oil, leaving at least 2 inches between them. (If frying frozen alcapurrias, peel off the parchment and gently place the alcapurria in the oil.) As soon as the alcapurrias touch the oil, they should sizzle gently and hold their shape. If the oil smokes, it's too hot; reduce the heat and wait for the temperature to come down. Fry until golden and crispy all around and slightly chewy inside (if it's chalky, it needs to cook a bit longer), 5 to 10 minutes (or 10 to 15 minutes from frozen), flipping them over halfway through. Transfer to the paper towel–lined plate and repeat with the remaining alcapurrias. Let cool for 5 to 10 minutes before serving.

FOR SAVORY WAFFLES: As a hack, I use leftover alcapurria masa to make savory waffles, a hassle-free, open-faced version of alcapurrias. Simply coat a waffle iron liberally with olive oil and add your masa like you would waffle batter. Press it until it looks crispy. Plate it and top it with anything—any alcapurria filling, guac (page 145), or any of my Grandmother Sauces (pages 40–51). Have fun with it!

SOPAS Y ASOPAOS

SOUPS AND ASOPAOS

One of the most valuable lessons I've learned from Abuela is how to economize—a skill she actively implements in her day-to-day cooking. I put what I'd learned to good use when I found myself advising friends and family on how to maximize the limited ingredients they had on hand during COVID lockdown in 2020. Having this skill helped me get through that time, and I felt grateful for my ability to contribute to others. If mindset is everything, then internalizing *How can I make the most of this?* has set me up for success, not just in my own cocina, but in life. I think many Puerto Ricans share that view. Our resilient nature derives from adversity, and it reflects in our cooking. That's what this chapter is about.

I'll teach you how to make Abuela's heartwarming Sopita de Pollo Cura-Tó' (cure-all chicken noodle soup, page 177), for those days you feel under the weather; her Caldo de Pescado (fish broth, page 173), using fish carcasses and stray veggies that would otherwise go to waste; and Sancocho con Bollitas (root veggie stew with plantain dumplings, page 187), an inexpensive one-pot meal that feeds the hungriest crowd. I also introduce you to *asopaos* (page 179), rice-thickened soups home cooks prepare when there's an *aguacero* (downpour) or a *temporal* (hurricane), displaying how to turn unpredictable situations—or humble ingredients—into delicious meals.

CALDO DE PESCADO

FISH BROTH

MAKES ABOUT 2½ QUARTS

1 or 2 fresh fish heads and carcasses (about 2 pounds total)

1 small onion, quartered

1 bell pepper (any color), quartered and seeded

2 or 3 sweet ajíes or sweet mini peppers, halved and seeded

3 large garlic cloves, smashed and peeled

15 culantro leaves, or a handful of cilantro stems (about 1 cup), coarsely chopped

1 teaspoon whole black peppercorns

1 teaspoon salt, plus more as needed

Cooked white rice (page 205), for serving

Diced avocado, for serving

A cup of hot caldo with a scoop of white rice is one of Abuela's go-to power snacks. I think it's one of the reasons why, at ninety years old, she is, as we say, *como coco* (strong as a coconut). Caldo de pescado is loaded with essential omega-3 fatty acids and vitamins, and provides many more nutritional health benefits. For Abuela, caldo de pescado is a given any time we're preparing fresh fish fillets, Grouper Nuggets (page 223), or Ceviche (page 119). If we're buying whole fish, she always saves the head and carcass to make this light, wholesome broth—nothing goes to waste. Make sure it's as fresh as the meat itself—it shouldn't smell fishy, the eyes should be clear (not cloudy), it should feel cold to the touch, and it shouldn't be slimy. You can use any snapper (like red, queen, or yellowtail), or any non-oily white fish, like cod or grouper.

In a large pot, combine the fish head and carcass, onion, bell pepper, ajíes, garlic, culantro, peppercorns, salt, and 3½ quarts water. Bring to a boil over high heat (this may take 15 to 20 minutes). As soon as it boils, reduce the heat to medium and simmer gently, using a spoon or ladle to skim the foam off the top, until the veggies are soft, 30 to 45 minutes. Strain through a fine-mesh sieve set over a bowl, gently pushing down on the veggies with the back of a spoon to extract all the broth and flavor.

If you have the time (and patience), using clean hands, pick the remaining meat off the fish head and carcass, discarding any pin bones you find, and set aside it for serving. Taste the broth. It should have sweet hints of pepper and herbaceous culantro and cilantro, and a mild fish flavor. If necessary, add more salt pinch by pinch, stirring and tasting after each addition until you get there.

Serve hot, with a few scoops of rice, some of the picked fish meat, and some diced avocado. Or let cool to room temperature, transfer to an airtight container, and store in the fridge for up to 4 days (it will look gelatinous when cold—this is normal) or freeze for up to 2 months.

SOPITA DE PLÁTANO

VELVETY PLANTAIN SOUP

SERVES 3 OR 4

¼ cup olive oil

2 large green plantains, peeled and cut into ¼-inch dice

½ teaspoon salt, plus more if needed

1 small onion, cut into ¼-inch dice

1 tablespoon grated or chopped garlic (from about 2 large cloves)

4 cups chicken broth

1 chicken bouillon cube

I'm a soup lover, even in the hottest, most humid tropical weather. I attribute that love of soup to Abuela, who prepared my baby foods with fresh viandas (see pages 25–31) Abuelo harvested from their backyard. They made me appreciate the importance of fresh, wholesome, local ingredients. Yes, I was spoiled, but in the best way. This sopita is as comforting as swinging on Abuela's hammock on a rainy afternoon. It's creamy, starchy, and delicately flavored, which makes it a good canvas for mix-ins and toppings—think potato soup. You can swirl in some coconut milk, drizzle it with chimichurri (page 47), add avocado, freshly ground black pepper, crushed *platanutres* (plantain chips) or croutons, some fresh herbs, or all of the above. It's a great opportunity to chef-up an otherwise plain dish.

In a medium pot, heat the olive oil over medium heat. Add the plantains and ¼ teaspoon of the salt and cook, stirring, until they're light golden brown, 3 to 5 minutes. Add the onion and the remaining ¼ teaspoon salt and cook, stirring, until the onion is translucent and tender, 3 to 5 minutes. Add the garlic and cook just until the garlic is fragrant, up to 1 minute.

Add the broth and bouillon cube, raise the heat to high, and bring to a boil. Immediately reduce the heat to maintain a low simmer, cover, and cook for 10 minutes, until the plantains are soft. Carefully transfer everything to a blender and puree on low speed, gradually increasing to high, until smooth, creamy, and homogeneous, about 1 minute. (Alternatively, blend the soup directly in the pot with an immersion blender.) Adjust the consistency by adding more water 1 to 2 tablespoons at a time, if necessary. Return the pureed soup to the pot and taste it. It should have subtle, sweet hints of plantain and garlic followed by a lingering chicken-y umami flavor from the bouillon. If necessary, adjust the seasoning with more salt. Serve hot, topped with the mix-ins of your choice (see headnote).

SOPITA DE POLLO Y FIDEOS CURA-TÓ'

CURE-ALL CHICKEN NOODLE SOUP

SERVES 4 TO 6

3 pounds bone-in, skin-on chicken thighs, drumsticks, and/or wings

3 tablespoons adobo, homemade (page 36) or store-bought

4 tablespoons olive oil

1 cup small-diced celery (about 2 stalks)

1 cup small-diced onion (about 1 small)

2 tablespoons grated or chopped garlic (from about 4 large cloves)

½ cup Sofrito (page 38)

1 tablespoon sazón, homemade (page 39) or store-bought

3 quarts chicken broth

Salt (optional)

2 cups 2-inch-diced peeled yellow, gold, or Yukon Gold potatoes (about 3 small)

1½ cups 1-inch-diced carrots (about 3 medium)

2 ears corn, cut crosswise into six 2-inch-wide pieces each (optional)

This is a classic, no-frills Puerto Rican chicken noodle soup. It's the one mamis and abuelitas make us when we stay home from school because we're sick (or faking it—like my sister would). Whenever I feel my immune system fighting something, I make a big ol' batch of this. I use bone-in, skin-on dark meat chicken for added flavor and protein, which I'll take a hundred times over a shot of penicillin. I load it with tons of sofrito and extra garlic for an anti-inflammatory immune kick that's gotten me through flus/colds, NYC winters, COVID, even heartbreaks—and trust me, I've had many. It sits well in the fridge for a few days, so if you're actually feeling under the weather, it's as easy popping it in the microwave.

Place a rack in the middle of the oven and preheat to 400°F. Line a large baking sheet with parchment paper.

Place the chicken on the prepared baking sheet and sprinkle it evenly on all sides with the adobo. Drizzle with 2 tablespoons of the olive oil and, using clean hands, rub it all over the chicken and between the skin and the flesh. Space the chicken pieces at least an inch apart on the baking sheet and bake for 20 to 30 minutes, until golden brown.

Meanwhile, in a large pot, heat the remaining 2 tablespoons olive oil over medium heat for 30 seconds to 1 minute. Add the celery and onion and cook, stirring, until they are soft and translucent but have not taken on any color, 4 to 5 minutes. Add the garlic and sofrito and cook, stirring, until the garlic is fragrant and all the moisture from the sofrito has evaporated, 2 to 3 minutes. Add the sazón and stir until all the veggies have an orangey tinge. Add the broth, increase the heat to high, and bring to a boil, about 10 minutes.

recipe and ingredients continue

8 ounces thin egg noodles, such as angel hair or vermicelli pasta, broken into 1- to 2-inch pieces (about 3 cups)

¼ cup chopped fresh cilantro

Sliced avocado, for garnish (optional)

Lime wedges, for serving (optional)

Add the chicken and all the pan drippings to the pot with the broth. To lift residual drippings from the pan, ladle in some broth and stir with a large spoon or wooden spatula, scraping the bottom of the pan, then add that to the pot. Reduce the heat to medium, cover, and simmer until the chicken is tender enough to pull away from (but not falling off) the bone, about 20 minutes.

When the chicken is ready, taste the broth. It should be chicken-y, with hints of sweet garlic and onion from the sofrito. If necessary, adjust the seasoning with salt.

Remove the chicken from the pot, pick the meat off the bones (to make it easier to eat in the soup later), and return it to the soup, or leave it on the bone, if you prefer—I like a mix of picked chicken and whole pieces.

Add the potatoes, carrots, and corn (if using) and simmer over medium heat until the potatoes are fork-tender, about 15 minutes more. Add the noodles and simmer until the noodles are tender, 3 to 5 minutes. Add the cilantro and taste the soup. If necessary, add more salt a pinch at a time until it tastes savory from the chicken and slightly sweet from the corn and carrots, with grassy hints of cilantro. Serve hot, as is, or top with slices of avocado and serve with a lime wedge alongside for squeezing.

FOR A PRESSURE COOKER OR INSTANT POT: While the chicken is baking, heat the remaining 2 tablespoons olive oil in a pressure cooker over medium heat or in an Instant Pot on the Sauté setting. Add the celery and onion and continue as directed. After adding the chicken and pan drippings to the pot, seal the lid and cook on high pressure for 5 minutes. Release the pressure and remove the lid. Pick the chicken meat from the bones, if you like, then add the potatoes, carrots, and corn. Set the heat to medium or select the Sauté setting and continue as directed.

ASOPAOS

HEARTY RICE-THICKENED SOUPS

Asopao is an unassuming soup that has all the creamy, hearwarming comfort of risotto minus all the stirring and fussy steps. It's also one of my favorite Puerto Rican meals and Abuela's rainy-day go-to, cure-all, and solution for using leftover rice. It's thick, savory, and flavorful without being rich and heavy. I love eating it on snowy winter evenings in New York and imagining I'm swinging on the hammock at Abuela's house on a rainy, breezy, tropical afternoon. When Abuela makes her pigeon pea version with plantain "buoy" dumplings (recipe follows), she keeps an eye on my sister and me, ensuring we don't scoop them from the surface of the soup, where they float like bouys. She refers to that as *cegar la sopa* ("blinding the soup").

If you want to enjoy asopao like a pro, top it with avocado and make some Arañitas (crispy plantain fritters, page 153) for dipping.

ASOPAO DE GANDULES CON BOLLITAS DE PLÁTANO

PIGEON PEA AND RICE SOUP WITH PLANTAIN "BUOY" DUMPLINGS

SERVES 4 TO 6

DUMPLING MASA

2 medium green plantains, peeled and cut into 1-inch chunks

2 teaspoons adobo, homemade (page 36) or store-bought

ASOPAO

¼ cup olive oil

1 cup ½-inch-diced ham steak (about 6 ounces; optional)

¾ cup Sofrito (page 38)

Make the dumpling masa: In a blender or food processor, combine the plantains and the adobo. Blend or process on high speed until a smooth paste forms, 2 to 4 minutes, scraping the sides with a rubber spatula as necessary. Use the blender tamper to help things along, if needed, but don't add water or liquid. (Alternatively, grate the plantain in a circular motion on the zesting side of a box grater until a smooth, slimy paste forms. Transfer it into a bowl, add the adobo, and stir until homogeneous.)

Make the asopao: In a large pot, heat the olive oil over medium-high heat. Add the ham (if using) and cook, stirring,

recipe and ingredients continue

2 cups small-diced fresh tomatoes (about 1 large), or 1 (14.5-ounce) can stewed tomatoes

4 pimento-stuffed olives, minced

1 (15.5-ounce) can pigeon peas, undrained

2 quarts chicken broth

½ cup uncooked medium-grain white rice, or 2 to 3 cups cooked (page 205)

Salt (optional)

¼ cup chopped fresh cilantro, plus more for serving

2 ripe Hass avocados, sliced

until it's golden, 2 to 4 minutes. Add the sofrito and cook, stirring, until the moisture has evaporated, 2 to 4 minutes more. Add the tomatoes and olives and cook, stirring, until the moisture has evaporated, 2 to 4 minutes more. Add the pigeon peas with their liquid, broth, and uncooked rice (if that's what you're using) and bring to a boil, then immediately reduce the heat to maintain a simmer. Taste for seasoning. It should have hints of the herbaceous sofrito and sweet tomatoes. If necessary, add salt pinch by pinch, stirring and tasting after each addition, until the flavor is to your liking.

Using a scoop (or two small spoons), drop teaspoon-size portions of the masa directly into the hot broth until you've used all the masa. If you're using cooked rice, add it now. Stir the soup gently, cover, and cook over low heat until the rice is fully cooked and the soup has thickened, 15 to 20 minutes. Taste again and adjust the seasoning with salt, if necessary. Stir in the cilantro.

Serve the asopao in large bowls with a slice or two of avocado and some cilantro on top.

ASOPAO DE CAMARONES O LANGOSTA

SHRIMP OR LOBSTER AND RICE SOUP

SERVES 4 TO 6

2 quarts chicken broth

4 tablespoons olive oil

1½ pounds shrimp, peeled (shells reserved), deveined, and cut into 1-inch chunks, or 1½ pounds lobster tails, shells removed (and reserved), meat cut into 1-inch chunks

1 cup small-diced white or yellow onion (about 1 medium)

1 cup small-diced yellow or red bell pepper (about 1 pepper)

½ cup Sofrito (page 38)

½ teaspoon salt, plus more if needed

2 cups small-diced fresh tomatoes (about 1 large), or 1 (14.5-ounce) can stewed tomatoes

4 pimento-stuffed olives, minced

¾ cup uncooked medium-grain white rice, or about 2 cups cooked (page 205)

¼ cup chopped fresh cilantro, plus more for serving

2 ripe Hass avocados, diced, for serving

2 to 3 limes, cut into wedges, for serving

In a medium pot, bring the broth to a boil over medium-high heat, then immediately reduce the heat to maintain a low simmer and cook for 8 to 10 minutes.

In a large pot, heat 2 tablespoons of the olive oil over medium-high heat. Add the reserved shrimp shells or lobster shells and cook, stirring, until they're bright red, slightly golden on the edges, and fragrant, 1 to 2 minutes. Transfer them to the pot with the simmering broth.

In the pot you used for the shells, combine the remaining 2 tablespoons olive oil, the onion, bell pepper, sofrito, and salt. Cook, stirring, until the onion is translucent, the bell pepper is soft, and the moisture from the sofrito has evaporated, 8 to 10 minutes. Add the tomatoes and olives and cook, stirring, until the moisture from the tomato has evaporated, 6 to 8 minutes.

Carefully strain the broth through a fine-mesh sieve into the pot with the tomato mixture. Taste it. It should taste shrimpy or lobstery. If not, add salt pinch by pinch as needed. Add the rice, stir, and reduce the heat to medium-low. Simmer, stirring occasionally, until the rice is fully cooked and the soup has thickened and looks like gumbo, 15 to 20 minutes if using cooked rice, 25 to 30 minutes for uncooked rice. Taste again. It should have hints of the herbaceous sofrito and sweet tomatoes. If necessary, add salt pinch by pinch. Turn off the heat, stir in the shrimp or lobster meat, and let stand until the shrimp or lobster is pink and opaque, 2 to 3 minutes. Stir in the cilantro. Serve hot, in large bowls, with avocado and more cilantro on top and lime wedges for squeezing.

ASOPAO DE POLLO CON CHICHARRONES

CHICKEN AND RICE SOUP WITH CRISPY CHICKEN SKIN

SERVES 4 TO 6

1½ pounds bone-in, skin-on chicken thighs or drumsticks

3 teaspoons adobo, homemade (page 36) or store-bought

¼ cup olive oil

1 cup small-diced white or yellow onion (about 1 medium)

1 cup small-diced yellow or red bell pepper (about 1 pepper)

½ cup Sofrito (page 38)

2 cups small-diced fresh tomatoes (about 1 large), or 1 (14.5-ounce) can stewed tomatoes

4 pimento-stuffed olives, minced

½ teaspoon salt, plus more if needed

2 quarts chicken broth

¾ cup uncooked medium-grain white rice, or about 2 cups cooked (page 205)

¼ cup chopped fresh cilantro

2 ripe Hass avocados, sliced, for serving

Preheat the oven to 400°F. Line a baking sheet with parchment paper.

Remove the skins from the chicken pieces and stretch them out in a flat, single layer on the prepared baking sheet. Sprinkle the skins evenly with 1 teaspoon of the adobo. Bake for 10 to 15 minutes, until the skin is golden brown and crispy. Transfer the skin to a paper towel–lined plate to drain and let cool to room temperature. Resist the urge to eat the chicharrones by placing them out of sight in a dry airtight container.

Sprinkle the chicken with the remaining 2 teaspoons adobo. Using clean hands, massage the adobo into the chicken until it's well coated. Let stand at room temperature for 15 to 20 minutes or refrigerate for up to 2 hours.

In a large pot, heat the olive oil over medium-high heat. Add the chicken and cook until golden brown on all sides, about 10 minutes. Transfer the chicken to a large plate. Reduce the heat to medium and add the onion, bell pepper, and sofrito to the pot. Cook, stirring, until the onion is translucent, the bell pepper is soft, and the moisture from the sofrito has evaporated, 8 to 10 minutes. Add the tomatoes, olives, and salt and cook, stirring, until the moisture from the tomato has evaporated, 6 to 8 minutes. Add the broth and rice and return the chicken to the pot. Increase the heat to high and bring to a boil, then immediately reduce the heat to medium-low and simmer for 8 to 10 minutes. Stir the soup, reduce the heat to low, cover, and cook until the rice is fully cooked and the soup has thickened, 15 to 20 minutes if using cooked rice, 25 to 30 minutes for uncooked rice.

Remove the chicken from the pot, pick the meat off the bones (to make it easier to eat in the soup later), and return the meat to the soup, or leave it on the bone, if you prefer—I like a mix of picked chicken and whole pieces. Taste the soup for seasoning. It should have hints of the herbaceous sofrito and sweet tomatoes. If necessary, add salt pinch by pinch, stirring and tasting after each addition, until the flavor is to your liking. Stir in the cilantro and serve hot, in large bowls, with some sliced avocado (seasoned with salt) and some hand-crushed chicken skin chicharrones on top for a pop of salty, chicken-y crunch.

SANCOCHO DE ABUELA CON BOLLITAS DE PLÁTANO

ABUELA'S ROOT VEGGIE STEW WITH PLANTAIN DUMPLINGS

SERVES 5 OR 6

Sancocho is a hearty stew known throughout many Latin American countries that combines different viandas (see pages 25–31) and proteins. In Puerto Rico, there is no ultimate way to prepare it—every family has their own method and their preferred ingredients. Making sancocho is also a great way to maximize stray ingredients, which is why we often use the term *sancocho* to refer to a "melting pot" of anything. The amount of viandas required means it's tough to make a small portion, so plan on serving an army or having leftovers (which are even better the next day). I wrote this recipe per Abuela's loose guidelines, but the ingredients always vary based on the viandas we have on hand, so feel free to make swaps based on your preferences or what's available to you. I like to serve this humble dish with white rice (page 205), a large slice of avocado, and *maaaybe* some Pique (page 43), like a pro.

MEAT STEW

2 pounds bone-in beef or pork ribs, cut into 2-inch chunks (ask your butcher), or bone-in chicken thighs or drumsticks

2 tablespoons adobo, homemade (page 36) or store-bought

4 to 6 tablespoons olive oil

1 cup ½-inch-diced ham steak or chorizo (about 6 ounces; optional)

1 cup small-diced cubanelle or green bell pepper

⅓ cup Sofrito (page 38)

1 teaspoon dried oregano

½ teaspoon freshly ground black pepper

½ teaspoon salt

¼ teaspoon ground cumin

1 tablespoon tomato paste

1 cup small-diced fresh tomatoes (about 1 medium), or ½ (14.5-ounce) can stewed tomatoes

Make the meat stew: Place a rack in the middle of the oven and preheat the broiler to high.

Place the ribs (or chicken pieces) on a large baking sheet and sprinkle evenly on all sides with the adobo. With clean hands, rub the seasoning into the meat. Drizzle with 2 to 3 tablespoons of the olive oil and rub it in to evenly coat on all sides. Space the ribs (or chicken) 1 inch apart on the baking sheet. Broil for 20 to 30 minutes, flipping them over halfway through, until golden brown. Transfer the meat to a plate or bowl. Add 1 cup water to the baking sheet and, using a wooden spoon, stir and scrape the stuck-on bits from the bottom of the pan to release them. Reserve this liquid with the meat.

recipe and ingredients continue

DUMPLING MASA

1 large green plantain (about 1 pound), peeled and cut into 1-inch chunks

4 large garlic cloves, peeled

1 tablespoon olive oil

1 teaspoon salt, plus more if needed

SANCOCHO

½ cup 1-inch-diced carrot (about 1 small)

½ cup ½-inch-sliced celery (about 1 stalk)

1 cup 1-inch-diced peeled apio (about 1 tennis ball–size bulb)

1 cup 1-inch-diced peeled yuca (about ½ pound)

1 cup 1-inch-diced peeled yam or sweet potato (about ½ pound)

1 cup 1-inch-diced peeled white yautía (about ½ pound)

1 cup 2-inch-diced peeled calabaza (about ½ pound)

1 cup 1-inch-diced peeled chayote (about ½ pound)

2 ears corn, husked and cut into thirds

2 cups thinly shredded green cabbage (about ½ pound)

½ cup chopped fresh cilantro

In a large pot (see Note), heat the remaining 2 to 3 tablespoons olive oil over medium-high heat. Add the ham and cubanelle. Cook, stirring, until the ham is light golden brown and the cubanelle is soft, 4 to 6 minutes. Add the sofrito, oregano, black pepper, salt, and cumin. Cook until the moisture from the sofrito has evaporated and the spices are fragrant, 4 to 5 minutes. Add the tomato paste and cook, stirring to coat the vegetables, until it smells sweet and turns brickred in color, 4 to 5 minutes. Add the tomatoes and cook, stirring, until the moisture from the tomato has evaporated, 3 to 4 minutes. Pour in 3 quarts water, then add the ribs (or chicken) and the liquid from the baking sheet and bring to a boil over high heat.

Reduce the heat to medium-low, cover, and simmer gently for 2 to 4 hours for ribs (30 to 45 minutes for chicken), until the meat is tender enough to pull away from the bone with a fork.

Meanwhile, make the masa: In a blender or food processor, combine the plantains, garlic, olive oil, and salt. Blend or process on high speed until a smooth paste forms, 2 to 4 minutes, scraping down the sides with a rubber spatula as necessary. Use the blender tamper to help things along, if needed, but don't add water or liquid. Transfer the masa to a large bowl. (Alternatively, grate the plantain in circular motions on the zesting side of a box grater until a smooth, slimy paste forms. Transfer to a large bowl. Grate or mince the garlic into a paste and add it to the bowl with the plaintain. Add the olive oil and salt, and stir until well combined.)

Taste the masa. It should be savory and garlicky. If necessary, add more salt pinch by pinch until you get there. Set the masa aside at room temperature.

Clean out the blender jar by adding 1 cup water and blending it to pick up any remaining masa. Pour this water-masa mixture into the meat stew pot (as a thickener).

Finish the sancocho: Add the carrot, celery, apio, yuca, yam, yautía, calabaza, chayote, corn, and cabbage to the pot with the meat stew. Cover and bring to a boil over high heat, about 10 minutes. Uncover and reduce the heat to medium-

NOTE: *To cook the meat stew in an Instant Pot or pressure cooker, broil the ribs or chicken as directed and set aside. Heat the remaining olive oil in a pressure cooker over medium-high heat or in an Instant Pot on the Sauté setting, then continue as directed. After adding the broth, place the ribs or chicken in the pot, seal the lid, and cook at high pressure for 20 minutes for ribs, or 10 minutes if using chicken. Release the pressure and check for doneness—the meat should be tender enough to pull away from the bone with a fork. If it's not ready, reseal it and cook at high pressure for 5 to 10 minutes more. Transfer the meat stew to a larger pot and proceed with finishing the sancocho as directed.*

low so the stew simmers gently. Using a teaspoon (or two small spoons), scoop teaspoon-size portions of the masa directly into the stew until you've used all the masa. Cook until you see some of the dumplings floating to the top, about 10 minutes, then stir the soup gently. Reduce the heat to low and cook until the vegetables are fully cooked and all the dumplings are floating, about 20 minutes more. If you'd like a saucier/thicker consistency, ladle about 1½ cups of the veggies and broth into a blender and puree until smooth (or mash them in a bowl), then stir this mixture into the sancocho.

Add the cilantro, stir, and taste the sancocho. It should taste earthy from the viandas, with hints of herbaceous culantro and meaty savoriness. If needed, adjust the seasoning with more salt, adding it pinch by pinch and stirring and tasting after each addition. Serve hot.

HABICHUELAS Y ACOMPAÑANTES

BEANS AND SIDE DISHES

In many Puerto Rican homes, beans are a staple—served almost daily in some form. Whether stewed and spooned over rice, cooked into it (like in our Arroz con Gandules, page 211, or Arroz Mampostea'o, page 215), or stirred into a comforting asopao (like Asopao de Gandules, page 179), they show up at nearly every meal. Abuela usually buys them fresh or dried. I often reach for canned beans—they save time, require fewer dishes, and don't need advance soaking.

While rice and beans are often seen as a side to mains like Bistec Encebolla'o (page 242) or Camarones al Ajillo (page 227), in this chapter I focus on the beans themselves. You'll find recipes for preparing them as classic sides, rice toppers, and even standalone soups. I also include beloved side dishes made from viandas (see pages 25–31), which pair beautifully with any of the proteins or meats in this book for a wholesome Boricua meal.

HABICHUELITAS GUISADAS CON CALABAZA

STEWY BEANS WITH CARIBBEAN PUMPKIN

SERVES 4

1 tablespoon olive oil

1 cup ½-inch-diced ham steak (about 6 ounces), or ½ teaspoon smoked paprika

⅓ cup Sofrito (page 38)

1 cup small-diced fresh tomatoes (about 1 medium), or ½ (14.5-ounce) can stewed tomatoes

1 (15.5-ounce) can beans (such as pink, pinto, small white, navy, cannellini, or red kidney beans), undrained

2 chicken, ham, or vegetable bouillon cubes

1 cup ½-inch-diced peeled calabaza

2 tablespoons chopped fresh cilantro

Salt (optional)

This universal recipe using your choice of canned beans packs Abuela's sazón in a fraction of the time as dried. My favorites are pink beans or small white ones (like navy beans), but you can also use red kidney beans, pinto beans, or a combination. In my opinion, stewed beans are better the next day (or after a couple of days), so I like making a big batch to dip into throughout the week. It makes for an easy, tasty, wholesome weeknight meal I'm happy to repeat.

In a medium pot, heat the olive oil over medium heat. Add the ham (if using) and cook, stirring, until it turns golden, 3 to 4 minutes. Add the sofrito and cook, stirring, until most of the moisture evaporates, 3 to 4 minutes (if using paprika instead of ham, add it at this point). Add the tomatoes and cook, stirring, until the liquid looks saucy, 1 to 2 minutes. Add the beans (with their liquid) and the bouillon cubes, then fill the empty bean can with water and add that as well. Raise the heat to high and bring to a boil, then reduce the heat to low, cover, and simmer for 20 minutes.

Uncover, stir, and add the calabaza. Raise the heat to medium and cook, uncovered, until the squash is fork-tender, about 15 minutes more. Stir in the cilantro, then taste the beans. They should be savory, with sweet hints of calabaza and herbaceous cilantro. Adjust the seasoning with salt, if necessary.

Remove from the heat and serve, or let cool to room temperature, transfer to an airtight container, and store in the fridge for up to 5 days.

FRIJOLES NEGROS CON CERVEZA

BEER-BRAISED BLACK BEANS

MAKES ABOUT 3 CUPS

1 tablespoon olive oil

½ cup diced white or yellow onion

½ cup diced green bell pepper or cubanelle pepper

½ teaspoon salt, plus more if needed

½ teaspoon ground cumin

½ teaspoon dried oregano

½ cup Sofrito (page 38)

1 (15.5-ounce) can black beans, undrained

1 cup light beer (such as Medalla), chicken broth, or vegetable broth

1 cup chicken broth or vegetable broth

1 bay leaf

2 tablespoons chopped fresh cilantro, plus more for serving

Sliced avocado, for serving (optional)

In some Spanish speaking countries, the word *frijoles* (*free-hoh-lehs*) is used to refer to beans in general. In Puerto Rico, we're referring to black beans specifically. Any other beans or legumes are called habichuelas (*ah-bee-chu-eh-lahs*). Mama makes these especially well, adding her special touch: a splash of beer. This ups the savoriness, but I also think it was an excuse to crack open a beer midweek. She'd always say, "The rest is for the chef." These are great as a side atop white rice or served as a soup with fun toppings like pepper Jack cheese, plantain chips, avocado, sour cream, cilantro, chopped red onions, and/or limes. And if you're not into cooking with beer or want to keep them gluten-free, just swap in any type of broth.

In a medium saucepan, heat the olive oil over medium heat. Add the onion, bell pepper, and salt and cook, stirring continuously, until the onion is translucent, 3 to 5 minutes. Add the cumin and oregano and stir until the spices are aromatic, about 30 seconds. Add the sofrito and cook until most of its moisture has evaporated, 2 to 3 minutes. Add the beans (with their liquid), beer, broth, and bay leaf and stir. Raise the heat to medium-high and bring to a boil, then reduce the heat to medium-low. Simmer, uncovered, stirring occasionally, until the liquid has reduced by one-third, about 20 minutes.

Using the back of a spoon, mash about ¼ cup of the beans against the side of the pot (this will help thicken the sauce) and simmer for 5 minutes more. Stir in the cilantro, then taste the beans: They should have a slight sweetness from the onion and pepper, smokiness from the cumin, and savoriness from the beer. Adjust the flavor with salt, if necessary, and serve, topped with additional cilantro and some avocado, if desired.

YUCA AL MOJO

CITRUSY GARLIC YUCA

SERVES 4 TO 6

2 pounds yuca, peeled and cut into ½-inch-thick by 3-inch-long batons

1 tablespoon plus 1 teaspoon salt

¼ cup extra-virgin olive oil

¼ cup neutral oil, such as canola or sunflower oil

1 medium white onion (about 8 ounces), thinly sliced

2 tablespoons grated or chopped garlic (from about 4 large cloves)

Zest of 1 sour orange (see Note)

¼ cup fresh sour orange juice (see Note)

1 tablespoon chopped fresh cilantro, for serving (optional)

NOTE: *If you can't find a sour orange, use the zest and juice of 1 orange and 1 lime.*

Yuca's creamy, slightly chewy texture and mild flavor make it a gorgeous canvas for sazón and creativity. Yuca al mojo is from Cuba, our island neighbor. At Abuela's we have a surplus of yuca, so this dish was pretty standard when I was growing up, and later, when I lived in Miami, I redeveloped my taste for it. It's a sabor-packed alternative to the typical rice, potatoes, and other starches we're accustomed to. The yuca soaks up the citrusy garlic sauce and becomes so creamy, it sticks to the roof of your mouth. I like serving this with Pernil Asado (page 235) because the bright sauce from the yuca cuts through the pork's fattiness.

In a medium pot, combine the yuca, 1 tablespoon of the salt, and 2 quarts water. Bring to a boil over high heat, then reduce the heat to medium-high to maintain a gentle boil and cook until the yuca is tender and translucent, 20 to 30 minutes.

Meanwhile, in a medium pot, combine the olive oil and neutral oil and heat over medium heat for 1 to 2 minutes. Add the onion and remaining ½ teaspoon salt and cook, stirring continuously, until the onion is soft and translucent, 5 to 10 minutes. Add the garlic and cook until it's aromatic, 1 to 2 minutes. Add the orange zest, orange juice, and ⅓ cup of the hot, cooking starchy water from the yuca. Remove mojo from the heat and stir to combine. Spoon some of the liquid from the mojo over the bottom of a 9 by 13-inch baking dish.

Preheat the oven to 350°F.

Check the yuca. It should look creamy, soft, and translucent. Fish out the yuca batons and line them up in the prepared baking dish. If any pieces still look matte white or chalky, boil them in 2- to 4-minute increments until they're soft. (If you notice a fibrous string in the center of the yuca, remove and discard it.) Pour the rest of the mojo evenly over the yuca and cover the dish with foil. Bake for 15 to 20 minutes, until steamy. Garnish with the cilantro, if desired, and serve.

MAJADO DE PLÁTANO (MANGÚ)

BUTTERY PLANTAIN MASH

SERVES 6

2 pounds green plantains, peeled and cut into 1-inch-thick rounds (see Note)

1 tablespoon salt, plus more if needed

3 tablespoons cold unsalted butter

NOTE: *You can substitute other viandas like yautía, malanga, pana, or yuca—**see pages 25–31.*

I'd say *mofongo* (fried mashed plantain) is to Puerto Ricans what *mangú* (boiled mashed plantain) is to Dominicans. You won't find a recipe for mofongo in this book. I don't want mofongo to be the only meal that defines our cuisine. But I love plantains and I think *majado de plátano* (as Puerto Ricans call Dominican mangú) highlights all the things I love about them. They're starchy with a mild, earthy flavor and slight sweetness reminiscent of bananas. They just taste like the tropics. When you mash 'em up with a little butter and their own starchy water, they literally shine and turn into a creamy-chunky landing pad for any ingredients (like the fried egg, juicy tomatoes, crumbled queso fresco, tangy pickled onions, and fresh cilantro shown here) to assemble a delicious and wholesome breakfast, lunch, or dinner.

In a medium pot, combine the plantains, salt, and 4 cups water. Bring to a boil over high heat, then reduce the heat to medium and simmer until the plantains are tender and easily mashable (test one with a fork), 15 to 20 minutes. Drain the cooking liquid into a heatproof bowl. While they're hot, mash the plantains in the pot with a fork or potato masher. Add the butter and ½ cup of the reserved cooking water. Mash and stir, adding more starchy water ½ cup at a time as necessary, until the mixture looks creamy but still slightly chunky, like mashed potatoes. Taste it: It should be savory and buttery, with mild earthy sweetness from the plantains. If necessary, season with more salt.

Serve immediately, while it's hot, or let cool, transfer to an airtight container, and refrigerate for up to 2 days. To reheat, bring a few tablespoons of water to a simmer in a small pot over medium heat, add the desired amount of mash, and stir the water into the mash until it's creamy again, adding more water a few tablespoons at a time, if necessary. Taste and season with more salt, if needed.

GARBANZOS CRIOLLOS CON CHORIZO

CREOLE CHICKPEA STEW WITH CHORIZO

SERVES 2 OR 3

2 tablespoons olive oil

3½ ounces chorizo (see Note), casing removed, diced (about 1 cup)

½ cup diced red, orange, or yellow bell pepper

½ cup diced white or yellow onion (about 1 small)

1 (15.5-ounce) can chickpeas, drained (liquid reserved)

½ teaspoon sweet (or hot) smoked paprika (pimentón)

½ teaspoon red pepper flakes (optional; omit if using hot paprika)

¼ teaspoon salt, plus more if needed

⅓ cup Sofrito (page 38)

1 tablespoon grated or chopped garlic (from about 2 large cloves)

1 cup light beer (such as Medalla), chicken broth, or vegetable broth

2 tablespoons chopped fresh cilantro, scallion, or parsley

Cooked white rice (page 205), quinoa, or other starchy grain, for serving (optional)

Z, one of my best childhood friends from Puerto Rico (who also lives in New York), once invited me over to her house for dinner. When she greeted me, she expressed how nervous she felt about cooking for me. What she didn't know was that I'd been savoring her meal from the second I stepped off the elevator on her floor—the smell of the smoky chorizo and sweet peppers was intoxicating. The hearty stew she made was everything I needed on that chilly winter day. She generously set the pot on the table, which meant I could (and did) keep going back in for more. Z's tenacity has always inspired me. It wasn't until she made me this dish that I realized how much her food could, too. These chickpeas meant more than relieving hunger; they meant I had family here. This recipe calls for chorizo, but you can skip it—just add extra paprika for similar smokiness.

In a medium pot, heat the olive oil over medium-low heat. Add the chorizo and cook, stirring, until golden and crispy, 4 to 6 minutes. Add the bell pepper, onion, chickpeas, paprika, red pepper flakes (if using), and salt. Cook, stirring occasionally, until the onion and bell pepper look soft and translucent, about 10 minutes. Add the sofrito and garlic and cook, stirring occasionally, until most of the moisture evaporates, 3 to 4 minutes. Add the beer and the reserved chickpea liquid and stir. Raise the heat to high and bring the liquid to a simmer, then reduce the heat to medium-low. Simmer, stirring occasionally, until the liquid looks saucy, 25 to 30 minutes. If you want it thicker, scoop about 10 chickpeas onto a small plate, smash them with a fork, and return them to the stew, then cook until you

NOTE: *If you like, you can substitute diced bacon or ham steak for the chorizo or omit the meat and add an additional ½ teaspoon smoked paprika.*

achieve the thickness you like. If it gets too thick, add water 1 to 2 tablespoons at a time. Taste and, if and adjust the seasoning with more salt, if necessary. Stir in the cilantro and serve as is, like a soup, or over rice or quinoa.

ARROCES AL CALDERO

CAULDRON-STYLE RICE MAINS

Most of these dishes are meant to be prepared in a caldero (see page 16), the heart of Abuela Sara's cocina. Calderos are great for their durability and heat distribution, which yields the best *pega'o* (crispy stuck-on rice crust; see page 205), a delicious by-product of rice preparation we fight over in my family. Abuela's caldero serves a small army and looks like it's been through a war. Despite that, if she leaves me anything as an inheritance, I'd like it to be that.

Puerto Ricans have many ways of preparing rice, most of which use Sofrito (page 38), so you know they pack a punch of sabor. I'm sharing my recipes for composed rice dishes—soulful meals made up of rice and some form of protein cooked together in one or pot, like Arroz con Pollo (page 213). I usually serve these as mains, but you can serve them as sides and top them with beans if you want an extra boost of protein and sabor.

ARROZ BLANCO (CON PEGA'O)

WHITE RICE (WITH CRUNCHY STUCK-ON CRUST)

SERVES 3 OR 4

2 cups uncooked medium-grain white rice

2 tablespoons extra-virgin olive oil

1 teaspoon salt

2 tablespoons neutral oil, such as canola or sunflower oil (optional, for pega'o)

I LOVE rice. It's my favorite food. I could eat it every day and did just that for half of my life growing up in Puerto Rico. We sometimes prepare it as a standalone meal (like Arroz con Pollo, page 213) or as a side, often topped with beans, which is why rice deserves its own chapter. If done right, white rice is the perfect canvas to carry all the love and sazón from our food and culture. I've included an option to make this with pega'o (stuck-on)—the crispy, golden crust that forms at the bottom of the pot. It's a beloved part of the meal, so much so that my family sometimes fights over it. This is my old-faithful, no-fail recipe if followed to a T.

In a large pot, combine the rice, olive oil, and salt. If you want pega'o, add the neutral oil. Add 3 cups water and stir to distribute the ingredients, 5 to 10 seconds. Bring to a boil over high heat, then reduce the heat to low, cover with a lid, and cook for 15 minutes.

For arroz blanco (pale, fluffy white rice), remove from the heat, uncover, and stir, then cover again and let steam for 5 minutes. Stir again and serve hot.

For pega'o (crunchy stuck-on rice), uncover, increase the heat to medium-high, and cook, without stirring, for 5 to 10 minutes more, until it's hissing and sizzling and the rice coming up the sides looks golden. Turn off the heat, cover, and let steam for 5 minutes. Uncover and stir from the bottom up to release and distribute the crunchy bits. This will yield fluffy white rice with crispy, slightly chewy pieces. Serve hot or scrape up that pega'o and eat it straight from the pot.

ARROZ CON CEBOLLA Y TOCINETA

CARAMELIZED ONION RICE WITH BACON BITS

SERVES 4 TO 6

1 pound bacon, cut into small dice (optional; see Note)

4 cups small-diced white or yellow onions (about 2 large)

1 tablespoon honey

1½ tablespoons beef bouillon or vegetable bouillon powder (about 3 cubes)

2 cups uncooked medium-grain white rice

¼ cup thinly sliced scallion (optional)

Freshly ground black pepper (optional)

NOTE: *If pork isn't your thing, omit the bacon; instead, combine 2 tablespoons olive oil and 2 tablespoons unsalted butter in a large pot and heat over medium heat until the butter melts and sizzles. Add the onions and continue as directed.*

It was always a happy day when Mama made us arroz con cebolla. It's slightly sweet from the caramelized onions, with salty bacon bits scattered throughout . . . I mean, c'mon! As a busy working woman, she sometimes took shortcuts. Instead of caramelizing onions, she used *Campbell's* French onion soup—a flavorful cooking hack. The time she saved on caramelizing onions, she'd invest into rendering bacon. Knowing she went through this additional step made it extra special. This is my homage to Mama's arroz con cebolla, but instead we're caramelizing. The onions just get SO. MUCH. SWEETER.

In a large pot, cook the bacon (if using) over medium-low heat, stirring, until the fat has rendered and the bacon looks bright red and crispy, 10 to 15 minutes. Using a slotted spoon, transfer the bacon to a paper towel–lined plate. Set it aside, away from thieves.

Add the onions to the pot with the rendered fat and cook, stirring every 1 to 2 minutes, until they're soft, deep golden brown, and caramelized, 15 to 20 minutes. Add the honey and bouillon and cook until the moisture from the honey has evaporated, 1 to 2 minutes. Add 3½ cups water and the rice. Stir to combine and fully dissolve the bouillon. Raise the heat to high and bring to a boil, then immediately reduce the heat to low, cover, and cook for 17 minutes. Remove from the heat, stir, and cover again. Let stand, covered, for 10 minutes more, then uncover and stir. Garnish with the scallion (if you want some extra allium-y flavor), crispy bacon bits, and some cracked pepper, if desired, then serve.

ARROZ CON JUEYES

STEWED LAND CRAB RICE

SERVES 4 TO 6

1 recipe Salmorejo de Jueyes (crab stew, page 247; omit the cilantro garnish)

2 cups uncooked medium-grain white rice

1½ teaspoons salt

¼ cup chopped fresh cilantro

When I was a child, Abuelo would bring in live young *jueyes* (land crabs) that he purchased from local fishermen. He raised and fed them for about one month downstairs in his *bohío* (a hut he'd built to keep his tools and gardening equipment). My sister and I loved running down there to peek at the aggressive-looking animals clacking around in an inverted refrigerator. On "arroz day," Abuelo would bring them up to the kitchen for Abuela to cook. After boiling them, she'd spread newspaper over the dining table on the terrace and implore whoever was around to help her crack all the meat out. My sister and I loved using a *maceta* (pestle) to squish the meat out of the crabs' skinny legs. And Abuela kept a close eye to prevent us from eating the crabmeat that was meant for the rice. She'd throw that meat into a massive caldero along with her magical sofrito, rice, and some crab shells (for flavor). It took more than one month of effort and over four people to produce this dish, but the result was an aromatic pot of flavorful crabby rice. I won't have you raise crabs or pick their meat, but if you can source some fresh-picked crabmeat, then I promise to deliver the love and sazón of one of my most cherished meals and memories. I like to serve this with fish, lobster or shrimp *al ajillo* (page 227), or *a caballo* (with a runny egg on top).

In a large pot, bring the salmorejo to a simmer over medium heat. Add the rice and salt and cook, stirring with a large spoon, until the rice is hot to the touch and well coated in the saucy crab stew, 1 to 2 minutes. Stir in 2¾ cups water. Raise the heat to high and bring to a boil, then immediately reduce the heat to low. Stir it again, cover, and cook for 20 minutes—do not remove the lid at any point. Remove from the heat and stir the rice well. Cover the pot again and let stand for 10 minutes more. Uncover, stir in the cilantro, and serve.

ARROZ CON GANDULES CON JAMÓN AHUMADO

PIGEON PEA RICE WITH SMOKY HAM CHUNKS

SERVES 6 TO 8

¼ cup olive oil

1 cup ½-inch-diced ham steak (about 6 ounces), or ½ teaspoon smoked paprika

½ cup Sofrito (page 38)

1 tablespoon sazón, homemade (page 39) or store-bought

1 (15.5-ounce) can pigeon peas, drained and rinsed

2 cups uncooked medium-grain white rice

1½ teaspoons salt

¼ cup chopped fresh cilantro leaves, stems, or a mix

Arroz con gandules is a Christmas staple in Puerto Rico. *Gandules* (pigeon peas) are tiny legumes, similar in size to black-eyed peas, that grow in pods. Abuelo and Abuela grow them at home, so we always have grocery bags packed with fresh-picked gandules pods. If I'm caught lying around, Abuela plops a bag on my lap and tells me, *"Ponte a 'esgranar, nena—haz algo por la patria"* (Start shelling, girl—make yourself useful). She and her sisters turn shelling gandules into *la hora del bochinche* (gossip hour). Once they're through every pod, they'll cook a pot of rice for an army. Somehow, there are never any leftovers. I learned this from Abuela: When you have a house full of food made with love, you'll always have a house full of people to love. This recipe calls for ham, but you can skip it and use paprika for a similar smoky flavor. For a complete Boricua Christmas feast, serve this with Pasteles (page 267) and Pernil Asado (page 235).

In a medium pot, heat the olive oil over medium heat. Add the ham (if using) and cook, stirring, until it turns golden, 3 to 4 minutes. Add the sofrito and cook, stirring, until most of the moisture evaporates, 3 to 4 minutes (if using paprika instead of ham, stir it in at this point). Add the sazón, pigeon peas, rice, and salt and stir to coat the rice evenly with the sazón. Add 3 cups water, stir, and increase the heat to high. Bring to a boil, then immediately reduce the heat to its lowest setting, cover, and cook for 15 minutes. Remove from the heat and stir in the cilantro. Cover the pot again and let stand for 10 minutes more. Uncover, stir, and enjoy.

ARROZ CON POLLO Y CHICHARRONES

CHICKEN RICE WITH CRISPY CHICKEN SKIN

SERVES 4

Despite what the name suggests, *arroz con pollo* isn't rice served with chicken (or vice versa)—it's chicken rice: a one-pot dish where everything is cooked together so the rice soaks up all the flavor from the chicken. Arroz con pollo is a humble dish that punches above its weight on sabor. Reminiscent of paella, its influence in our cocina derives from postcolonial adaptations with the use of Spanish imports such as olives, olive oil, sazón made with saffron, and roasted red peppers, often used as a garnish. Its distinctive yellowish color comes from achiote (see page 19). Abuela walked me through how to make hers the night before I'd have to re-create it on *Beat Bobby Flay*. To elevate it, I used chicken skins to make crispy chicharrones that I sprinkled on top as a textural contrast. I served it with my sweet and tangy pique for a pop of bright acidity, feeling gratified to represent Puerto Rico with Abuela's heart and my cooking style. It wasn't just any old arroz con pollo, and—spoiler alert—it beat Bobby.

1½ pounds bone-in, skin-on chicken thighs or drumsticks

3 teaspoons adobo, homemade (page 36) or store-bought

3 to 4 tablespoons olive oil

1 cup Sofrito (page 38)

3 pimento-stuffed green olives, minced, plus 1 tablespoon brine from the jar

2 cups uncooked medium-grain white rice

2 teaspoons Sazón (page 39)

2½ cups chicken broth

¼ cup finely chopped fresh cilantro, plus more for serving

Pique (page 43), for serving (optional)

Preheat the oven to 400°F. Line a baking sheet with parchment paper.

Remove the skins from the chicken pieces and stretch them out flat in a single layer on the prepared baking sheet. Cut the meat from the bones and place the bones on the baking sheet as well. Cut the meat into 2-inch chunks and place in a large bowl. Sprinkle the skins and bones evenly with 1 teaspoon of the adobo. Bake for 10 to 15 minutes, until the skins are golden brown and crispy. Transfer the skins to a paper towel–lined plate to drain and let cool to room temperature. Resist the urge to eat the chicken skin chicharrones by placing them out of sight in a dry airtight container. Reserve the bones.

Sprinkle the chicken meat with the remaining 2 teaspoons adobo. Using clean hands, massage the adobo into the

recipe continues

chicken until it's well coated. Let stand at room temperature for 15 to 20 minutes or cover and refrigerate for up to 2 hours.

In a large pot, heat the olive oil over medium heat. Add the chicken and cook until golden brown on all sides, about 10 minutes. Transfer the chicken to a large plate. In the same pot, combine the sofrito, olives, and olive brine. Cook, stirring, until most of the moisture has evaporated, 2 to 5 minutes. Add the rice and sazón and cook, stirring, until the rice is hot to the touch, 2 to 4 minutes more.

Add the broth and reserved chicken bones and bring to a boil, then immediately reduce the heat to low. Stir, then arrange the chicken (and any juices collected on the plate) in an even layer on top of the rice. Cover and cook for 15 minutes—do not remove the lid at any point during that time. Remove from the heat and stir the chicken into the rice. Remove and discard the chicken bones. Cover the pot again and let stand for 10 minutes more. Uncover and stir in the cilantro.

Serve the rice in bowls. With your hands, crush some of the chicken skin chicharrones and sprinkle them over the top. Finish with more cilantro. And if you want to kick it up the way I did on *Beat Bobby Flay*, drizzle on a few drops of pique.

ARROZ MAMPOSTEA'O CON AMARILLITOS

STEWY BEAN RICE WITH SWEET PLANTAINS

SERVES 1 OR 2

2 or 3 slices thick-cut bacon, cut into small dice (optional; see Note)

1 cup diced sweet plantain (about 1 medium)

1 teaspoon sazón, homemade (page 39) or store-bought

2 cups cooked white rice (page 205)

1 cup hot Habichuelitas Guisadas con Calabaza (page 193)

Salt (optional)

2 tablespoons chopped fresh cilantro

In Puerto Rico, beans are cooked as a stew and usually served atop rice. *Arroz mampostea'o* means the rice and beans are cooked together, as one dish. In my house, it means the cook was tired and there were leftovers. In *restaurantes criollos* (Creole restaurants), arroz mampostea'o was my way to hack the system by getting two sides for the price of one . . . girl math. Cooking the rice in the bean stew makes it creamier—like a Creole risotto. People often throw in extra goodies, resulting in a chunky, flavor-packed rice dish that can stand on its own as a meal. I like to add some bacon and diced sweet plantains to contrast all the savory for THEE ultimate lazy-girl-with-sazón dinner.

In a medium pot, cook the bacon (if using; see Note) over medium heat, stirring continuously, until all the fat has rendered and the bacon looks crispy, 6 to 8 minutes. Using a slotted spoon, transfer the bacon to a paper towel–lined plate. Add the plantain to the pot with the rendered fat and cook, stirring continuously, until bright yellow and subtly caramelized, 3 to 4 minutes. Transfer the plantain to the plate with the bacon. Add the rice to the pot and sprinkle with the sazón. Cook, stirring, until the rice is tinted evenly from the sazón, 1 to 2 minutes. Add the habichuelitas and reduce the heat to medium-low. Cook, stirring, until the rice looks creamy, 4 to 6 minutes. Taste and season with salt, if needed. Return the bacon and plantains to the pot, stir, and

recipe continues

increase the heat to medium-high. Cook, without stirring, until the rice looks drier and the edges are starting to stick to the bottom of the pot, 2 to 4 minutes more.

Sprinkle with the cilantro and stir, scraping from the bottom up, then serve.

NOTE: *If you're not using bacon, heat 1 tablespoon olive oil in a medium pot over medium heat, then add the plantain and continue as directed.*

MAMA'S ARROZ RELLENO

PICADILLO "STUFFED" RICE WITH CRUSTY CHEESE

SERVES 6 TO 8

Olive oil spray

1 recipe Arroz con Cebolla (page 207; see Note)

1 recipe Picadillo (page 260)

8 slices Swiss cheese or another mild, melty cheese (such as mozzarella, cheddar, Muenster, or Monterey Jack), shredded or sliced

¼ cup thinly sliced scallion or chopped fresh cilantro or parsley (optional)

Freshly cracked black pepper (optional)

NOTE: *For this recipe, I prefer the rice without the bacon, but leave it in if you're feeling extra indulgent.*

This dish is naughty, and it's one of Mama's signatures. She layers sweet, caramelized onion rice with savory picadillo and tops it with a melty/crunchy layer of broiled Swiss cheese. It's how her mom (my other abuela, Oda) made it for Mama and her sisters, and how Mama made it for my sister and me— Boricua comfort food. To add some freshness, I serve mine with a side of Garlicky Cabbage Salad (page 121), which basically makes it fat-free. What I love most about this dish is that I can prepare it a day (or two) ahead and bake it when I'm ready to serve it. It's great for a fuss-free, casual dinner with family or friends, or a board game type of night.

Place a rack in the middle of the oven and preheat to 350°F. Coat a 9 by 13-inch baking pan with olive oil spray.

Add half the rice to the prepared baking pan and spread it into a flat, even layer with the back of a spoon, then add the picadillo and do the same. Repeat with the rest of the rice, then top it evenly with the cheese. (At this point, you can cover and refrigerate the rice until you're ready to bake it, up to 2 days.)

Cover the rice with foil and bake for 30 minutes (or 45 minutes, if refrigerated). Remove the foil and bake for 15 to 20 minutes more, until the top and edges look light golden. If it's taking longer, switch the oven to broil and broil for 2 to 4 minutes; this will speed up that browning process, but watch it, because it happens fast. Let cool for 10 to 15 minutes before serving.

Slice and serve like a lasagna, garnished with scallion or fresh herbs and cracked pepper, if desired.

CARNES Y MARISCOS

MEAT AND SEAFOOD

Restaurantes criollos (Creole restaurants) are the heart and soul of Puerto Rican dining. Here meat and seafood take center stage, celebrating the diversity and heritage of our land and sea. While the island's under-developed commercial fishing industry means grocery stores rely on flash-frozen seafood imported from the US, local fishermen sell their fresh catch directly to restaurants, which makes restaurantes criollos *the* place to enjoy our island's ocean bounty.

Some of recipes in this chapter, like Fried Red Snapper (page 225) and Grouper Nuggets (page 223), are inspired by family road trips along the coast. And the Grilled Skirt Steak (page 231), which I'd classify as the Puerto Rican steak of choice, is my niece's default pick.

I walk you through how to season and prepare them using adobo and sazón, and share techniques I picked up working in fine-dining kitchens—skills I still use in my own cocina today. I'll also suggest sauce pairings from the Grandmother Sauces chapter (pages 40–51)—all meant to add depth and sabor to your protein of choice. Whether I'm slicing into tender churrasco or tearing into crispy chunks of chillo frito with my bare hands, these *sabores* (flavors) bring me back to Puerto Rican dinner tables, surrounded by *los míos* (my people), again and again.

NUGGETS DE MERO

CRISPY GROUPER NUGGETS

MAKES ABOUT 40 NUGGETS

2 pounds skinless fresh grouper fillets (or other flaky white fish, such as cod), cut into 2-inch chunks

2 to 3 tablespoons adobo, homemade (page 36) or store-bought

1½ cups all-purpose flour

5 large eggs

2 cups plain breadcrumbs (see Note)

Olive oil spray

Salt

1 tablespoon chopped fresh cilantro leaves, stems, or a mix

3 limes

NOTE: *I like using Export soda crackers ground into crumbs in the food processor.*

This recipe brings back memories of family staycations in the coastal town of Río Grande, just 45 minutes away from San Juan. My parents and their *corillo* (friend crew) would rent a big beach house. For us kids, it was a one-weekend-only free-for-all on the discipline end, and we loved it. We'd head to the Kioskos de Luquillo (beachside kiosks located one town over)—the perfect casual spot for a big group of rowdy kids and boozed-up adults. The grown-ups would order an assortment of *frituras* (fritters), including baskets of these nuggets made with fresh-caught grouper. A squeeze of lime and a dunk in Mayo-Ketchup (page 45), and we were entertained and satisfied long enough for the grown-ups to let loose on beer and mojitos. (I also like them with Ájili-Mójili, page 46.)

Place a rack in the middle of the oven and preheat the broiler to high. Line a baking sheet with parchment paper.

Place the grouper in the large bowl and sprinkle with 2 to 3 teaspoons of the adobo. Toss gently, coating the fish evenly.

Place the flour, eggs, and breadcrumbs in three separate medium bowls. Sprinkle each with 1 teaspoon of the adobo and whisk the adobo into the flour and the breadcrumbs. Add ¼ cup water to the eggs and beat well. From left to right, place the bowl with the fish, followed by the flour, eggs, breadcrumbs, and prepared baking sheet. Using clean hands, dredge the pieces of fish one at a time in the flour to coat evenly, patting it gently to remove the excess. Dip them into the eggs, shaking off the excess, then place them in the breadcrumbs, pressing gently so they adhere well. Place in a single layer on the baking sheet and coat generously on both sides with olive oil spray. Bake on the center rack for 15 to 20 minutes, flipping them halfway through, until crispy, golden, and sizzling.

Season lightly with salt and sprinkle with the cilantro. Gate the lime zest over the fish, then quarter the limes and serve them on the side for squeezing.

CHILLO FRITO

FRIED RED SNAPPER

SERVES 1 OR 2

4 cups canola oil, plus more if needed

1 (2- to 2½-pound) whole chillo (red snapper), mero cabrilla (mutton snapper), colirubia (yellowtail snapper), or cartucho (queen snapper), scaled and gutted (see Note)

1 teaspoon salt, plus more as needed

½ teaspoon dried oregano

¼ cup all-purpose flour

2 to 4 lime wedges

This dish brings back fun memories of our road trips to Arecibo, Abuela Sara's native town, located on the northwest coast of Puerto Rico. On the way back to San Juan, we'd always stop at our favorite seafood restaurant that specialized in fresh-caught local fish. My *primas* (cousins) and I loved ordering sharing-sized portions of *chillo frito* (fried whole red snapper)—it was the perfect excuse to act like savages, tearing into its tender, juicy flesh with our bare hands, licking our fingers after each bite.

Though seemingly intimidating, chillo frito is relatively easy to prepare. Unfortunately, snapper is not necessarily easy to source fresh in Puerto Rico. But thanks to Papa's charming personality, we have the connections to (what feels like) black market contraband. So when he brings some home, we don't ask questions and leave the frying to him.

For this dish, timing is everything. Overcooking risks drying it out. It should be lightly crisp on the outside, with tender flesh that flakes off when lightly tugged and a glistening interior. The taste should be mild and sweet. A squeeze of lime juice is all it needs to bring out its delicate flavor. This is Papa's method. We like serving this with fresh arepas (see pages 163–164) and Mayo-Ketchup (page 45) or Ájili-Mójili (page 46). It's modest, unlike Papa, but highlights the quality and rarity of something that is truly special.

Pour the oil into a large, shallow, heavy-bottomed pan or deep fryer (check out my Guide to Frying on page 148 for tips). (If using a pan, there should be enough oil to come about halfway up the sides of the fish.) Heat over medium heat to 350°F.

Pat the fish completely dry with paper towels and place it on a cutting board. Using a sharp knife, score the fish on both sides in a diagonal crosshatch pattern, spacing the cuts about 1 inch apart.

In a small bowl, combine the salt and oregano, using your fingertips to crush the oregano into the salt until it's aromatic. Sprinkle this mixture all over the fish and gently

recipe continues

NOTE: *While 2 to 2½ pounds sounds like a lot for 1 to 2 servings, keep in mind that you won't eat the head or bones of the fish, which are factored into this weight. Depending on your appetite, it's easy to polish off one fish per person, but if you're having hearty sides like rice, beans, or tostones (page 151), you may want to consider splitting it with a loved one.*

rub it in, getting into the scored grooves in the flesh. Evenly sprinkle the fish with the flour to coat. Pat it lightly over the cutting board to remove excess flour.

Gently place the fish in the hot oil to avoid splattering. Fry until it looks golden and crisp on both sides, 3 to 5 minutes per side. Reduce the heat to medium-low to bring the oil temperature down to about 330°F and cook until the scored flesh looks flaky and the fish is a deep golden brown, 3 to 5 minutes more on each side. If your fish is bigger, at this stage, add 1 minute of cooking per side per extra pound of fish. Transfer the fish to a paper towel–lined plate to drain. While it's still hot and sizzling, season it with salt on both sides. Serve with the lime wedges on the side. Tear into it with your hands. Don't be shy.

RABOS DE LANGOSTA O CAMARONES AL AJILLO

GARLICKY LOBSTER TAILS OR SHRIMP

SERVES 4 OR 5

1½ to 2 pounds fresh lobster tails (about 4), halved lengthwise

1 recipe Ajillo (page 51), at room temperature

1 teaspoon salt

2 tablespoons chopped fresh cilantro, parsley, or chives

2 limes or lemons, quartered

If you can bite the bullet and get your hands on some fresh lobster tails, you need to try this recipe. Shrimp is a less expensive alternative that delivers the same sabor. The recipe looks intimidating, but it's foolproof, ready in less than 15 minutes, and will have you feeling like a pro chef—and the ingredients cost half what you'd pay for the dish at a restaurant. The mellow garlicky flavor complements the sweet, delicate lobster. If you're scared to crack your lobster tails, ask the person at the fish counter to do so—that's half the work. I like to serve this over Buttery Plantain Mash (page 199), a bed of plain white rice (page 205), or Arroz con Jueyes (land crab rice, page 209) to soak up all the garlicky goodness. Setting everything family-style in the middle of the table makes it a complete showstopper.

Place a rack in the middle of the oven and preheat the broiler to high. Line a large baking dish with foil.

Using clean hands, separate the lobster meat from the shell by pinching the chunkiest piece (the one opposite the fanned tail end) and gently pulling it toward you with one hand while you hold on to the shell with the other. Place the meat back in the shell and set it meat-side up on the prepared baking dish. Repeat with the remaining tail halves. Sprinkle the lobster meat lightly with the salt and, using a spoon, distribute the ajillo evenly among the tail halves, coating the lobster meat evenly. (The tails can be covered and refrigerated for up to 2 hours; uncover before broiling.)

When ready to serve, broil for 2 to 6 minutes (start checking after 2 minutes), until the shells are bright red, the ajillo is melted and sizzling, and the meat looks white and opaque.

recipe continues

Serve immediately, preferably while it's still sizzling. If any garlicky butter oozed out, spoon it back on top! Sprinkle with the cilantro and serve with the lime or lemon wedges on the side for squeezing.

FOR CAMARONES (SHRIMP) AL AJILLO: Peel (leaving the tails on) and devein 1½ to 2 pounds large (16/20-count) shrimp. Melt the ajillo in a large sauté pan over medium heat. When it's aromatic, about 1 minute, add the shrimp and sprinkle them with about half the salt. Raise the heat to medium-high. They should sizzle gently without the garlic or butter browning. Cook, lightly tossing or stirring continuously, until they're just pink on both sides and fully opaque and white in the center, 3 to 5 minutes. Finish and serve as directed.

CHURRASCO O SOLOMILLO DE CERDO A LA PARRILLA

GRILLED SKIRT STEAK OR PORK TENDERLOIN

SERVES 4 TO 6

3 pounds skirt steak or pork tenderloin

Adobo, homemade (page 36) or store-bought; Sazón, homemade (page 39) or store-bought; Adobo Mojado (page 36); or your favorite dry seasoning, wet rub, or salt and pepper (see Note)

2 to 3 tablespoons olive oil

NOTE: *For dry seasonings/rubs that contain salt, like sazón or adobo, I use about 1 tablespoon per pound of meat. For dry spice blends with no salt, I use about 2 teaspoons and add about 1 teaspoon salt per pound of meat. For wet rubs/marinades that contain salt, like adobo mojado, I use about ¼ cup per pound of meat.*

Grilled pork tenderloin was my first winning dish on *Hell's Kitchen*, and was described by Chef Gordon Ramsay as "Delicious. Pink . . . and again, pink." Grilled *churrasco* (skirt steak) was one of my last winning dishes during my final challenge. It was inspired by Papa and his casual cookout serving style—passing a cutting board with fresh-off-the-grill, juicy chunks of meat ready to be pinched with bare fingers. Both the pork and the churrasco involve the same trimming, seasoning, and cooking process. I like serving the pork with Salsita Criolla (page 48) and the skirt steak, inspired by Argentinean parrilladas, with chorizo chimichurri (page 47), as shown here.

Pat the meat dry thoroughly with paper towels and place it on a cutting board. Using a sharp knife, trim off any excess fat or white sinew (try to avoid trimming off the actual meat). If using skirt steak, cut it crosswise into individual portions if it's very long; otherwise, leave it whole. If using pork, cut the tenderloin crosswise into 1- to 2-inch-thick medallions (2 to 3 ounces per piece).

Sprinkle or spread the seasoning of your choice over the surface of the steak or pork, then massage it evenly into the meat. Cover and let stand at room temperature for up to 1 hour or refrigerate for up to 1 day (bring the meat to room temperature for 10 to 15 minutes before cooking if refrigerated).

Brush some olive oil over the rack of an outdoor grill or a stovetop grill pan until all the ridges are evenly coated. Heat

recipe continues

the grill to medium-high or heat the pan over medium-high heat until the rack or pan sizzles and steams when sprinkled with water.

If the meat looks wet, gently pat it dry with paper towels. Drizzle it lightly with the olive oil and rub it in on all sides. Place the meat on the grill or pan, spacing the portions at least ½ inch apart, and gently press down on each piece to create even contact with the grill. Cook, undisturbed, until you achieve brown grill marks, about 2 minutes. Rotate each piece 45 degrees and gently press down on it again—enough to get even contact on the grill, but not so much to squeeze out the meat's juices. Cook, undisturbed, until you achieve crosshatched grill marks, about 2 minutes more. Flip the meat over and repeat this process on the opposite side. Check for doneness with an instant-read thermometer. For skirt steak, I prefer medium-rare, between 125° and 135°F. If you prefer it more cooked, leave it on the grill for an additional minute or two on each side. For pork medallions, I like medium doneness, between 150° and 155°F.

Transfer the meat to a cutting board and let rest for 5 to 10 minutes before serving. After resting, it should look pink throughout in the center and should have a bouncy, tender texture when poked with a finger. Slice it into bite-size pieces (across the grain, if it's steak) and serve it Papa's way (see headnote).

PERNIL ASADO CON CUERITO

GARLICKY ROAST PORK SHOULDER WITH CRISPY CRACKLING

SERVES 5 TO 7

⅓ cup salt, plus more if needed

1 recipe Adobo Mojado (page 36)

5 pounds bone-in, skin-on pork shoulder (pernil; see Note)

1 tablespoon olive oil

NOTE: *Keep in mind the weight of your pork shoulder. If it's heavier or lighter than mine, you'll need to scale all the ingredients up or down accordingly, including the adobo.*

Pernil is a must at any Puerto Rican holiday, especially Noche Buena (Christmas Eve). When I walk into Abuela's house, I first inhale the unmistakable aromas of sweet garlic and earthy oregano. Then I make my way to the oven and peek at the bronzed hunk of meat sizzling away inside. Abuela always nails the *cuerito*—the top layer of pork skin, so crispy it snaps. That piece is highly coveted, but Abuela, my angel on earth, always saves me the biggest chunk.

Preparing this roast takes two days, one for marinating and one for baking. For holidays, we serve this with Arroz con Gandules (page 211) and Pasteles (page 267)—pernil's partners in crime. On any other occasion, I'd serve this with any of the arroces on pages 202–219 or sides on pages 190–201. If you have leftovers, use them to make Papa's Lifesaving Medianoche Sandwich (page 91).

You're about to get down and dirty with this meat, so *prepárate* (get prepped)! Stir 1 tablespoon of the salt into the adobo—this is your marinade. Grab a 9-inch square baking pan, paper towels, a long sharp knife, a spoon, your marinade, the rest of the salt, and some gloves if you want (I go bare-handed). Hair in a bun? Great. Now you're ready. For step-by-step visuals, see page 238. Using clean hands, rub the marinade into the flesh of the pork all around (avoiding the skin), using your fingers to push the marinade into all those slits you created. Don't be coy. Get in it, then on it.

Place the pork in the pan and pat it dry well with paper towels. With the knife, separate the thick layer of skin from the meat, gliding it horizontally between the skin and the meat just until you get to the edge but leaving the end attached so the skin folds out like a book. Working around

recipe continues

the bone, cut deep slits in the flesh from top to bottom and side to side, spacing them about 2 inches apart, creating large pockets throughout the meat that will hold the garlicky marinade. (Essentially, stab the meat, get any anger out on it.)

When you've used up all the marinade, place the pork skin-side up and fold the skin back over the top like a blanket. Using paper towels, pat that skin completely clean and dry again, rubbing off any marinade that has gotten on it. (This step may sound excessive, but trust me, you'll thank me when you taste that cuerito.) Sprinkle the skin with the remaining salt, 1 to 2 tablespoons at a time, using your hands to spread it evenly into a thin layer over the entire surface of the skin. (This will dehydrate the skin, which will help achieve that snappy, shattery, golden crust.) Loosely cover the pan with foil and refrigerate overnight or for up to 24 hours.

Take the pernil out of the fridge and let it come to room temperature for 1 hour. Place a rack in the middle of the oven and preheat to 350°F.

Scrape the salt off the top of the skin using a spoon, spatula, or knife; discard the salt. Using paper towels, wipe off any remaining salt until the skin looks clean and dry. There will be liquid pooling around the pork. Transfer the pork skin-side up to a clean pan or rinse out the one it was in and discard the liquid, then return the pork to the pan. Rub the olive oil over the skin. (This will promote even tanning.) Bake, uncovered, for 3 to 4 hours, or about 30 minutes per pound of meat, until the center of the meat, close to the bone, registers 185° to 200°F on an instant-read thermometer. (If you don't have a thermometer, check the doneness of the meat by tugging it away from the bone with a fork. It should shred off easily and look pink.) Start checking about 1 hour before it's supposed to be ready, then every 15 to 20 minutes after that—you don't want to overcook it. The cuerito should look crispy; do the tap test by tapping the cuerito with the back of a knife or spoon. It should sound like you're tapping a hard, hollow shell. If it

recipe continues

Separate the skin from the meat.

Pierce slits into the flesh.

Stuff marinade into the slits.

Rub marinade onto the flesh.

Sprinkle the skin with salt.

Spread and press the salt onto the skin.

doesn't, increase the oven temperature to 450°F and roast in 10- to 15-minute increments until the cuerito looks deeply bronzed, like it went beach-hopping around Puerto Rico for a couple of weeks. Remove from the oven and let rest, uncovered, for 30 minutes.

Transfer the meat to a large baking sheet or cutting board. If there are juicy drippings in the pan, save those, but pour off any excess fat. Peel the cuerito off the roast and set it aside—you may need to hide it from thieves. If the meat is cool enough to handle, use clean hands to pull it apart. (If not, use two forks.) Discard any excess fat that feels soft and flabby. Transfer the pulled meat and the reserved drippings (if you had any) to a baking pan or oven-safe container and taste it. It should be very porky, savory, garlicky, smoky from the cumin in the adobo, and mildly peppery, with herbaceous hints of oregano. Add salt little by little, if needed, tasting after each addition until you bring out all those flavors. Cover with foil and keep warm in the oven on the lowest heat setting (about 170°F) for up to 1 hour, or until you're ready to serve it. Don't forget to serve everyone a chunk of that cuerito you stashed away.

POLLOCHÓN

LECHÓN-FLAVORED ROAST CHICKEN

SERVES 4 TO 6

3 pounds bone-in, skin-on chicken thighs and/or drumsticks

½ to ¾ cup Adobo Mojado (page 36)

Pavochón is roast turkey seasoned the same way we would season a lechón (pork roast). The name is a mash-up of two words: *pavo* (turkey) + *chón* (from *lechón*). *Pollo*chón (*pollo* = chicken) is my lazy-girl version that I make with chicken thighs or drumsticks. It brings all the punchy flavors and aromas of that Boricua holiday roast, with the *best* parts of the bird (dark meat—duh!) in a fraction of the time.

Even though Thanksgiving is a North American tradition, we still observe it in Puerto Rico and classify it as the beginning of our (VERY) long Christmas celebration. At Abuela's, we could always count on having pavochón stuffed with mashed viandas (see pages 25–31). This recipe is inspired by that menu, but made for a very busy, single, working girl who, despite being a pro chef, can't be bothered to prepare a whole bird (even on a holiday). I like serving this over rice (page 205) or plantain mash (page 199), drizzled with some of the pan drippings and chimichurri (page 47).

Place the chicken pieces and the adobo in a large bowl. Using clean hands, massage the adobo into the chicken, trying to get it underneath the skin so it's evenly coated. Cover and marinate at room temperature for 45 minutes or in the fridge for up to 6 hours (bring to room temperature before roasting if refrigerated).

Place a rack in the middle of the oven and preheat to 400°F. Line a large baking sheet with parchment paper.

Place the pieces of chicken 1 inch apart on the prepared pan (skin-side up if using thighs). Scrape all the adobo from the bowl onto the chicken. Roast for 30 minutes, or until light golden and sizzling on the pan. Switch the oven to broil on high and broil for 3 to 5 minutes, until the skin turns deep golden and starts to blister on top. Remove from the oven and let rest for 5 to 10 minutes before serving.

BISTEC ENCEBOLLA'O

BEEF STEAK WITH VINEGARY ONION GRAVY

SERVES 4 OR 5

2 pounds cube steak (minute steak) or chicken breasts, pounded with a meat mallet to ¼-inch thickness

1 tablespoon adobo, homemade (page 36) or store-bought

1 teaspoon freshly ground black pepper

3 tablespoons apple cider vinegar

4 tablespoons olive oil, plus more if needed

2 medium white or yellow onions, sliced into ½-inch-thick rounds

Salt

Bistec encebollado, or steak and onions, is a homey dish prepared in different Latin American countries, including Mexico, Dominican Republic, and Puerto Rico. Each country has their own way of seasoning and preparing it. Its origin is unclear, though many believe it derives from a dish brought by our Spanish colonizers called *carne con cebollas* (meat with onions). The word *bistec* is an anglicism of the words "beef steak," also reflecting US influences in our dialect.

In Puerto Rico, we use inexpensive cuts of meat like cube steak (also known as minute steak) that we tenderize by pounding with a meat mallet and marinating in vinegar. We top it with caramelized onions cooked with the steak, often alongside white rice (page 205) with *habichuelas* (beans; see pages 190–201). It's a quick, hearty, and flavorsome meal. I've also offered the option to prepare this with chicken breasts, which makes the dish lighter but no less flavorful.

Place the meat flat in a large, shallow container or bowl. Sprinkle it evenly on both sides with the adobo and pepper. Drizzle with 2 tablespoons of the vinegar and 2 tablespoons of the olive oil. With clean hands, rub the vinegar and oil into the meat, cover, and marinate at room temperature for 20 to 30 minutes or in the fridge for up to 8 hours.

In a large sauté pan, heat 1 tablespoon of the olive oil over medium heat. Add the onions and cook, stirring occasionally, until they begin to soften and caramelize, about 10 minutes. Add ½ teaspoon salt and the remaining 1 tablespoon vinegar and cook until the onions are soft and translucent, 4 to 7 minutes more. Transfer the onions to a plate and keep it close by. Add the remaining 2 tablespoons olive oil to the pan (or enough to coat the surface) and raise the heat to medium-high. When the oil starts smoking, working in batches, if needed, to avoid overcrowding, place the steaks side by side in the pan and cook until browned on both sides, 1 to 2 minutes per side. They're thin, so they'll cook fast; don't step away and risk overcooking them. Transfer the cooked steaks to the plate with the onions and repeat with the remaining steaks. When you've browned all the meat, return the steaks to the pan and top with the onions and any juices accumulated on the plate. Reduce the heat to medium-low and cook for 1 minute more (or 3 minutes more if using chicken). Remove from the heat and serve immediately.

GUISOS

STEWS

Stewing is a cooking method that requires slow, gentle heat. For me, stews are the perfect way of luxuriating cuts of protein that may be considered undesirable or cheap, resulting in unctuous, melt-in-your-mouth, fall-apart-tender meat. As a culture, we often have to tolerate being dealt crappy cards and playing at disadvantages. But we're resilient—we use what's available to us, and in our cocinas, we won't let inexpensive ingredients limit our creativity and touch of sabor.

In Puerto Rico, we serve these guisos atop rice any time of year, but they also make a cozy, heartwarming winter meal for people like me who deal with snowy weather. Pastelón (page 255), Canoas (page 263), and Pasteles (page 267) combine viandas (see pages 25–31) and stewed meat in one. You can also use them as fillings for Frituras (see pages 146–169).

You can cook any of these stews in a caldero (see page 16) or heavy-bottomed pot, but I'll offer shortcuts and options (like oven-searing or using a pressure cooker) along the way to make things even easier.

SALMOREJO DE JUEYES

SAUCY CRAB STEW

SERVES 4 TO 6

5 tablespoons Achiote Oil (page 37) or olive oil

1 cup diced onion

½ cup small-diced jarred roasted red peppers (pimientos morrones)

½ cup Sofrito (page 38)

1 pound jueyes (land crab) or blue crab meat

1 teaspoon adobo, homemade (page 36) or store-bought

6 pimento-stuffed olives or pitted green olives, finely chopped, plus 1 tablespoon brine from the jar

2 teaspoons drained brined capers, finely chopped, plus 2 teaspoons brine from the jar

2 cups small-diced fresh tomatoes (about 1 large), or 1 (14.5-ounce) can stewed tomatoes

Salt

FOR SERVING (OPTIONAL)

Cooked white rice (page 205)

2 or 3 avocados, halved

2 tablespoons chopped fresh cilantro

This versatile stew makes a delicious filling for Alcapurrias (page 168), Pastelillos (page 165), arepas (pages 163–164), and even a less traditional take on Pasteles (page 267). You can also serve it with tostones (page 151) as a dip—a hearty snack or a true Boricua girl-dinner. Abuela uses it as the base for her Arroz con Jueyes (page 209). And for a showstopping lunch or dinner, nestle a halved avocado over a bed of fluffy white rice, then spoon the stew into the center so it spills over the sides, as shown here.

In a large pot, heat the achiote oil over medium heat. Add the onion, roasted peppers, and sofrito and cook, stirring with a spatula, until the onion looks soft and translucent and the moisture from the sofrito has evaporated, 5 to 8 minutes. Add the crab, sprinkle it with the adobo, and use the spatula to break it up and stir it into the sofrito. Add the olives and their brine, capers and their brine, and the tomatoes, increase the heat to medium-high, and cook, stirring, until the liquid from the tomatoes has reduced by half and looks saucy but not soupy, 5 to 10 minutes. Taste it. It should be slightly savory, enough to taste the sweet crab, with mild acidity from the tomatoes and brininess from the olives. If you can't taste the crab, add salt pinch by pinch, stirring and tasting after each addition. Simmer gently for 2 to 5 minutes more to allow the flavors to combine. Remove from the heat.

Serve as suggested in the headnote, or if desired, spoon some rice onto each serving plate to make a bed, then set an avocado half on top and season with salt. Spoon the crab stew into the avocado, garnish with the cilantro, and serve.

FRICASÉ DE POLLO CON CHICHARRONES

STEWED CHICKEN FRICASSEE WITH CRISPY CHICKEN SKIN

SERVES 4 OR 5

4 chicken drumsticks (about 1½ pounds)

4 bone-in, skin-on chicken thighs (about 1½ pounds)

2 tablespoons adobo, homemade (page 36) or store-bought

¼ cup olive oil

½ cup Sofrito (page 38)

2 cups small-diced fresh tomatoes (about 1 large), or 1 (14.5-ounce) can stewed tomatoes

7 pimento-stuffed olives, minced, plus 1 tablespoon brine from the jar

4 cups chicken broth

1 tablespoon sazón, homemade (page 39) or store-bought

2 large Yukon Gold potatoes, cut into large, golf ball–size chunks

2 large carrots, cut into 1-inch cubes

¼ cup chopped fresh cilantro leaves, stems, or a mix

Salt (optional)

Once upon a time, Papa and I capped off a successful beach day with a visit to Abuela's house for dinner. We were famished, and when we opened the door, we were smacked by the aroma of Abuela's pollo en fricasé, an unassuming chicken stew that surprises you with layers of deep Creole flavor, simmering away on the stove. Still in my bikini top and shorts, but desperate to savor it, I grabbed a spoon and dug in. I broke off a piece of chicken and scooped up some of its sauce. As I blew on my bite over the pot, Abuela walked in and caught me. Pissed, she yelled "*¡Eso no está!*" (That's not ready!) She startled me, and I dropped my perfectly constructed bite back into the simmering pot, splattering hot fricasé sauce on my exposed chest. She exclaimed "*¡Quémate! ¡Quémate las tetas ahora!*" (Burn! Burn your tits now!) Papa and I laughed hysterically as she shooed me away from the kitchen while I wiped the sauce off me. Now, whenever anyone scavenges from Abuela's pots on the stove, we say, "You're gonna burn your tits," which just means don't mess with her food.

I like to serve this over fluffy white rice (page 205) with some crushed chicken skin chicharrones on top for crunch. And if you add a slice of ripe avocado lightly sprinkled with salt, you'd be having our Puerto Rican version of a cherry on a sundae.

Remove the skin from the drumsticks and thighs and place them in a medium bowl or airtight container. Add the drumsticks and thighs. Sprinkle with the adobo and toss to coat the chicken pieces and skins. Cover and let stand at room temperature for 20 to 30 minutes or refrigerate for 1 to 2 hours.

Preheat the oven to 400°F. Line a baking sheet with parchment paper.

Stretch out the chicken skins flat in a single layer on the prepared baking sheet. Bake for 10 to 15 minutes, until the

recipe continues

chicharrones are golden brown and crispy. Transfer to a paper towel–lined plate to drain and let cool to room temperature. Resist the urge to eat the chicken skin chicharrones by placing them out of sight in a dry airtight container.

In a large heavy-bottomed pot, heat the olive oil over medium heat or until it sizzles when you place the chicken on it. Add half the chicken pieces and sear until light golden on all sides, 2 to 3 minutes per side. Transfer to a plate and repeat with the remaining chicken. Add the sofrito to the pot and cook, stirring, until all the moisture has evaporated, 2 to 3 minutes. Add the tomatoes and olives. Cook, stirring, until the moisture has evaporated, 2 to 3 minutes more. Add the olive brine, broth, and sazón, return the chicken to the pot, and stir to combine.

Bring to a boil over high heat. Reduce the heat to medium-low to maintain a soft simmer, cover, and cook until the chicken is tender and easily pulls off the bone with a fork, 20 to 25 minutes.

Add the potatoes and carrots and cook until the potatoes are fork-tender, 10 to 15 minutes more. Take out 2 or 3 pieces of potato, mash them with the fork, and return them to the stew to thicken it. Raise the heat to medium and cook until the stew has a saucy consistency, 3 to 5 minutes more. Stir in the cilantro and taste the stew. It should have a mild sweetness from the tomatoes, a slight funkiness from the olives, and savoriness from the chicken. If needed, add salt pinch by pinch, stirring and tasting after each addition, then serve.

FOR A PRESSURE COOKER OR INSTANT POT: Bake the chicken skin as directed. Heat the olive oil in a pressure cooker over medium heat or in an Instant Pot on the Sauté setting. Add half the chicken pieces and continue the recipe as directed. After returning the chicken to the pot, seal the lid and cook on high pressure for 8 minutes. Release the pressure and remove the lid. Add the potatoes and carrots to the pot, and set the heat to medium-low or select the Sauté setting. Continue the recipe as directed.

CARNE GUISADA

BROTHY BEEF STEW

SERVES 4 OR 5

3 pounds beef eye round or beef stew meat, cut into 1-inch cubes

2 tablespoons adobo, homemade (page 36) or store-bought

¼ cup olive oil

¼ cup neutral oil, such as canola or sunflower oil

1 medium green bell pepper, cut into small dice

1 medium onion, cut into small dice

½ cup Sofrito (page 38)

2 cups small-diced fresh tomatoes (about 1 large), or 1 (14.5-ounce) can stewed tomatoes

7 pimento-stuffed olives, minced, plus 1 tablespoon brine from the jar

4 cups beef broth

2 large carrots, cut into 1-inch cubes

2 large Yukon Gold potatoes, cut into large, golf ball–size chunks

¼ cup chopped fresh cilantro

Salt (optional)

Carne guisada is an inexpensive, hearty, and homey Puerto Rican classic that feeds a crowd and tastes even better the next day. It's also a favorite of Titi Myrna, Papa's sister. She's a working entrepreneur with a hectic and demanding schedule. Abuela likes to pamper her by making an obscenely large pot, sending her home with a full belly and a to-go bag of leftovers. We serve this over fluffy white rice (page 205) with tons of broth for the rice to sop. A slice of avocado (lightly seasoned with salt) on the side would also be perfectly appropriate.

Place the beef in the bowl or airtight container and sprinkle with the adobo. Rub the adobo into the meat with clean hands to evenly coat on all sides. Cover and let stand at room temperature for 20 to 30 minutes.

In a large heavy-bottomed pot, heat the olive oil and neutral oil over medium-high heat. When the oil starts smoking, working in two or three batches to avoid overcrowding, add the beef (it should sizzle when it hits the pan) and sear until light golden on all sides, 1 to 2 minutes per side. Transfer the seared beef to a bowl and repeat with the remaining meat. Reduce the heat to medium, add the bell pepper and onion, and cook, stirring, until the onion looks translucent and soft, 3 to 4 minutes. Add the sofrito and cook until the moisture has evaporated, 1 to 2 minutes more. Add the tomatoes, olives, and olive brine. Cook, stirring, until the moisture from the tomato has evaporated, 2 to 3 minutes more. Add the broth and return the beef (along with any juices accumulated in the bowl) to the pot.

Bring to a boil over high heat, then reduce the heat to medium-low, cover, and simmer until the beef is tender and pulls apart easily with a fork, 2 to 3 hours.

Add the potatoes and carrots and simmer, uncovered, until the potatoes are fork-tender, 10 to 15 minutes more. Take

recipe continues

out 2 or 3 pieces of potato, mash them with the fork, and return them to the stew to thicken it. Simmer for 3 to 5 minutes more, until the broth becomes saucier. Stir in the cilantro and taste the stew. It should have a mild sweetness from the tomatoes, a slight funkiness from the olives, and beefy savoriness. If needed, add salt pinch by pinch, stirring and tasting after each addition, then serve.

FOR A PRESSURE COOKER OR INSTANT POT: Heat the olive oil and neutral oil in a pressure cooker over medium heat or in an Instant Pot on the Sauté setting. Working in batches, add the beef and continue with the recipe as directed. After returning the beef to the pot, seal the lid and cook at high pressure for 15 minutes. Release the pressure and remove the lid. Add the potatoes and carrots, and set the heat to medium-low or select the Sauté setting. Continue the recipe as directed.

PASTELÓN DE AMARILLO

SWEET PLANTAIN LASAGNA

SERVES 12

Olive oil spray

5 or 6 large sweet plantains, peeled and sliced lengthwise into ¼-inch-thick slices

Salt

1 recipe Picadillo (page 260)

8 ounces mozzarella, mild cheddar, Monterey Jack, or Muenster cheese, shredded

3 eggs, beaten

2 tablespoons chopped fresh cilantro (optional)

Pastelón (also known as piñón in some regions of Puerto Rico) is often compared to a lasagna due to its layers. Slices of ripe plantain are soft and sweet. Briny, savory picadillo contrasts the plantain's sweetness. Cheese contributes creamy richness and binds the layers together. Pastelón was only ever on the menu at Abuela's when she had plantains that were on their last leg. That's the beauty of plantains—every stage of their life is filled with purpose. With some techniques I tweaked from Abuela's, it's a breeze to make and accidentally gluten-free, but full of sazón and indulgence. You can serve this as you would any protein. In mi casa, we serve it with white rice (page 205) and Habichuelitas Guisadas (stewy beans, page 193), a slice of avocado, and Abuela's garlicky cabbage salad (page 121).

Preheat the oven to 400°F. Line a baking sheet with parchment paper and coat it evenly with olive oil spray.

Place the plantain slices side by side in a single layer on the prepared baking sheet (work in batches if you can't fit all the slices). Sprinkle them with salt and coat them evenly with olive oil spray. Bake for 15 to 20 minutes, until they are light golden brown and sizzling. Remove from the oven and transfer to a plate. (Alternatively, cook the plantain slices in a large, preferably nonstick sauté pan over medium-low heat until they're light golden, 1 to 2 minutes per side.)

Reduce the oven temperature to 350°F. Coat a 9 by 13-inch baking pan liberally with olive oil spray.

Using the back of a spoon, spread some sauce from the picadillo over the bottom of the prepared baking pan. Place slices of the plantain side by side over the bottom of the pan, covering it. Spoon half the picadillo on top of the plantain, top with half the cheese, then drizzle one-third of the eggs

recipe continues

evenly over all of it. Repeat these layers, then finish with a layer of plantain. Drizzle the remaining egg over the top. Cover with foil and bake for 40 minutes. Remove the foil and bake for 10 to 15 minutes more, until the top looks golden brown. Remove from the oven and let rest at room temperature for 15 to 20 minutes before slicing. Garnish individual slices with cilantro, if desired, and serve.

PATITAS DE CERDO CON GARBANZOS

PIG'S FEET STEW WITH CHICKPEAS

SERVES 4 OR 5

3 pounds fresh pig's feet (see Note), rinsed with cold water

¼ cup salt, plus more as needed

3 tablespoons olive oil

½ cup small-diced white or yellow onion (about 1 small)

¼ cup small-diced sweet ajíes or sweet mini peppers

¼ cup Sofrito (page 38)

1 teaspoon Achiote Oil (page 37), or ½ teaspoon sazón, homemade (page 39) or store-bought

2 tablespoons grated or chopped garlic (from about 4 large cloves)

1 teaspoon dried oregano

¼ teaspoon freshly ground black pepper

1 cup small-diced fresh tomatoes (about 1 medium), or ½ (14.5-ounce) can stewed tomatoes

2 (15.5-ounce) cans chickpeas, undrained

¼ cup chopped fresh cilantro leaves, stems, or a mix

Patitas means "little (animal) feet." Don't be put off by the name. I know—it's feet—but if you think about it from a different angle, it's pork and beans. Pig's feet are severely underrated. This is my favorite Abuela meal. She slowly simmers them with garbanzos in an aromatic, tomatoey broth. The result is fall-off-the-bone, unctuous meat, and addictively porky chickpeas. Pig's feet are loaded with collagen, which gives them a lip-smacky mouthfeel. You get to pick them up with your hands and gnaw on them. At least, I hope you will—that's where all the flavor is. Serve it over fluffy white rice (page 205) to soak up the broth, with Abuela's Garlicky Cabbage Salad (page 121) alongside, as shown on the following page, for freshness, and go to town on the bones.

Place the pig's feet in a large heavy-bottomed pot, then add cold water to cover by 2 inches and the salt (if you used salted pig's feet, omit the salt here). Bring to a boil over high heat, about 10 minutes, skimming off the foam that forms on the surface. Reduce the heat to medium-low, cover, and simmer gently until the meat is tender enough to pull away from the bone with a fork, 2 to 4 hours. Add water to the pot as needed to keep the pig's feet completely submerged as they cook.

About 20 minutes before the pig's feet are ready, in a separate large pot, heat the olive oil over medium heat. Add the onion, ajíes, and sofrito. Cook, stirring, until the onion is translucent, the ajíes are soft, and the moisture from the sofrito has evaporated, 8 to 10 minutes. Add the achiote oil, garlic, oregano, and black pepper and cook until aromatic, about 1 minute. Add the tomatoes and ½ teaspoon salt and cook, stirring, until the moisture from the tomato has evaporated, 6 to 8 minutes. Add the chickpeas (with their liquid) and raise the heat to high. Bring to a boil, then

recipe continues

NOTE: *If you can't find pig's feet at a regular grocery store, head to a Latin grocery store. Like any cut of pork, the meat should look light pink and should have no odor or gooey liquid or blood pooling in the bag or container. Pig's feet are bony, so try to pick whichever package has more meat. If you can only find salted pig's feet, you can use those instead of fresh, but they will need to be desalted first. To do so, place them in a large bowl and rinse under cold running water, using your hands to rub off the excess salt until they feel smooth. Transfer to a large airtight container or deep bowl with a lid and add cold water to cover by at least 2 inches. Cover and refrigerate for at least 8 hours or up to overnight, changing the water three times. Drain and rinse again before using.*

immediately reduce the heat to medium-low and simmer until the liquid looks saucy, 10 to 15 minutes. Remove from the heat and cover to keep it hot while the pig's feet finish cooking.

Pour the broth from the pot with the pig's feet into a container or large measuring cup. Skim the fat off the top and set the broth aside. Pour the chickpea stew into the pot with the pig's feet and add enough of the reserved broth to cover them. Stir and bring to a simmer over medium-high heat, 5 to 10 minutes, then simmer until the liquid has reduced by one-third and looks saucy, 20 to 30 minutes. Taste the stew. It should be porky, with sweet hints of onion, tomato, and garlic, and aromatic oregano and black pepper. If needed, add more salt pinch by pinch, stirring and tasting after each addition. Stir in the cilantro and serve.

FOR A PRESSURE COOKER OR INSTANT POT: Place the pig's feet in the pressure cooker or Instant Pot and add cold water to cover and ¼ cup salt (if you used salted pig's feet, omit the salt here). Bring to a boil over high heat if using a pressure cooker or on the Sauté setting. Skim off the foam that forms on the top and discard it. Seal the lid and cook at high pressure for 15 minutes, or until the meat is tender enough to pull away from the bone with a fork. Release the pressure and check the meat; if it's not ready, reseal and cook at high pressure in 5-minute increments until tender. Release the pressure. Cook the chickpea stew as directed. Pour the broth from the pig's feet into a measuring cup. Skim the fat off the top and set the broth aside. Add the chickpea stew to the pressure cooker or Instant Pot and add enough of the reserved broth to cover them. Bring to a simmer over medium-high heat or on the Sauté setting, then continue the recipe as directed.

PICADILLO

BEER-BRAISED SAVORY GROUND MEAT STEW

SERVES 4 TO 6

¼ cup olive oil

1 pound ground beef (90/10), ground chicken, or ground turkey

1 tablespoon adobo, homemade (page 36) or store-bought

½ cup Sofrito (page 38)

6 pimento-stuffed olives or pitted green olives, finely chopped, plus 1 tablespoon brine from the jar

1 cup small-diced fresh tomatoes (about 1 medium), or ½ (14.5-ounce) can stewed tomatoes

1 cup light beer (like Medalla), beef broth, chicken broth, or vegetable broth

1 tablespoon adobo sauce (from a can of chipotles in adobo) or sriracha (optional)

1 to 2 tablespoons honey, or as needed

Salt (optional)

¼ cup chopped fresh cilantro

Picadillo (*pee-kah-dee-joh*) was one of Mama's *resuelves*, go-to dishes or recipes that are easy to make and ready in a flash. It's mostly made up of pantry ingredients that she always keeps on hand and she batches it out to last through the week. I remember sitting on the counter as a kid and picking out browned bits of seasoned ground beef from the pan while she hustled to finish cooking.

Most families have their own recipe. This is Mama's, with a few cheffy embellishments of my own. There's an ongoing debate about adding/omitting raisins. I'm Team No Raisins. I dislike them and believe there's no place for them in a picadillo—it's a savory dish. In my family, we never added them, and if I find them in someone else's picadillo, I will politely eat them but will most likely lose respect for the chef. You can serve this over white rice (page 205), or use it as a *relleno* (filling) for frituras (see pages 146–169) or baked casseroles like Pastelón (sweet plantain lasagna, page 255), Arroz Relleno (stuffed rice with crusty cheese, page 219), or Canoas (sweet plantain canoes, page 263).

In a large sauté pan, heat the olive oil over medium-high heat. Add the ground beef and sprinkle it evenly with the adobo. Break it up with a flat wooden spatula until there are no visible large clumps. Cook, stirring continuously, until all the meat is browned and looks slightly crispy, 5 to 10 minutes. Add the sofrito and olives and cook, stirring, until all the moisture from the sofrito has evaporated, about 2 minutes. Add the tomato and cook, stirring, until the moisture from the tomato evaporates and the tomato turns darker in color and starts smelling sweet. Add the olive brine, beer, and adobo sauce (if using) and stir to combine. Reduce the heat to medium-low and cook, stirring occasionally, until the liquid reduces by half and looks saucy, not runny, 10 to 20 minutes more.

Taste the picadillo. It should be savory and meaty with slight sweetness from the tomato and brininess from the olives. If it's too acidic, add honey 1 tablespoon at a time to balance it. If it's not savory enough, add salt pinch by pinch, stirring and tasting after each addition. Simmer gently for 5 minutes more to allow the flavors to combine. Stir in the cilantro and serve hot, or let cool to room temperature, transfer to an airtight container, and store in the fridge for up to 3 days.

CANOAS

SWEET PLANTAIN CANOES WITH MEAT STEW

MAKES 1 CANOA

1 sweet plantain, peel-on

½ to 1 cup Picadillo (page 260) or Mama's Life-Saving Chili (page 141), preferably cold

1 large egg, beaten

¼ cup shredded mozzarella, mild cheddar, Monterey Jack, or Muenster cheese (optional)

Canoas (*kah-noh-ah*, Spanish for "canoes") are baked sweet plantains stuffed with a meat stew, sometimes cheese, and coated with egg. I use stray overripe plantains as a vehicle for leftovers, which results in an effortless weeknight dinner for one. I often have extra picadillo or some form of stewed meat on hand. When laziness strikes, and an innocent sweet plantain is in sight, I'll sacrifice it to stuff full of premade fridge goodies. It's not something I batch out—that's what Pastelón (page 255) is for; this is more of a solo rescue mission for random leftovers. If you *really* want to make it next level, drizzle over some Pique (page 43) or Chimichurri (page 47), or top with Pickled Red Onions (page 50) to paddle your palate through a flavor expedition.

Preheat the oven to 350°F. Line a baking sheet with parchment paper.

Place the plantain on the prepared baking sheet. Bake for 20 to 25 minutes, until the skin has turned completely black and the plantain looks puffy and slightly oozy (from the caramelized sugar) and is soft to the touch. Remove from the oven and let cool for 10 to 15 minutes. Keep the oven on.

Using the tip of a small sharp knife, make a shallow lengthwise slit along the inside curve of the plantain, cutting through the peel and most of the flesh, but not all the way through to the other side. Split the plantain open gently from end to end and stand it split-side up on the baking sheet. Using a spoon, press out the sides from the center to widen the opening into a canoe shape. Loosely fill with the picadillo, using more or less as needed, spreading it from end to end until the cavity is full. Drizzle the egg over and into any crevices in the filling. Bake for 20 to 25 minutes, until the top looks golden brown and sizzly. (If you're using the cheese, sprinkle it on top after 20 minutes and bake for 5 minutes more, or until the cheese melts fully.) Remove from the oven and let cool for 5 to 10 minutes before serving.

Using clean hands, gently peel off the skin. Carefully transfer the canoa to a large plate and serve.

PICADILLO DE CERDO O POLLO

DICED PORK OR CHICKEN STEW

SERVES 4 TO 6

This stew is packed with flavor and a nice, meaty bite from dicing (rather than grinding) the meat. This is Abuela's go-to filling for Pasteles (page 267), but you can also use it to fill Alcapurrias (page 168) or Pastelillos (page 165), or spoon it over some fluffy white rice (page 205) to absorb the sweet and savory tomatoey sauce.

2 pounds boneless, skinless pork shoulder or chicken thighs

¼ cup olive oil

1 tablespoon Achiote Oil (page 37) or ½ teaspoon sazón, homemade (page 39) or store-bought

2 tablespoons adobo, homemade (page 36) or store-bought

2 cups small-diced white or yellow onion (about 1 medium)

1 cup small-diced cubanelle peppers, sweet ajíes (about 10), or bell pepper (about 1 small)

2 tablespoons grated or chopped garlic (about 4 large cloves)

1 teaspoon salt, plus more if needed

1 teaspoon freshly ground black pepper

1 teaspoon dried oregano

¼ teaspoon ground cumin

3 tablespoons tomato paste

10 pimento-stuffed green olives, coarsely chopped

2 tablespoons capers, coarsely chopped

¼ cup chopped fresh cilantro

Using a sharp knife, remove any excess fat or sinew from the meat. Freeze the meat for about 1 hour, until firm but not solid. Pat it dry with paper towels and cut it into ½-inch cubes. In a large pot, heat the olive oil and achiote oil over medium-high heat. Add the meat and sprinkle it evenly with the adobo. Cook, stirring continuously and breaking up the meat with a spatula, until the meat is evenly browned and any moisture has evaporated, about 10 minutes.

Reduce the heat to medium, add the onion and cubanelles, and cook, stirring, until the onion is translucent and the cubanelles are soft, about 5 minutes. Add the garlic, salt, black pepper, oregano, and cumin. Cook, stirring, until the garlic and spices are fragrant, about 1 minute. Add the tomato paste and stir until it turns brickred in color and starts smelling sweet, about 3 minutes. Add the olives, capers, and 2 cups water and stir. Simmer, uncovered, until the liquid has reduced by two-thirds and looks saucy, not runny, about 15 minutes. Stir in the cilantro and taste the stew. It should taste meaty, slightly sweet from the tomato paste, briny from the olives and capers, and herbaceous from the sofrito. If necessary, add more salt pinch by pinch, stirring and tasting after each addition. Serve, or let cool to room temperature, transfer to an airtight container, and store in the fridge for up to 3 days.

PASTELES

MAKES ABOUT 24 PASTELES

12 cups 1-inch-diced peeled yuca or green bananas, or, in a pinch, green plantains (from about 6 pounds unpeeled)

6 cups 1-inch-diced peeled white yautía or, in a pinch, malanga (from about 3 pounds unpeeled)

10 large garlic cloves, peeled

½ cup Achiote Oil (page 37), plus more if needed

2 to 3 tablespoons salt

2 pounds saucy meat filling, such as Picadillo de Cerdo o Pollo (page 265), Picadillo (page 260), or Salmorejo de Jueyes (page 247)

24 to 30 plantain or banana leaves (see Notes)

½ to 1 cup thinly sliced roasted red peppers (pimientos morrones; optional)

½ to 1 cup cooked chickpeas, drained (optional)

NOTES: *Plantain and banana leaves impart a subtle earthy flavor to the pasteles and keep them from sticking to the paper. In a pinch, you can use foil, but you won't get the same flavor.*

You can find pasteles paper (papel para pasteles) or butcher paper online or in some Latin food markets. Please don't substitute parchment paper; it will disintegrate when boiled.

Pasteles are little parcels of starchy vegetable *masa* (dough) filled with chunks of stewed meat and wrapped in banana or plantain leaves. We boil them until they firm up into a dumpling with a custardlike texture. Pasteles are one of three must-haves on our traditional Noche Buena plate, which includes Arroz con Gandules (page 211) and Pernil Asado (page 235), as shown here.

For the masa, I prefer yuca's bouncy texture over green banana's softness. Pork or chicken picadillo are standard fillings, but you can get creative with the protein. There's an ongoing debate about adding ketchup. For me, if it's good, it doesn't need it. But a little tangy Pique (page 43) never hurts. Try them with either or both and decide.

This recipe requires planning ahead and many different steps. But if you make a day of it with loved ones, you can turn it into a fun and memorable holiday tradition that ends with a freezer full of pasteles.

Working in small batches, in a high-speed blender or food processor, combine the yuca, yautía, and garlic. (These roots, especially the yuca, are tough, so only fill your blender or food processor halfway.) Blend or process on high speed until you achieve a smooth paste, 2 to 4 minutes, stopping occasionally to scrape down the sides with a spatula. Use the blender tamper to help things along, if needed, but don't add water or liquid. Transfer the pureed mixture to a large bowl and repeat until you've pureed all the vegetables, adding each batch to the bowl as you work.

Add the achiote oil and 1 tablespoon of the salt to the puree and stir well to combine; you should have a homogeneous paste that's pale yellow in color (like corn). Taste the masa—it should be slightly salty and garlicky. If not, add more salt ½ teaspoon at a time, stirring and tasting after each addition. If it's not yellow enough, add more achiote oil 1 tablespoon at a time until you achieve the desired color. Add about ½ cup of the liquid from the meat filling to the

recipe continues

Spread liquid from the filling on a leaf.

Spread some masa over the liquid.

Top with the filling and garnishes.

Fold the leaf over the filling.

Press the filling into a 2-inch strip.

Continue folding over the leaf and paper.

Fold in the ends to seal.

Secure the packet with twine.

Set aside and repeat.

masa and stir to combine it. Cover and refrigerate for at least 4 hours or up to overnight to thicken and firm up.

Using a sharp knife or a pair of kitchen shears, cut lengthwise along the tough inner core of each plantain leaf to remove it, then cut the leaves into 6 by 12-inch rectangles. Wipe them thoroughly with a damp paper towel or clean kitchen towel. Turn the largest burner on your stovetop (gas or electric) to medium heat. Using tongs, gently place one leaf directly over the burner. You'll see it will turn from opaque to shiny, about 5 seconds. If necessary, using the tongs, rotate it until every corner shines. Set it aside on a plate and repeat with the remaining leaves. (If using foil, skip this step.)

Cut twenty-four 12-inch squares of pasteles paper or butcher paper (see Notes) and twenty-four 30-inch-long pieces of kitchen twine. Form an assembly line with all the components: pasteles paper, plantain leaves, masa, filling, roasted peppers and/or chickpeas (if using), twine.

Place a square of pasteles paper in front of you and place a plantain leaf on top of it horizontally so it covers the half of the paper closest to you. Spoon about ½ teaspoon of the liquid from the filling and spread it around the center of the leaf to lubricate it (this will enable the pastel to easily slide out once it's cooked). Scoop out about ⅓ cup of masa and, with the back of a large spoon, spread it in an even layer over the saucy portion of the leaf so it covers an area of about 6 by 3 inches. Scoop out about ¼ cup of filling, draining off most of the liquid. Scatter the filling in a horizontal line across the center of the masa from edge to edge. Place 1 or 2 strips of roasted pepper horizontally over the filling and/or add 3 or 4 chickpeas.

To fold the pasteles, grab the two corners of the plantain leaf and paper closest to you and fold it over the filling horizontally. Hold the folded edge down with one hand, and with the back of your other hand, gently press the filling into a 2-inch-wide strip. Folding the paper over itself, like folding a letter, until you reach the end—you should have a long roll about 2 inches wide and 12 inches long. Pinch one

recipe continues

end of the roll and fold it in about 3 inches to push the filling toward the center. Then, stand the pastel upright with the open end facing up and give it a gentle shake to slide the filling down. Pinch and fold in that remaining open end, also about 3 inches. You should now have a neat packet, about 6 inches long by 2 inches wide, with both ends folded in.

Take a piece of kitchen twine and fold it in half. Place it vertically on the counter with the folded loop farthest from you and the two loose ends closest to you. Lay the folded pastel packet horizontally on top of the twine, with the folded ends facing down. Bring each side of the twine up and over the ends of the so they sit underneath the folds. Grab the looped (folded) end of the twine with one hand, and with the other, thread the two loose ends through the loop. Hold the twine in place under the folds, and gently pull the right end to the right and the left end to the left to tighten and secure the packet. Carefully flip the packet over, keeping it horizontal. Take the loose ends (now underneath), bring them to the center, and tie them together firmly but gently to hold everything in place. Set the finished packet aside and repeat until you've used up all the masa. (If you don't plan on cooking the assembled pasteles right away, store them in an airtight container in the fridge for up to 3 days or freeze for up to 6 months. Cook them directly from the fridge or freezer.)

Bring a large pot of water to a rolling boil. Add the pasteles and boil for 20 minutes (or 30 minutes if frozen). Carefully fish them out of the water, allowing them to drain slightly, and place them on a plate. Cut off the twine and carefully unwrap the paper and plantain leaf to reveal the pastel. Lift it from one end and let it slide onto the plate or transfer the pastel on the leaf directly to a plate for a more organic presentation. (Don't eat the leaf, though.)

RABO ENCENDIDO CON GUAYABA

SPICY GUAVA OXTAIL STEW

SERVES 4 OR 5

3 pounds oxtails, trimmed of excess fat

Salt and freshly ground black pepper

½ cup olive oil

1 cup small-diced onion

½ cup small-diced bell pepper

½ cup Sofrito (page 38)

1 cup small-diced fresh tomatoes (about 1 medium), or ½ (14.5-ounce) can stewed tomatoes

1 cup dry red wine

2 quarts beef broth

6 bay leaves

1 cup diced celery

1 cup diced carrots

1 spicy ají (see page 19) or serrano chile, minced (with seeds), or ½ habanero pepper, or 3 Fresno peppers or jalapeños, seeded and minced

3 cups chopped peeled Yukon Gold potatoes (1-inch chunks; about 2 large)

6 ounces guava paste (see page 20)

¼ cup chopped fresh cilantro

In the 1960s and '70s, an influx of our Cuban neighbors established communities in Puerto Rico, influencing our cuisine with their own vibrant culture. Technically Cuban in origin, *rabo encendido* ("tail on fire") is a rich stew of slowly simmered oxtails, red wine, and hot peppers. It involves a lot of prepping, technical steps, and a long cooking time to tenderize the tough oxtails. The result is the reward—silky meat, so tender it falls off the bone, in a mouthwatering sauce packed with spicy personality. It's also one of Papa's favorite dishes to prepare. It benefits from assertive seasoning, which allows Papa's bold personality (and heavy hand with heat and spices) to shine. I added my own little twist (which I learned from a valued mentor in Miami, Chef Kris Wessel): guava paste. It melts into the sauce, adding a tropical sweetness that rounds out the spiciness from the peppers and the acidity from the wine and tomatoes.

Place a rack in the middle of the oven and preheat the broiler to high.

Place the oxtails on a baking sheet and sprinkle them generously and evenly on all sides with about 1 tablespoon salt and 1 tablespoon black pepper. Rub the seasoning into the oxtails with clean hands. Drizzle them with 2 to 3 tablespoons of the olive oil and rub it in. Space the oxtails 1 inch apart on the baking sheet. Broil for 20 to 30 minutes, flipping them halfway through, until deep golden brown in color.

Meanwhile, in a large, heavy-bottomed pot, heat 2 to 3 tablespoons of the olive oil over medium heat. Add in the onion and bell pepper and cook, stirring, until the onion is soft, slightly golden, and translucent, 4 to 6 minutes. Raise the heat to medium-high, add the sofrito, and cook, stirring, until the moisture has evaporated, 4 to 5 minutes. Add the tomato, ½ teaspoon salt, and ½ teaspoon black pepper and

recipe continues

cook, stirring, until the moisture has evaporated, 4 to 5 minutes. Pour in the wine and simmer until it has reduced by two-thirds, 7 to 10 minutes. Pour in the broth and add the bay leaves. Increase the heat to high and bring to a boil, then immediately reduce the heat to maintain a simmer. Cook for 5 to 10 minutes.

Add the oxtails to the broth. Pour ½ cup water onto the baking sheet and stir with a spoon or wooden spatula, scraping up any beefy bits left behind, then pour this into the pot as well. Bring to a boil over high heat, then reduce the heat to medium-low, cover, and simmer until the meat is tender enough to pull away from the bone with a fork, 3 to 5 hours.

Adjust the heat to medium and cook, uncovered, until the liquid has reduced by half and looks saucy and shiny, about 20 minutes. Skim off the fat from the top using a ladle or large spoon. Add the celery, carrots, ají, potatoes, and guava paste to the pot with the oxtails. Reduce the heat to medium-low and simmer gently until the potatoes are fork-tender and the guava paste has dissolved completely, 15 to 20 minutes. If you'd like it saucier or thicker, ladle about 1½ cups of the veggies and broth into a blender and puree until smooth, then stir the puree into the stew.

Taste the stew. It should have a mild sweetness from the guava, a fruity spiciness from the ají, and beefy savoriness. If needed, season with more salt and pepper. Stir in the cilantro and serve.

FOR AN INSTANT POT/PRESSURE COOKER: While the oxtails are in the oven, heat 2 to 3 tablespoons of the olive oil in a pressure cooker over medium heat or in an Instant Pot on the Sauté setting. Add the onion and bell pepper and continue the recipe as directed. After adding the oxtails and pan drippings to the pot, seal the lid and cook on high pressure for 30 minutes. Release the pressure and check the meat; it should be tender enough to pull away from the bone with a fork. If it's not, reseal and cook at high pressure in 5-minute increments until tender. Release the pressure and remove the lid. Add the celery, carrots, ají, potatoes, and guava paste, set the heat to medium or select the Sauté setting, and continue as directed.

POSTRES

DESSERTS

All the desserts here are traditional favorites you'll find on Puerto Rican restaurant menus or made at home by abuelas and *titis* (aunties). Some benefit from cheffy twists based on my experience as a professional chef. Flan de Café (page 286) is a variation on our classic flan, featuring Puerto Rican coffee, while Flan de Calabaza (page 284) is my fall version. I make Tembleque (page 295), a traditional Christmas coconut pudding, with fresh ginger. For Budín (page 297), or bread pudding, I use stale Mallorcas (page 89) and stud the pudding with guava, which adds complexity and Puerto Rican sabor. Caribbean Passion Pie (page 313) is a tropical twist on a key lime pie that combines some of my favorite ingredients from home, like Holsum coconut cookies and fresh passion fruit. Finally, limbers (see pages 321–323), frozen "cupsicles," are nostalgic, easy-to-make childhood treats that are perfect for summer, and taste bright and tropical, like Puerto Rico.

FLAN PRO TIPS

When I think of Puerto Rican desserts, the first that comes to mind is flan—a richer, more flavorful cousin of the classic French **crème caramel**. It's a delicate custard made with evaporated milk, condensed milk, and eggs, gently baked in a caramel-coated pan inside a steamy water bath. Flans are a foundational dessert in Puerto Rican gastronomy and are notoriously tricky—even **Abuela and Titi** won't make them because they've had too many go sideways.

After making more flans than I can count (and messing up a fair share), I've put together this set of troubleshooting tips to help you avoid potential pitfalls at each stage—from caramel to custard to unmolding. These apply to all the flan recipes in this chapter and are here to help you master the dreaded flan.

FOR THE CARAMEL

- Start with a clean, dry pan, and keep it next to the stove so you're ready to pour as soon as the caramel is done.
- I use the "wet" method (adding water to sugar), which gives more control and helps prevent burning. Gently pour the water around the sugar, then shimmy the pot to hydrate it evenly–avoid stirring and splashing.
- Once it starts cooking, stand by and keep a close eye on it. Stir only stir if you notice the caramel is browning unevenly, and if crystals form, lower the heat and gently dissolve them with the back of a spatula before continuing.
- I think I'm stating the obvious, but just in case, the caramel is HOT, so don't get any ideas about tasting it in its liquid state. You'll sear your tongue–again, experience here.
- The color is up to you: lighter caramel is milder; darker caramel has a more robust flavor. I like mine deep golden, like maple syrup. You can test the color by dropping a few drops onto a white plate.
- As soon as you achieve your desired shade, quickly pour the caramel into your baking pan and, using oven mitts, rotate the pan immediately to coat the bottom and some of the sides before it hardens.

FOR THE CUSTARD

The key to that smooth, creamy flan texture is blending just enough and timing.

- **Overblending** adds air, which can lead to bubbles and a spongy surface. Blend the dairy ingredients first until smooth, then add the eggs and blend briefly. Always skim any foam off the top, and strain the custard through a fine-mesh sieve—don't press anything through.

- **Undercooking** results in a runnyy custard when unmolded.
- **Overcooking** results in a firm, eggy custard filled with holes throughout.
- **Perfectly timing** the custard means removing it from the oven while it still has a soft jiggle in the center, like Jell-O. To check, gently shimmy the pan—if the edges are set but the center wobbles slightly, it's ready. Take it out at that point—it will continue to cook as it cools. Let it sit in the water bath to room temperature, then discard the water bath and transfer it to the fridge to chill until fully set, preferably overnight.

FOR THE WATER BATH

Place the roasting pan in the oven first, then set the covered flan pan inside and pour hot water around it until it reaches halfway up the sides. This helps avoid spills, which can affect the texture of the custard. Covering the custard pan protects it from spills and helps it cook gently and evenly without browning. Make sure the flan pan sits flat and doesn't float.

FOR UNMOLDING

- Unmold just before serving. If transporting, keep it cold and bring your own serving plate if needed.
- Run a thin knife around the edges, then dip the bottom of the pan in warm water for 10 to 15 seconds to loosen the caramel. If you hear a crack, don't panic—it's just hard caramel.
- Place a rimmed plate that can catch the caramel over the mold. With one hand on the plate and the other under the mold, flip it swiftly and confidently.
- If the flan sticks, gently press on the mold or slide a knife in slightly to break the air seal.

FOR INDIVIDUAL PORTIONS

- One batch of flan yields ten to twelve 4-ounce ramekins. Bake for 15 to 20 minutes (for aluminum ramekins) or 20 to 30 minutes (for glass or ceramic). Because they'll cook faster, there's no need to cover them, but be careful not to let water splash into the custard, or it may not set properly.

FLAN DE VAINILLA

VANILLA BEAN FLAN

SERVES ABOUT 10

1 cup sugar

¾ teaspoon salt

1 (12-ounce) can evaporated milk

1 (14-ounce) can sweetened condensed milk

a cup whole milk

¼ cup (2 ounces) mascarpone cheese or full-fat cream cheese

1 tablespoon vanilla bean paste or pure vanilla extract

5 large eggs

This recipe is a nod to Mama's classic "flan de Mami," which she made from a recipe handwritten on a mint-green letter-size sheet of paper. I knew it would be a good day when I'd see her bust it out of her dusty recipe drawer. I'd hover around her in the kitchen like a fly, waiting for her to put down the spoon she used to stir the caramel. After it cooled and hardened, I'd lick the amber-colored candy like a lollipop.

While the ingredients are simple—eggs, milk, sugar—this dessert requires precise technique and attention to detail. It makes sense that Mama mastered this skill, given her detail-driven personality. I like a deeply colored caramel, which adds bitter notes and provides a good flavor contrast to the sweet, mild custard. This recipe calls for a touch of mascarpone cheese, which adds an extra-silky texture, and vanilla bean paste, which results in cute vanilla bean freckles scattered throughout.

Before starting, check out my Flan Pro Tips on page 276. Place a rack in the middle of the oven and preheat to 325°F. Bring 4 cups water to a boil in a medium saucepan or teakettle over high heat. Place a straight-sided 8- to 9-inch round aluminum baking pan and a small white plate near the stovetop. Make sure the pan is dry.

In a medium saucepan, combine the sugar and ¼ teaspoon of the salt. Gently pour ⅓ cup water around the sugar and shimmy the pot just enough to flatten and hydrate the sugar. Bring to a gentle simmer over medium heat and cook, without stirring, until the sugar dissolves and caramelizes to the desired color, 10 to 15 minutes. Test the color of the caramel by spooning a few small drops onto the white plate (I like it deep golden, like maple syrup). Remove from the heat. Quickly but carefully pour the hot caramel into the baking pan and, using a kitchen towel or oven mitts, carefully pick up the pan and slowly rotate it to distribute the caramel evenly over the bottom and sides. If necessary,

recipe continues

use a spatula to guide it up the sides. Set aside to cool while you work on the custard.

In a blender, combine the evaporated milk, condensed milk, whole milk, mascarpone, vanilla, and remaining ½ teaspoon salt. Blend on medium speed until there are no visible lumps of mascarpone, 10 to 15 seconds. Add the eggs and blend on low speed until just incorporated, about 5 seconds. Gently tap the blender a few times to encourage air bubbles to rise to the surface and use a large spoon to skim off any foam that may have formed.

Pour the custard through a fine-mesh sieve into the caramel-coated pan; discard any solids in the sieve. Gently tap the pan against the counter a few times again to force air bubbles to the surface and pop any that appear with a toothpick.

Place a 10- to 12-inch, 3-inch-deep roasting pan on the middle rack in the oven. Cover the custard pan with a lid or piece of foil and place it in the roasting pan. Gently pour enough hot water around the custard pan to come halfway up the sides of the pan, being careful not to splash any water into the custard. Bake for 50 minutes to 1 hour, until the custard is jiggly in the center (like Jell-O) when the pan is lightly shimmied. If it is still liquid and runny, bake, uncovered, in 5-minute increments until you've achieved the desired consistency. If it's firm in the center, it's overcooked.

Carefully remove the water bath from the oven and place it on the stovetop. Leave the flan in the water bath to cool completely, about 1 hour, then refrigerate, covered, for at least 6 hours or up to overnight before serving.

Unmold the flan onto a serving plate, scraping any residual caramel from the pan on top—don't waste that liquid gold! Slice and serve cold, with plenty of caramel. Store leftovers, covered, in the fridge for up to 1 week.

FOR FLAN DE QUESO (CREAM CHEESE FLAN): Substitute one 8-ounce package full-fat cream cheese, at room temperature, for the 2 ounces mascarpone.

FLAN DE COCO CARAMELIZADO

CARAMELIZED COCONUT FLAN

SERVES ABOUT 10

1 cup sweetened coconut flakes

1½ cups sugar

¾ teaspoon salt

¾ cup barrel-aged rum, such as Ron del Barrilito

1 (12-ounce) can evaporated milk

1 (15-ounce) can cream of coconut

½ cup (4 ounces) mascarpone cheese or full-fat cream cheese

5 large eggs

2 large egg yolks

Coconut is a common flavor found in Puerto Rican holiday desserts, which is why I like making this dessert when I'm home for the holidays, but this variation is a unique way to keep the island-vibes going all year long. I toast coconut flakes on a pan to bring out their nutty aroma, fold them into the caramel, and add some aged rum for more depth of flavor. This results in a glistening amber film of chewy coconut speckles.

Before starting, check out my Flan Pro Tips on page 276. Place a rack in the middle of the oven and preheat to 325°F. Bring 4 cups water to a boil in a medium saucepan or teakettle over high heat.

In a medium sauté pan, toast the coconut over medium heat, stirring continuously with a rubber spatula, until it turns golden in color and starts smelling coconutty, 5 to 10 minutes. Transfer to a shallow plate and keep it close by.

Place a straight-sided 8- or 9-inch round aluminum baking pan and small white plate near the stovetop. Make sure the pan is dry.

In a medium saucepan, combine the sugar and ¼ teaspoon of the salt. Gently pour ½ cup of the rum and ½ cup water around the sugar and shimmy the pot just enough to flatten and hydrate the sugar. Bring to a gentle simmer over medium heat and cook, without stirring, until the sugar dissolves and caramelizes to the desired color, 10 to 15 minutes. Test the color of the caramel by spooning a few small drops onto the white plate (I like it deep golden, like maple syrup). Remove the caramel from the heat, add the toasted coconut, and stir to combine. Quickly but carefully pour the hot caramel into the baking pan and, using a

recipe continues

kitchen towel or oven mitts, carefully pick up the pan and slowly rotate it to distribute the caramel evenly over the bottom and sides. If necessary, use a spatula to guide it up the sides. Set aside to cool while you work on the custard.

In a blender, combine the evaporated milk, condensed milk, cream of coconut, cream cheese, remaining ½ teaspoon salt, and remaining ¼ cup rum. Blend on medium speed until there are no visible lumps of cream cheese, 10 to 15 seconds. Add the eggs and egg yolks and blend on low speed until just incorporated, about 5 seconds. Gently tap the blender a few times to encourage air bubbles to rise to the surface and use a large spoon to skim off any foam that may have formed.

Pour the custard through a fine-mesh sieve into the caramel-coated pan; discard any solids in the sieve. Gently tap the pan against the counter a few times again to force air bubbles to the surface and pop any that appear with a toothpick.

Place a 10- to 12-inch, 3-inch-deep roasting pan on the middle rack in the oven. Cover the custard pan with a lid or piece of foil and place it in the roasting pan. Gently pour enough hot water around the custard pan to come halfway up the sides of the pan, being careful not to splash any water into the custard. Bake for 50 minutes to 1 hour, until the custard is jiggly in the center (like Jell-O) when the pan is lightly shimmied. If it is still liquid and runny, bake, uncovered, in 5-minute increments until you've achieved the desired consistency. If it's firm in the center, it's overcooked.

Carefully remove the water bath from the oven and place it on the stovetop. Leave the flan in the water bath to cool completely, about 1 hour, then refrigerate, covered, for at least 6 hours or up to overnight before serving.

Unmold the flan onto a serving plate, scraping any residual caramel from the pan on top—don't waste that liquid gold! Slice and serve cold with plenty of caramel. Store leftovers, covered in the fridge for up to 1 week.

FLAN DE CALABAZA Y ESPECIAS CON BROWN BUTTER

SPICED PUMPKIN FLAN WITH BROWN BUTTER

SERVES ABOUT 10

1 cup sugar

¾ teaspoon salt

3 tablespoons unsalted butter, cubed

1 teaspoon pumpkin pie spice

1 cup canned or fresh calabaza puree or pumpkin puree (see Note)

1 (12-ounce) can evaporated milk

1 (14-ounce) can sweetened condensed milk

¼ cup (2 ounces) mascarpone cheese or full-fat cream cheese

1 tablespoon pure vanilla extract

5 large eggs

Puerto Ricans, for the most part, are purists. We like our classic desserts. Flan is one of them. Though not the traditional American Thanksgiving dessert, you'll most likely spot it at our holiday dessert table. This was the case in my family. And if there was flan, no one touched the pumpkin pie. Thus, pumpkin flan was born—a solution to a decades-long problem that went unnoticed at my family holiday celebrations. It merges classic American thanksgiving flavors with a Puerto Rican staple. This one's a hit to bring to your next Thanksgiving or Friendsgiving, just make sure to unmold it when you get there!

Before starting, check out my Flan Pro Tips on page 276. Place a rack in the middle of the oven and preheat to 325°F. Bring 4 cups water to a boil in a medium saucepan or teakettle over high heat. Place a straight-sided 8- to 9-inch round aluminum baking pan and a small white plate near the stovetop. Make sure the pan is dry.

In a medium saucepan, combine the sugar and ¼ teaspoon of the salt. Gently pour ⅓ cup water around the sugar and shimmy the pot just enough to flatten and hydrate the sugar. Bring to a gentle simmer over medium heat and cook, without stirring, until the sugar dissolves and caramelizes to the desired color, 10 to 15 minutes. Test the color of the caramel by spooning a few small drops onto the white plate (I like it deep golden, like maple syrup). Remove from the heat. Quickly but carefully pour the hot caramel into the baking pan and, using a kitchen towel or oven mitts, carefully pick up the pan and slowly rotate it to distribute the caramel evenly over the bottom and sides. If necessary, use a spatula to guide it up the sides. Set aside to cool while you work on the custard.

NOTE: *To make fresh calabaza or pumpkin puree, place a rack in the middle of the oven and preheat to 350°F. Chop about 1 pound of peeled, seeded calabaza or pumpkin into 1-inch pieces. Toss with 1 to 2 tablespoons melted unsalted butter and place in a small roasting pan. Cover with foil and bake for 20 to 30 minutes, until fork-tender and mashable. Mash the calabaza or pumpkin until smooth. This yields 1½ to 2 cups puree. Let it cool to room temperature and use as directed, or transfer it to an airtight container and store in the fridge for up to 3 days.*

In a blender, combine the evaporated milk, condensed milk, whole milk, mascarpone, vanilla, and remaining ½ teaspoon salt. Blend on medium speed until there are no visible lumps of mascarpone, 10 to 15 seconds. Add the eggs and blend on low speed until just incorporated, about 5 seconds. Use a large spoon to skim off any foam that may have formed on the surface.

Pour the custard through a fine-mesh sieve into the caramel-coated pan; discard any solids in the sieve. Gently tap the pan against the counter a few times to force air bubbles to the surface; pop any that appear with a toothpick.

Place a roasting pan on the middle rack in the oven. Cover the custard pan with a lid or piece of foil and place it in the roasting pan. Gently pour enough hot water around the custard pan to come halfway up the sides of the pan, being careful not to splash any water into the custard. Bake for about 50 minutes to 1 hour, until the custard jiggles (like Jell-O) in the center when the pan is shimmied. If it is still runny, bake, uncovered, in 5-minute increments until you've achieved the desired consistency. If it's firm in the center, it may be overcooked.

Carefully remove the water bath from the oven and place it on the stovetop. Leave the flan in the water bath to cool completely, about 1 hour, then refrigerate, covered, for at least 6 hours or up to overnight before serving.

Unmold the flan onto a serving plate, scraping any residual caramel from the pan on top—don't waste that liquid gold! Slice and serve cold, with plenty of caramel. Store leftovers, covered, in the fridge for up to 1 week.

FLAN DE CAFÉ

COFFEE FLAN

SERVES ABOUT 10

1 cup sugar

¾ teaspoon salt

¼ cup Puerto Rican coffee beans or a dark-roast, robust-flavored type

1 (12-ounce) can evaporated milk

½ cup whole milk

1 (14-ounce) can sweetened condensed milk

¼ cup (2 ounces) mascarpone cheese or full-fat cream cheese

5 large eggs

With coffee being an integral part of Puerto Rican culture, I'm unsure as to why we don't have more coffee flavored desserts. Milk, coffee, and caramel are a match made in heaven. Integrating the robust, complex flavor of coffee beans, along with a milky custard, and rich, toasty caramel seemed obvious to me: a harmonious marriage of flavors that just belong together.

Before starting, check out my Flan Pro Tips on page 276. Place a straight-sided 8- to 9-inch round aluminum baking pan and a small white plate near the stovetop. Make sure the pan is dry.

In a medium saucepan, combine the sugar and ¼ teaspoon of the salt. Gently pour ⅓ cup water around the sugar and shimmy the pot just enough to flatten and hydrate the sugar. Bring to a gentle simmer over medium heat and cook, without stirring, until the sugar dissolves and caramelizes to the desired color, 10 to 15 minutes. Test the color of the caramel by spooning a few small drops onto the white plate (I like it deep golden, like maple syrup). Remove from the heat. Carefully pour the hot caramel into the baking pan and set the saucepan aside (do not wash it). Using a kitchen towel or oven mitts, carefully pick up the baking pan and slowly rotate it to distribute the caramel evenly over the bottom and sides. If necessary, use a spatula to guide it up the sides. Set aside to cool.

Place the coffee beans in a pilón (mortar and pestle) and smash to crack them all gently. (You can also place them in a gallon-size zip-top bag and use a rolling pin or bottom of a heavy pot to crack them.) In the saucepan you used for the caramel, combine the evaporated milk and the whole milk. Bring to a gentle simmer over medium heat, 2 to 4 minutes. Remove from the heat, add the cracked coffee beans, cover, and let steep for 20 minutes.

Place a rack in the middle of the oven and preheat to 325°F. Bring 4 cups water to a boil in a medium saucepan or teakettle over high heat.

Strain the coffee-infused milk mixture through a fine-mesh sieve directly into a blender; discard the coffee beans. Add the condensed milk, mascarpone, and remaining ½ teaspoon salt to the blender. Blend on medium speed until there are no visible lumps of mascarpone, 10 to 15 seconds. Add the eggs and blend on low speed until just incorporated, about 5 seconds. Gently tap the blender a few times to encourage air bubbles to rise to the surface and use a large spoon to skim off any foam that may have formed.

Pour the custard through a fine-mesh sieve into the caramel-coated pan; discard any solids in the sieve. Gently tap the pan against the counter a few times again to force air bubbles to the surface and pop any that appear with a toothpick.

Place a 10- to 12-inch, 3-inch-deep roasting pan on the middle rack in the oven. Cover the custard pan with a lid or piece of foil and place it in the roasting pan. Gently pour enough hot water around the custard pan to come halfway up the sides of the pan, being careful not to splash any water into the custard. Bake for 50 minutes to 1 hour, until the custard is jiggly in the center (like Jell-O) when the pan is lightly shimmied. If it is still liquid and runny, bake, uncovered, in 5-minute increments until you've achieved the desired consistency. If it's firm in the center, it's overcooked.

Carefully remove the water bath from the oven and place it on the stovetop. Leave the flan in the water bath to cool completely, about 1 hour, then refrigerate, covered, for at least 6 hours or up to overnight before serving.

Unmold the flan onto a serving plate, scraping any residual caramel from the pan on top—don't waste that liquid gold! Slice and serve cold, with plenty of caramel. Store leftovers, covered, in the fridge for up to 1 week.

ARROZ CON DULCE CON RON Y PASAS

CANDIED COCONUT RICE PUDDING WITH RUM-SOAKED RAISINS

SERVES 4 TO 6

½ cup raisins

¼ cup aged rum (optional)

½ cup uncooked medium-grain white rice

1 cinnamon stick, or ½ teaspoon ground cinnamon

2 thumb-size knobs fresh ginger, peeled

1 (13½-ounce) can full-fat coconut milk

½ cup sugar

1 teaspoon salt

Arroz con dulce is a Christmas staple for Puerto Ricans, and it's one of Abuela's secret weapons. Every year she makes a colossal batch that she portions into disposable containers to gift to loved ones. One of the most amusing and endearing sights is Abuela stirring a pot of arroz that's big enough to fit her. I love when she makes it because the entire house smells of cinnamon and ginger that she dug up herself.

Place the raisins in a small bowl and pour over the rum (if using). Cover and set aside at room temperature for about 4 hours or overnight. (If you're not rum-soaking your raisins, skip this step.)

In a small pot, combine the rice, cinnamon stick, and 2 cups water. Bring to a boil over high heat, then immediately reduce the heat to low, cover, and cook for 17 minutes.

Meanwhile, place the ginger in a blender with 1 cup water. Blend on high speed until smooth, 30 seconds to 1 minute. Strain the mixture through a fine-mesh sieve into a medium pot, pressing on the solids to extract all the flavor, then discard the solids. Add the coconut milk, sugar, salt, and rum-soaked (or plain) raisins to the pot with the ginger.

When the rice is ready, transfer it (with the cinnamon stick) to the pot with the rest of the ingredients and stir to combine. Bring just to a boil over medium-high heat, about 5 minutes. Reduce the heat to medium-low so it bubbles gently and cook, uncovered, stirring every 2 to 3 minutes, until it looks thick, creamy, and goopy, 30 to 40 minutes.

While it's hot, portion the rice pudding into single-serving ramekins or into a mold of your choice. Refrigerate, covered, for at least 6 hours or up to overnight. Unmold it, if you wish, slice it or scoop it, and serve cold.

BIZCOCHO MOJADITO

MOIST CAKE

MAKES ONE 10-INCH ROUND CAKE

1 cup (2 sticks) plus 1 tablespoon unsalted butter, at room temperature

2 cups plus 3 tablespoons all-purpose flour

1 tablespoon baking powder

½ teaspoon salt

1½ cups sugar

6 large eggs, separated, at room temperature

1¼ teaspoons almond extract

½ cup whole milk, at room temperature

1 recipe Almíbar (recipe follows), warmed

½ recipe Merengue Sedoso (page 309), for frosting (optional)

Ever-present at Puerto Rican birthday parties and weddings, bizcocho mojadito (moist cake) gets its name from the *almíbar* (sugary syrup) that's poured over it to keep it moist and tender. Abuela LOVES it and makes it the reason to accept any wedding invitation—except when her niece Edzy is in town. Abuela has a special place in her heart for Edzy, not just because she visits often and cares for her and Abuelo, but because for no other reasons than kindness, she always makes this cake for her—no special occasion required. *Edzy, gracias por cuidármelos y por compartirnos tu rica receta.*

Place a rack in the middle of the oven and preheat to 350°F. Grease a 10-inch round cake pan with 1 tablespoon of the butter, coating the sides, corners, and bottom completely. Dust it with the 3 tablespoons of the flour, rotating the pan to coat, then tap out any excess flour. Set it aside while you work on the batter.

In a medium bowl, whisk together the remaining 2 cups flour, the baking powder, and the salt until evenly incorporated.

In the bowl of a stand mixer fitted with the paddle attachment (or in a large bowl using a handheld mixer), beat the remaining 1 cup (2 sticks) butter on medium-low speed until creamy, fluffy, and pale yellow, 3 to 4 minutes. Slowly, in about 1-tablespoon increments, add 1 cup of the sugar. Stop the mixer and scrape down the sides and bottom of the bowl with a rubber spatula. Beat on medium-low until the mixture looks pale (almost white), creamy, and fluffy (like whipped cream), about 10 minutes. Reduce the speed to low and add the almond extract, then add the egg yolks one at a time and mix until evenly incorporated. With the mixer on low, slowly add half the flour mixture, then slowly stream in half the milk. Repeat with the remaining flour mixture and

recipe continues

milk. Scrape down the bowl again and beat on low until everything is evenly incorporated, smooth, and homogeneous, 2 to 4 minutes. If you're using a stand mixer, transfer the batter to a separate large bowl, thoroughly clean and dry the mixer bowl, and switch to the whisk attachment, then place the egg whites in the mixer bowl. (If you're using a handheld mixer, clean and dry the beaters thoroughly and place the egg whites in a separate large bowl.) Whip the egg whites on medium speed until they start getting foamy and turning white, about 1 minute. With the mixer running, add the remaining ½ cup sugar, 1 tablespoon at a time, then whip until the egg whites hold medium-stiff peaks (when you lift the whisk or beaters out, the tip of the whites should hold a peak) and look glossy, 4 to 7 minutes. Using a rubber spatula, gently fold the whites into the batter in three additions until just incorporated (some streaks are fine)—do not overmix.

Using the spatula, scrape the batter into the prepared pan, holding the bowl close to the pan to avoid deflating the egg whites, and gently level the top. Bake on the center rack for 50 minutes to 1 hour, until the cake looks fluffy and evenly golden on top and a toothpick inserted into the center comes out clean. (This cake is very temperamental and sensitive to drastic temperature fluctuations, so avoid opening the oven door or cooking on the stovetop while it's baking and don't start checking for doneness before 50 minutes to avoid deflating it.) Remove from the oven and let cool for about 20 minutes.

Using a serrated knife, slice a thin layer off the top of the cake to level it. I run the knife along the top of the pan to guide myself, ensuring the top is even and level all around. (I also like to unmold the cake, trim off the browned sides and bottom, leaving the pale center exposed, then return it to the pan. This is purely for aesthetic reasons and entirely optional.)

Using a spoon or pastry brush, dab the warm almíbar evenly over the warm cake, waiting for the cake to absorb it before adding more. The quantity will depend on how moist (and sweet) you want your cake to be (I don't like it sopping, so I use about 2 cups). Let cool to room temperature, about 30 minutes. Cover with plastic wrap and refrigerate until it's completely cold, about 4 hours.

Find a large plate that's 2 to 3 inches wider than the cake. Run a butter knife or offset spatula around the edge of the cake to separate it from the pan. Place the plate upside down over the pan, then, holding the pan and plate together, flip them in one smooth motion to release the cake onto the plate. If the cake doesn't plop down right away, lift one side of the pan and use the butter knife or offset spatula to guide the cake out.

If using the meringue, use a spatula or offset spatula to spread it evenly over the top and sides of the cake. Try to work with thick layers of meringue to avoid lifting crumbs off the cake. Feel free to be creative with the pattern or design of the meringue frosting.

Slice and serve cold or at room temperature. The cake will keep, covered, at room temperature for up to 4 days or in the fridge for up to 1 week.

ALMÍBAR

CAKE SOAK

MAKES 2½ CUPS

1½ cups sugar

½ cup brandy

½ teaspoon almond extract

In a medium pot, combine the sugar, brandy, and 1½ cups water. Bring to a boil over high heat, then immediately reduce the heat to maintain a low simmer and cook, stirring with a spoon, until the sugar has dissolved, about 5 minutes. Remove from the heat and stir in the almond extract. Use immediately or let cool to room temperature, transfer to an airtight container, and store in the fridge for up to 1 month. Rewarm before using.

TEMBLEQUE

TREMBLY COCONUT PUDDING

SERVES 8 TO 10

3⅓ cups fresh coconut milk (page 77), or 2 (13½-ounce) cans full-fat coconut milk

½ cup sugar

1 teaspoon salt

1 cinnamon stick (optional)

2 slices fresh ginger (about 1 inch wide and ¼ inch thick; optional)

⅓ cup plus 2 tablespoons cornstarch

Ground cinnamon, for garnish (optional)

Tembleque is a Puerto Rican Christmas staple. It's a delicate, cornstarch-thickened coconut pudding, which means it's naturally vegan and gluten-free. Its name comes from the verb *temblar*, meaning "to tremble," because when set, that's just what it does. Abuela makes her own coconut milk (page 77) and loves its clean, pure flavor, so she skips the spices in her tembleque. I use canned (cracking coconuts in a NYC apartment? No, gracias) and steep it with ginger and cinnamon for extra warmth. Either way, this Boricua Christmas classic is easy to make—and welcome any time of year.

In a medium pot, combine the coconut milk, sugar, salt, cinnamon stick (if using), and ginger (if using). Bring to a boil over high heat, then immediately reduce the heat to low and simmer for 2 minutes. Remove from the heat, cover, and steep for 20 minutes. (You can skip the steeping if you aren't using the cinnamon and ginger.)

If you're making single servings, line up about ten 3- to 4-ounce ramekins, or have a 1½-quart nonstick mold or glass storage container ready to go.

In a small bowl, whisk together the cornstarch and ⅓ cup water until well combined to make a slurry. If you used the cinnamon and ginger, pick them out of the steeped coconut milk and bring the coconut milk to a simmer over medium heat. While whisking, slowly stream in the cornstarch slurry. Don't step away now! Cook, whisking continuously, until the mixture thickens, looks like mayonnaise, and produces slow, thick bubbles, 3 to 5 minutes.

Remove from the heat and use a rubber spatula to quickly pour/scrape the mixture into the mold(s) (it will start setting quickly). Immediately cover with a lid or plastic wrap to prevent a skin from forming and refrigerate for at least 6 hours or up to 1 week.

recipe continues

You can serve this straight from the ramekins, but it's more fun to see it wiggle when it's unmolded. To unmold it, gently run a knife around the sides. Place a serving plate over the mold. With one hand on the plate and the other under the mold, flip it swiftly and confidently. If it sticks, slide the knife in slightly to push it away from the sides and break a possible air seal. If it's still not coming out or your mold is more intricate, dip the bottom in warm water for 10 to 15 seconds to loosen the pudding, then invert again. Garnish with a light sprinkle of cinnamon, if desired. Slice (if you used one large mold) and serve.

BUDÍN DE MALLORCA CON GUAYABA

GUAVA-STUDDED MALLORCA BREAD PUDDING

SERVES ABOUT 10

4 tablespoons (½ stick) cold unsalted butter, cut into pea-size cubes, plus 2 tablespoons room-temperature butter for greasing

4 large Mallorcas (page 89; about 12 ounces total), cut into 1-inch cubes (see Note)

2 (12-ounce) cans evaporated milk

1 (14-ounce) can sweetened condensed milk

¼ cup sugar

6 large eggs

2 teaspoons pure vanilla extract

1 teaspoon ground cinnamon

½ teaspoon salt

7 ounces guava paste, cut into pea-size pieces

Pure maple syrup or vanilla ice cream, for serving (optional)

I once cared about a man who was incapable of effectively communicating; his solution to arguments was to give me days-long silent treatments. On one of those occasions, to break a 3-day-long streak of tense silence, instead of getting me flowers (his usual MO), he baked me a bread pudding. This is not his recipe. I wrote it (and improved it), but he inspired it and it's the only positive contribution he made to my life, so I'd like to thank him. This one will inundate your house with the intoxicating aroma of warm cinnamon and tropical guava—better than any "I'm sorry" flowers. The edges get crispy and golden, some slightly chewy from the guava, with a soft, custardy center and craggy crevices on top that beg for maple syrup or vanilla ice cream.

Spread the room-temperature butter evenly over the bottom and sides of a 9 by 13-inch baking pan. Scatter the bread in an even layer over the prepared pan.

In a blender, combine the evaporated milk, condensed milk, sugar, eggs, vanilla, cinnamon, and salt. Blend on medium-low speed until the mixture is well combined and the sugar has dissolved, about 1 minute.

Pour the custard evenly over the bread. Using clean, dry hands, gently push down on the bread (without squishing it) to mostly submerge it. Gently shimmy the pan to distribute the bread into an even layer. Stud the bread pudding with the pieces of guava paste one by one, place them in the crevices between the bread cubes and on top. Do the same with the 4 tablespoons (½ stick) cubed butter. Cover with foil and refrigerate for at least 20 minutes or up to overnight.

Place a rack in the middle of the oven and preheat to 350°F.

recipe continues

NOTE: *Stale bread is just an excuse to make bread pudding; I wouldn't go through the trouble of baking fresh mallorcas just to make this recipe. However, if you did prepare them, and for some sacrilegious reason they turned stale, this is how you should use them up. Otherwise, you can purchase them. If you can't source them, you can substitute any sweet, eggy bread like brioche, challah, or Hawaiian rolls.*

Bake the bread pudding, covered, for 30 minutes. Remove the foil, rotate the pan, and bake for 10 to 15 minutes more, until the top looks light golden brown, bubbly, puffy, and slightly wobbly when jiggled.

Serve hot or warm for breakfast or brunch, topped with a little maple syrup, or as dessert, topped with vanilla ice cream. The bread can be stored, covered, in the fridge for up to 5 days; reheat in the microwave or oven before serving.

MILKIEST TRES LECHES

SERVES 12 TO 16

Nonstick cooking spray

1½ cups all-purpose flour

1½ teaspoons baking powder

1½ teaspoons salt

8 large eggs, separated, at room temperature

1 cup sugar

2 tablespoons vanilla bean paste or pure vanilla extract

1 (13½-ounce) can full-fat coconut milk

1 (12-ounce) can evaporated milk

1 (14-ounce) can sweetened condensed milk

1 recipe Silkiest Meringue (page 309) or Fluffy Coconut Cloud Whip (page 315; see Note)

½ teaspoon ground cinnamon

NOTE: *The Silkiest Meringue holds its structure for days—ideal if you're unmolding the cake or making it ahead. The Fluffy Coconut Cloud Whip is much looser and is best served immediately as a topping (not for unmolding), so it stays put and doesn't run off the cake.*

Tres leches (three milks) is a beloved Latin American dessert: sponge cake soaked with a sweetened milky mixture topped with silky meringue or whipped cream. This is Papa's favorite. In essence, it's a sheet cake, which means you bake, assemble, and serve it from the same pan. This makes it portable and convenient to bring to parties or get togethers. But, if you want a more elegant/formal presentation, I've also included directions on how to unmold and frost it.

Place a rack in the middle of the oven and preheat to 350°F. If you plan to unmold the cake, lightly coat the bottom of a 9 by 13-inch baking dish or two 8- or 9-inch round cake pans with nonstick spray and line them with parchment paper cut to fit. Don't spray or line the sides. If you don't plan on unmolding it, don't spray or line the baking dish or pans at all.

In a medium bowl, whisk together the flour, baking powder, and ½ teaspoon of the salt until well combined.

In the bowl of a stand mixer fitted with the whisk attachment (or in a large bowl using a handheld mixer), combine the egg yolks, ½ cup of the sugar, and 1 tablespoon of the vanilla and whip on medium-high speed until the yolks are pale yellow in color, tripled in size, and glossy-looking, 2 to 5 minutes, stopping and scraping down the bowl with a rubber spatula halfway through. Reduce the speed to low and whisk in ⅔ cup of the coconut milk until just incorporated. Gently transfer the mixture to a large bowl. Using a sifter or fine-mesh sieve, sift the flour mixture evenly over the yolk mixture and fold it in gently by hand until just incorporated.

Wash and dry the bowl of the stand mixer and the whisk attachment (or large bowl and beaters) thoroughly. Place the egg whites in the clean bowl and whip on medium-high

recipe continues

speed until they start getting foamy and begin to turn white, about 1 minute, then begin adding the remaining ½ cup sugar, 1 tablespoon at a time. Whip until the egg whites hold medium-stiff peaks (when you lift the whisk or beaters out, the tip of the egg whites should just hold its peak) and look glossy, 4 to 7 minutes. Using a rubber spatula, gently fold the egg whites into the yolk-flour mixture in three additions until just incorporated (some streaks are fine); do not overmix.

Using the spatula, scrape the batter into the prepared pan(s), holding the bowl close to the pan(s) to avoid deflating the egg whites. Bake on the center rack for 24 to 29 minutes, until the cake looks light golden and fluffy and a toothpick inserted into the center comes out clean. Remove from the oven and let cool for at least 30 minutes or up to 2 hours.

Meanwhile, in a blender, combine the evaporated milk, condensed milk, and the remaining coconut milk, 1 teaspoon salt, and 1 tablespoon vanilla. Blend on medium speed until the ingredients are just combined and the condensed milk has dissolved, 30 seconds to 1 minute. Don't overblend; you don't want it to become frothy. Set aside while the cake cools.

When the bottom of the cake pan is cool to the touch, poke the cake all over with a fork or skewer, leaving no more than about ½ inch between each poke. Pour about one-third of the milk mixture from the blender over the cake. Be intentional when you pour, making sure to especially get it in the corner edges, which can sometimes end up dry. Allow the cake to drink up the milk, rotating the pan or tapping it gently, if necessary, to distribute the milk mixture evenly. Repeat until you've used up all the milk mixture, 5 to 10 minutes. Cover the cake with foil or plastic wrap and refrigerate for at least 6 hours or preferably overnight.

If you're not unmolding the cake, you can skip to frosting it with the meringue. To unmold the cake, find a large plate (with a lip) that's 2 to 3 inches wider than the cake. Run a butter knife or offset spatula around the edge of the cake to separate it from the pan. Place the plate upside down over the pan, then, holding the pan and plate together, flip them in one smooth motion to release the cake onto the plate. If the cake doesn't plop down right away, lift on side of the pan and use the butter knife or offset spatula to try to guide the cake out. Remove the parchment from the cake.

Use a spatula or offset spatula to spread the meringue evenly over the top and sides (if unmolded) of the cake. Try to work with thick layers of meringue to avoid lifting crumbs off the cake. Feel free to be creative with the pattern or design of the meringue frosting (I like to go around the top and sides of the cake in a circular motion to create a spiral pattern). Sprinkle the cinnamon on top.

Slice and serve cold. The cake will keep, covered, in the fridge for up to 5 days.

BIZCOCHO DE COCO Y ZANAHORIAS

COCONUTTY CARROT CAKE

MAKES 1 BUNDT CAKE OR TWO 9 BY 5-INCH LOAF CAKES; SERVES ABOUT 10

Abuela has been making this recipe for years, sometimes for our birthdays and sometimes just-because. It's one of those cakes you can place on the middle of the living room table and enjoy for breakfast, as a snack, or later, after dinner for dessert. I add virgin coconut oil and cream of coconut into the cake batter. This amps up the tropical notes in the cake and makes me day-dream about swinging on Abuela's patio hammock with cake crumbs all over my chest, a cup of hot, fresh brewed cafecito in hand, and the sound of palm trees swaying with the breeze.

This bizcocho can stand alone with no icing. In fact, Papa and Abuelo prefer it that way. But if you're slightly more indulgent, like me, you can smear it with Coconut Mascarpone Icing or serve a dollop of it on the side.

4 cups shredded carrot (from 1 pound peeled carrots, about 5 large carrots)

1 cup sweetened coconut flakes, loosely packed

½ cup coarsely chopped toasted pecans or walnuts (optional)

2 cups all-purpose flour

2 teaspoons baking powder

1½ teaspoons baking soda

½ teaspoon ground cinnamon

½ teaspoon salt

½ cup (1 stick) unsalted butter, cut into 8 cubes and chilled

1½ cups sugar

1 cup virgin coconut oil, melted

1 cup cream of coconut, melted

1 teaspoon pure vanilla extract

4 large eggs, at room temperature

Nonstick cooking spray

Coconut Mascarpone Icing (recipe follows; optional)

Place a rack in the middle of the oven and preheat to 325°F.

In a large bowl, combine the carrots, coconut flakes, and nuts (if using) and, using clean hands, toss gently to combine.

In another large bowl, whisk together the flour, baking powder, baking soda, cinnamon, and salt to combine them evenly. Transfer the flour mixture to the bowl with the carrot mixture and, using clean hands, toss to coat the carrots and coconut evenly with the flour mixture; set aside. Set the bowl you used for the flour mixture close to the stovetop.

In a small saucepan, melt the butter over medium heat, then cook, swirling the saucepan continuously, until it browns, gets foamy, and has a toasty, nutty aroma, 1 to 2 minutes. Using a rubber spatula, immediately scrape the brown butter into the empty bowl. Don't leave any of those butter bits behind! Add the sugar, melted coconut oil, cream of coconut, and vanilla and whisk until homogeneous. Add the

recipe continues

eggs one by one, whisking until each is well incorporated before adding the next. Add half the flour-carrot mixture, using the spatula to gently fold them into the wet ingredients until just incorporated, then repeat with the remaining flour-carrot mixture. Do not overmix.

Very generously coat a Bundt pan with cooking spray to cover all the sides, ridges, and center. If using loaf pans, spray them lightly, then line with parchment paper, pressing it into the sides and bottom and leaving 2 to 3 inches overhanging the long sides. Spray them again, this time generously, especially the exposed shorter sides.

Scrape the batter into the pan(s) (if using loaf pans, distribute it evenly between them) and spread it to flatten it evenly. Bake on the center rack for 45 minutes to 1 hour, until a toothpick inserted into the center comes out clean. Let cool for 1 to 2 hours before unmolding it.

Slice and serve at room temperature. If desired, smear it with a dollop of softened Coconut Mascarpone Icing and serve it with a cup of fresh-brewed cafecito (see page 55). This cake (un-iced) will keep, covered, at room temperature for up to 4 days or in the fridge for up to 1 week.

COCONUT MASCARPONE ICING

MAKES 4 CUPS

1 cup (2 sticks) unsalted butter, at room temperature

3 tablespoons powdered sugar

½ teaspoon salt

1 cup (8 ounces) cold mascarpone cheese or full-fat cream cheese, at room temperature

¾ cup (6 ounces) cream of coconut, at room temperature, well shaken

In a large bowl using a handheld mixer (or in the bowl of a stand mixer fitted with the paddle attachment), beat the butter, powdered sugar, and salt on medium speed until light and fluffy, about 2 minutes. Using a rubber spatula, scrape down the sides of the bowl. Add the mascarpone and beat on medium-low speed until just combined and smooth, 30 to 45 seconds. Avoid overmixing the mascarpone, which can result in it breaking. With the mixer on low, slowly stream in the cream of coconut and mix until combined, then increase the speed to medium and beat until the mixture is smooth and fluffy, about 1 minute. Check the texture—if it feels too soft to spread, refrigerate it for 10 to 15 minutes to firm it up slightly before using. Store in an airtight container in the fridge for up to 1 week. Let stand at room temperature for 10 to 15 minutes before using, then stir gently before spreading.

MERENGUE SEDOSO

SILKIEST MERINGUE

MAKES ABOUT 12 CUPS

⅔ cup egg whites (about 6 large), at room temperature

2 cups plus 1 tablespoon sugar

1 teaspoon cream of tartar or lemon juice

½ teaspoon salt

1 tablespoon vanilla bean paste or pure vanilla extract

This meringue is a great topping for desserts that are meant to last days (either refrigerated or at room temperature). It's sturdy and remains silky smooth and so-creamy-it's-almost-chewy even after a few days. I love frosting Tres Leches (page 301) and Bizcocho Mojadito (moist cake, page 291) with it, but I've also used it to frost chocolate cake, fill sandwich cookies, and top citrus-meringue pies, like Caribbean Passion Pie (page 313). Time is crucial when you work with hot sugar because it goes from clear to burnt in seconds, so before you start preparing it, make sure you have all the ingredients you need measured out and all your equipment accessible.

Place the egg white in the bowl of a stand mixer fitted with the whisk attachment (or in a large bowl if using a handheld mixer). Have 1 tablespoon of the sugar, the cream of tartar, salt, and vanilla ready to go right next to the mixer.

Place the remaining 2 cups sugar in a small pot and pour ⅔ cup water around the sugar without splashing. Bring to a boil over medium-high heat, then reduce the heat to medium and cook until the sugar syrup reaches soft-ball stage, or 230°F (if you don't have a thermometer, drop a little syrup into a cup of cold water; if it forms a soft, malleable ball, it's ready), 10 to 15 minutes. Remove from the heat.

In the meantime, begin beating the egg whites on medium speed. Add the 1 tablespoon sugar, the cream of tartar, and the salt. Whip until the egg whites get foamy and start looking white and meringue-y, about 5 minutes. Reduce the speed to medium-low and carefully, in a slow, steady stream, pour in the sugar syrup. If it splashes up the sides of the mixer, reduce the speed. Avoid pouring too much too fast or you'll scramble your egg whites. Continue until you've poured in all the syrup, 1 to 2 minutes.

Raise the speed to high and beat until the sides of the bowl are completely cool to the touch, about 10 minutes; the meringue should look creamy and shiny and feel almost tacky. Use immediately.

PANETELA

BROWN BUTTER GUAVA BARS

MAKES 15 BARS

½ cup (1 stick) unsalted butter, cut into 8 cubes and chilled

1 small ice cube

Nonstick cooking spray

1½ cups all-purpose flour

1½ teaspoons baking powder

½ teaspoon salt

1 cup granulated sugar

1 teaspoon pure vanilla extract

¼ teaspoon almond extract

3 large eggs, at room temperature

6 to 8 ounces guava paste (see page 20), thinly sliced (about ⅛ inch thick)

¼ to ½ cup powdered sugar, for dusting

Panetela is a Puerto Rican dessert or snack, often accompanied with coffee. I sandwich slices of guava paste between the buttery, almondy cake batter, bake it, and finish it with a generous dusting of powdered sugar. My twist on this traditional recipe involves the extra step of making brown butter, which imparts a deep, toasty aftertaste. Panetela is portable and has a long shelf life, which makes it great to bring to gatherings or for gifting.

In a small saucepan, melt half the butter over medium heat, then cook, swirling the saucepan continuously, until it browns, gets foamy, and has a toasty, nutty aroma, 1 to 2 minutes. Using a rubber spatula, immediately scrape the brown butter into the bowl of a stand mixer fitted with the paddle attachment (or into a large bowl if using a handheld mixer). Add the ice cube and the remaining unmelted butter and mix with the spatula until they melt completely. Let cool to room temperature, 20 to 30 minutes. (To speed up the process, you can place the butter in the fridge for 5 to 10 minutes, until it has hardened to a soft, creamy, spreadable texture.)

Place a rack in the middle of the oven and preheat to 350°F. Spray a 9-inch square baking pan with nonstick spray, then line it with parchment paper, leaving 2 to 3 inches overhanging two sides. Spray the exposed sides again.

In a medium bowl, whisk together the flour, baking powder, and salt.

Add the sugar to the cooled brown butter and beat on medium-high speed until the mixture looks light, fluffy, and pale in color (it will look slightly grainy, like a whipped body scrub), 3 to 5 minutes, stopping and scraping down the sides and bottom of the bowl halfway through. Scrape down the bowl again, then add the vanilla, almond extract, and eggs

recipe continues

one by one, beating on medium-low speed until each is completely incorporated before adding the next. Beat on high speed until it looks fluffy but silky, 1 to 2 minutes, then scrape down the bowl again. With the mixer on its lowest speed, add half the flour mixture and beat until just incorporated, then repeat with the remaining flour mixture—do not overmix.

Scoop half the batter into the prepared pan and use the back of a spoon to spread it into an even layer that covers the bottom of the pan. Place the guava paste side by side in a single layer over the batter, cover it. Scoop the rest of the batter into the pan and spread it evenly to cover the guava. Bake for 30 to 35 minutes, until the surface is evenly light golden in color and a toothpick inserted into the center comes out clean. Remove from the oven and let cool completely, 30 to 40 minutes.

Dust the cake liberally with the powdered sugar. Using the overhanging parchment as handles, lift the cake out of the pan onto a cutting board. Using a serrated knife, cut it into small squares (I like cutting the edges off) and enjoy with Cafecito (see page 55).

PIE DE PARCHA CARIBEÑA

CARIBBEAN PASSION PIE

MAKES ONE 8- TO 10-INCH PIE; SERVES 8 TO 12

Nonstick cooking spray

7 ounces coconut cookies (such as Holsum) or graham crackers

1 cup sweetened coconut flakes, plus more if needed

½ cup (1 stick) unsalted butter, melted

1 teaspoon salt

1 (14-ounce) can sweetened condensed milk

6 large egg yolks

1 cup passion fruit pulp (see page 21)

½ recipe Silkiest Meringue (page 309), or 1 recipe Fluffy Coconut Cloud Whip (recipe follows)

This is not a traditional Puerto Rican recipe. I mean, it's a pie. It tastes like home though—tangy, tropical passion fruit with toasty hints of coconut. I was inspired to make it after preparing a key lime pie for my New York clients. I made a standard key lime pie base: condensed milk, egg yolks, and lime juice. It sounds stupidly easy, and it is. But there's something almost magical that happens when you whisk together those three ingredients. The acid from the lime immediately thickens the mixture into a luscious custardy base. I thought of sour passion fruit and just had to attempt it. I was right. If you're a citrus pie lover and want to try a Caribbean spin on one, this recipe is for you.

For topping, you can go the classic citrus meringue pie route with silky meringue or, for a lighter creamy version in line with the tropical theme, use Fluffy Coconut Cloud Whip.

Place a rack in the middle of the oven and preheat to 350°F. Spray an 8- or 10-inch springform pan with nonstick spray and line the bottom with parchment paper cut to fit.

Crush the cookies into fine crumbs by pulsing them in a food processor or placing them in a large zip-top bag and smashing them with a pan or rolling pin. Place the cookie crumbs in a medium bowl and add the coconut flakes, melted butter, and ½ teaspoon of the salt. Using clean, dry hands to combine until the mixture resembles wet sand and the crumbs hold together in a ball when you compress them in your fist. (Alternatively, combine the ingredients in a food processor and pulse 4 to 6 times, until you achieve the same wet sand texture.) Transfer the crumb mixture to the prepared pan and lightly press it over the bottom and up the sides (about 3 inches up the sides of an 8-inch pan or 2 inches for a 10-inch pan). Bake on the middle rack for 10 to 15 minutes, until the crust is lightly golden in color and

recipe continues

the kitchen smells sweet and toasty. Remove from the oven and set aside while you work on the filling; keep the oven on.

In a medium bowl, whisk together the egg yolks, condensed milk, and remaining ½ teaspoon salt to combine. Add the passion fruit pulp and whisk until homogeneous, 30 seconds to 1 minute. Gently pour the filling into the crust (it doesn't have to be completely cooled). Bake on the center rack for 12 to 15 minutes, until the filling looks set but jiggles slightly when the pan is wiggled. Remove from the oven and let cool to room temperature, then cove with foil and refrigerate for at least 4 hours or up to overnight.

Pile the meringue on top of the chilled pie for a luxurious lacquered look, or top with coconut cloud whip for a lighter texture and a more down-to-earth look. To decorate, spread or tap it with the back of a spoon to create swirls or fun peaks. Sprinkle with more coconut flakes, if you wish, and serve. Store leftovers, covered, in the fridge for up to 5 days.

FLUFFY COCONUT CLOUD WHIP

MAKES ABOUT 4 CUPS

2 cups cold heavy cream

½ teaspoon salt

½ (14-ounce) can cold cream of coconut, well shaken

Chill a large bowl or stand mixer bowl until cold, at least 20 minutes. Combine the heavy cream and salt in the chilled bowl and, using a handheld mixer or the stand mixer whisk attachment, beat on medium-low speed until it holds soft peaks, 5 to 8 minutes. Slowly add the cream of coconut and beat until the whip holds medium peaks (if you lift out the whisk or beaters, the peaks should hold their tip), 2 to 4 minutes. Serve immediately, while cold, or store in an airtight container in the fridge for up to 5 days. If necessary, rewhip to medium peaks before using. Use leftovers for sundaes or hot or iced lattes, or as a topping for cakes or pies.

COCOTADITOS CON GUAYABA

GUAVA-STAINED COCONUT SHORTBREAD COOKIES

MAKES 32 COOKIES

¼ cup virgin coconut oil, at room temperature

¾ cup (1½ sticks) unsalted butter, at room temperature

1 small ice cube

2¼ cups plus 2 tablespoons all-purpose flour

½ cup

1 teaspoon almond extract

½ teaspoon salt

7 ounces guava paste (see page 20), chilled and cut into ½-inch cubes

1 large egg

1 cup sweetened shredded coconut

1½ teaspoons flaky sea salt

This recipe is an adaptation of the Puerto Rican legend C. A. Valldejuli's Mantecaditos recipe from her 1983 cookbook *Cocina Criolla*. Mantecaditos are thumbprint shortbread cookies made with *manteca* (lard or shortening), hence the name. I tweaked the original recipe by adding brown butter and coconut oil (instead of manteca). Thus, cocotaditos were born. I add guava paste and roll them up in sweet-and-salty coconut flakes. Yes, they're a bit fussier than the original, but the result is a crumbly, buttery, melt-in-your-mouth cookie with a stunning stained-glass effect from the guava paste. They look dainty and elegant served with coffee and make a thoughtful gift for loved ones.

Place the coconut oil in the bowl of a stand mixer fitted with the paddle attachment (or in a large bowl if using a handheld mixer).

In a small pot, melt 4 tablespoons (½ stick) of the butter over medium heat, then cook, swirling the pot continuously, until it gets foamy and starts turning light brown and smelling nutty, 2 to 4 minutes. Pour the brown butter into the bowl with the coconut oil. Add the ice cube and swirl the bowl around until the ice cube melts and the fats have turned an opaquer color. Refrigerate for at least 20 minutes, or until the fats are visibly solid but still soft to the touch.

Meanwhile, place the chilled guava paste in a dry medium bowl and sprinkle with 2 tablespoons of the flour. Using clean, dry hands, separate the guava pieces, dredging them in the flour to coat evenly on all sides. Shake the coated guava pieces to remove any excess flour, place them on a plate, and refrigerate while you work on the dough.

recipe continues

To the bowl with the coconut brown butter, add the remaining ½ cup (1 stick) butter, the sugar, the almond extract, and the salt. Beat on medium-high speed until it looks light and fluffy, like whipped cream, 4 to 7 minutes, stopping and scraping down the bowl halfway through. Add the remaining 2¼ cups flour and pulse 5 to 10 times on the lowest speed until the dough looks craggy and crumbly. Add the guava paste. If using the stand mixer, pulse 3 or 4 more times, until the guava is evenly(ish) distributed; do not pulse too much, or you risk blending the guava into the dough, which will destroy the stained-glass effect. (If you're using a handheld mixer, set it aside at this point and use a rubber spatula to gently distribute the pieces of guava paste into the dough without overmixing it.)

Place a 24 by 13-inch piece of parchment paper horizontally in front of you. Scrape the dough onto the parchment, distributing it lengthwise. If you notice pockets of dough with more guava, gently move the dough around to distribute the pieces more evenly. Fold the top edge of the parchment over the dough toward you, then use your hands to shape it into a rough log about 16 inches long and 2 inches thick. To achieve a smooth, cylindrical shape, hold down the edge of the parchment underneath the log with one hand to steady it. With the other hand, use a bench scraper or something flat (like a small baking sheet or a ruler) to gently press along the length of the log, pushing the parchment toward the dough to compact and round it as you go. Once shaped, roll the parchment tightly around the log to enclose the dough, then twist the ends like a candy wrapper to compact and seal the log. Refrigerate for 1 hour, or until firm enough to hold its shape when you pick it up.

In a food processor or blender, combine the shredded coconut and ½ teaspoon of the flaky salt. Pulse 10 to 15 times, until the coconut looks like coarse meal and the salt is evenly distributed within it. In a separate bowl, beat the egg vigorously until it's foamy.

Unwrap the chilled dough but leave it on the parchment. Using the pastry brush, coat the log evenly with a thin layer of beaten egg. Scatter the coconut mixture over the top and sides of the log and use your palms to press down so the flakes adhere evenly. (I also like to roll the log while gently pressing on it to ensure those flakes are crusted on.) Reroll the log in the parchment and twist the ends closed. Refrigerate for another hour. You're almost there, I promise! (The dough can be refrigerated for up to 2 days or frozen for up to 1 month for slice-and-bake-fresh cookies.)

Place a rack in the middle of the oven and preheat to 350°F. Line a large baking sheet with parchment

Unwrap the log of dough, place it on a cutting board, and slice it crosswise into ½-inch-thick rounds. If the rounds fall apart, push the pieces back together. Place them out about 2 inches apart, with their prettiest side facing up, on the prepared baking sheet. Bake for 14 to 20 minutes, rotating the pan halfway through, until the sides look lightly golden and crispy. As soon as they come out of the oven, sprinkle the bubbly guava with the remaining 1 teaspoon flaky salt. Let cool for 30 to 40 minutes so the guava can firm back up instead of oozing out of the cookies. Store in an airtight container at room temperature for up to 1 week.

Tamarind Limber
Sweet Milk Limber
Coconut Limber
Passion Fruit Limber

LIMBERS DE COCO DE ABUELA

ABUELA'S COCONUT "CUPSICLES"

MAKES 12 TO 15 LIMBERS

8 cups fresh coconut milk (see page 77) or full-fat canned coconut milk

1½ cups sugar

½ teaspoon salt

Limbers are nostalgic childhood treats in Puerto Rico. Tropical (often local) fruit juice frozen in a cup, they're our better version of ice pops. Yep, I said it. If you've ever had a limber, you probably have fond memories of it. I think of the limber operation I ran when I was a kid. I sold them to passing cars from my house through a window that led to the sidewalk, and outsourced help by rallying neighborhood kids to do door-to-door deliveries, increasing sales. After paying them and subtracting costs, I made a profit—successfully running my first business at ten years old. I've included my favorite flavors here, but you can use any fruit juice. I hope you're inspired to make your own memories.

In a blender, combine the coconut milk, sugar, and salt and blend on low speed until the sugar and salt have dissolved, about 1 minute. Distribute the liquid evenly among 10 to 12 (6- to 7-ounce) disposable cups, filling them to about 1 inch from the top. Freeze until solid, about 6 hours, stirring with a long skewer, knife, or fork every hour. This will help to break up the ice crystals and distribute the coconut fat throughout them as they freeze, resulting in a creamier limber. Cover the cups with foil if you won't be serving them right away. They'll keep in the freezer for about 1 month.

When ready to eat, place both hands around the cup to melt the sides a bit, then squeeze the sides gently or push on the bottom to pop it out. Using your hand, invert the limber in the cup so it sticks out of the top. Enjoy immediately.

recipe continues

FOR LIMBERS DE PARCHA (PASSION FRUIT LIMBERS): Replace the coconut milk with 2½ cups passion fruit pulp (see page 21) and 5 cups water; increase the sugar to 1¾ cups. Proceed with the recipe as directed.

FOR LIMBERS DE TAMARINDO (TAMARIND LIMBERS): Replace the coconut milk with 1¾ cups tamarind puree (see page 67) and 5 cups water; increase the sugar to 1¾ cups. Proceed with the recipe as directed.

FOR LIMBERS DE LECHE (SWEET MILK LIMBERS): Replace the coconut milk with 3 (12-ounce) cans evaporated milk and 1½ (14-ounce) cans sweetened condensed milk; omit the sugar and add 1½ teaspoons ground cinnamon. Proceed with the recipe as directed.

ACKNOWLEDGMENTS

This project came with late nights, sacrifices, curveballs—and more than its share of bruises, sweat, and many, many tears. In the midst of the overwhelming stress, I often lost sight of the end goal, convinced I wouldn't make it.

During the whirlwind of the photoshoot (which took place at Abuela's house in Puerto Rico), and with a tight prop budget, I turned to *los míos*—my people—asking if anyone had Abuela-ish artifacts or props I could borrow. I was overwhelmed by their generosity. Some dusted off their own abuelas' lace tablecloths and carefully stored tapestries. Others offered vintage china, crystal glasses from their family curio cabinets, and everyday tools they snagged from their own cocinas—pilones, grecas, calderos, and mixers. Local designers and restaurant colleagues even lent their handmade pieces—ceramic plates, surfaces, and dominoes.

I've always been a bit of a hermit, and I thought writing would suit me for that reason. This being my first book—and first professional writing project—I had no idea how lonely the process could feel, sometimes forgetting along the way that I had a community. Their contributions reminded me what that word truly means, especially in Puerto Rico, where sometimes having each other's backs is all we have. And while I'm beyond grateful for the help, what moved me most was the shared nostalgia—the collective desire to see their abuelas reflected in these pages. They reminded me of my purpose and gave me the push I needed to keep going.

This book lives on the shoulders of many—it's just as much theirs as it is mine. It wouldn't exist without the love, support, and generosity of my community. I'm endlessly grateful to the following people who—despite my refusal (or really, not knowing how) to ask for help—just showed up. Stood by me. Tolerated me. And helped bring this dream to life—each in their own meaningful way:

My writing coach, **Dianne Jacob**, author of *Will Write for Food*: Thank you for taking me on as a student, for preparing me for this monumental project, and for your patience every step of the way. I truly couldn't have done this without your coaching and guidance.

My agent, **Amy Collins:** Thank you for understanding my vision for this cookbook from the very start. Short of physically holding my hand, your guidance and mentorship made the entire process feel possible. Thank you for brainstorming with me and listening to every idea (and rant). Beyond an agent, you were an advocate, a mediator, a therapist. I hope we can sit down over cafecito soon, in person, and talk about anything *but* this cookbook.

The team at Union Square & Co., my publisher: My editors, **Caitlin Leffel** and **Amanda Englander**, thank you for seeing the potential in this project, for the opportunity to bring it into the world, and for helping shape it along the way. **Ivy McFadden**, your attention to detail surpassed even mine. I appreciate it. And to the design team, namely **Renée Bollier**, thank you for translating my creative vision of Old San Juan so thoughtfully onto these pages.

My creative DreamTeam: Finding you wasn't easy, but I'm so glad I did. My photographer, **Johnny Miller**, thank you for bringing your positive attitude, chill energy, and deep passion to this project. For insisting that we could make it happen. You were right. For bringing to life—through your unique lens—the love I hoped to see in these pages: love for my family, my community, and my Puerto Rico. My food stylist, **Rebecca Jurkevich**, thank you not just for bringing your culinary talent, but for your eye for the beauty in imperfection, and for your down-to-earth, honest approach to food. You were a calming presence throughout the shoot—thank you for grounding me. And for your hustle behind the scenes—it felt like magic, the sheer amount of food we prepared and the images we captured in the time we had. Also—for loving Abuela. You're welcome at our house anytime. I promise we won't make you cook. My prop stylist, **Marina Bevilacqua**, thank you for saying yes, and for scrambling on short notice (before we even set foot in Puerto Rico). Acquiring all our beautiful props and transporting them safely was a mission, and you were a trooper. Thank you for respecting my vision while gently nudging me to stretch beyond my comfort zone.

Chef Giovanna Huyke, *la Julia Child Boricua*: Thank you for inspiring me from the very beginning—as a kid, glued to the tiny TV in Abuela's cocina, tuned into *La Cocina de Giovanna* on Telemundo, scribbling down your recipes like they were gospel. I could've never imagined where that early inspiration would take me, but one thing was always clear: the person who had to introduce these recipes—who embodies the very spirit of *Cocina Puerto Rico*—was *you*. Gracias for your generosity in lending your voice to these pages, and for representing our cultura through the power of something as honest and essential as food. *Un abrazo fuerte*.

Chef Gordon Ramsay: Thank you for challenging me (because—let's be honest—I wouldn't be the "Challenge Queen" without you). Beyond that, thank you for seeing me and supporting me, and for your generosity in sharing your platform and words. Working in your cocina changed the course of my career—and gave me the confidence to tell these stories, to write about mi cultura, and to share my voice on my own terms. I'm still learning just how much that opportunity meant.

Chef Mark Hopper: While much of your work happens behind the scenes, I hope you know how deeply your mentorship shaped me. From my very green days as a chef de partie, chopping parsley at Bouchon, your words, your high standards, and your belief in me made a lasting impact—not just professionally, but personally. Thank you for pushing me to grow, for holding me to a higher standard, and for continuing to support me fifteen-plus years later. I will always hold the utmost respect for you.

Laura Serrano, Lau Pottery Studio: Your hand-built ceramics—elegant, organic, and deeply refined—grace some of the best tables in Puerto Rico, so I never imagined you'd say yes to this deeply personal project. But you did, with such genuine enthusiasm that it reenergized me. I'm so proud to showcase your pieces in these pages, and I only hope the food does justice to the care and artistry you bring to the table (pun intended).

Ana Cristina Quiñones, founder of Materia Madura: Thank you for lending your tasteful, waste-based pieces to this book—from dominoes to tabletop surfaces—all crafted from ingredients like coffee, plantain, and bread that might've otherwise ended up in a landfill. It feels poetic that the very foods we prepared are reflected in the materials that carried them. I'm so proud to showcase work like yours—proof that world-class design and innovation can come straight from Puerto Rico.

Chef Francis Guzmán, executive chef and owner of Vianda, fellow CIA alum, and one of Puerto Rico's most visionary chefs: Thank you for trusting me with the beautiful plates from Vianda during your peak season (I know what a big ask that was). Your generosity speaks volumes, and I'm proud to feature a small piece of your craft in these pages. You've helped redefine Puerto Rican cuisine on a global stage, and it means so much to have your support.

Clarissa Llenza (@HomeCookingTherapy): You inspire us with your sophisticated approach to our Caribbean cocina. It's been a joy getting to know you, first as a colleague and, over time, as a friend. Thank you again for sharing your network with me.

Marisol Pesquera, brilliant Puerto Rican photographer and artist: Thank you for graciously connecting me to your network in Puerto Rico and helping make the shoot possible. I deeply admire your work and hope we get to collaborate directly in the future.

Mairym "Monti" Carlo (@TheMontiCarlo): Thank you for being a voice of our islita and for kindly connecting me with Dianne, showing through action that there's room for all of us at the table.

La vecina, **Tere:** Por traer tacitas de azúcar cuando hacen falta. Por llegar con plátanos y carambolas. Por tu conocimiento que nutrió el capítulo de viandas. Y, más que todo, por siempre estar pendiente de mis viejitos.

Mi primito, **Adrián:** Gracias por compartir tu red de contactos y por ofrecer tu valioso *feedback* creativo, por aportar ideas frescas y una pasión genuina por nuestra cultura. Trabajar contigo, tanto directa como indirectamente, es una fuente de inspiración.

Mis sous chefs, **Cora y Marr:** Por ser mis *guinea pigs* y atreverse a probar mis recetas una y otra vez. Por llegar escandalosas con pompones a animar, por poner a Bad Bunny a to' volumen y encender el party. Por ponerse los delantales bien lindos que les di y ensuciarse las manos con rellenos de papa. Por siempre estar, cerca o lejos.

Mi vecinita de la vida, **Zo:** Por enseñarme. Uno de los consejos de Mama era: "Rodéate de gente que admires para que se te peguen sus cosas." Aunque . . . fuiste tú la que pasó por mi patio con esa bici roja. Tantos años después, sigo aprendiendo de ti y admirando tu tenacidad. Gracias por inspirarme, escucharme y por aconsejarme durante momentos bien difíciles.

Tío y Debbie: Por llegar con los benditos ajíes caballeros. Por enrollarse las mangas y meterle al tiburón de trastes. Por mantenerme el vasito lleno de sangría. Debbie, todavía te debo una manicura.

NaHOmi: Gracias por estar pendiente. Por escuchar mis perretas y sentir mis corajes conmigo —a veces, incluso, más que yo. Gracias por ser oído y pañuelo de lágrimas.

Titi Maggie: Por las carreras a buscar muebles, por sacudirle el polvo a los tesoros de tu Abuela y por confiármelos. Por siempre estar. Verdaderamente, le haces honor a tu apodo de *Golden Girl*—porque tu corazón es de oro. Afortunada yo que formes parte de mi familia.

Las *Gilmore Girls* Boricuas, **Ale y Emma:** Por llegar juntas como tornado a ayudar, a fregar, a estar. **Ale**, por tu tech-support y por prestarme tu vida de *supermom* como molde para estas recetas. Crear platos que funcionaran para ti—y para quienes leerán este libro—fue fundamental. **Emma**, te botaste. Me hiciste sentir sumamente orgullosa al ver tu admirable ética de trabajo. Gracias por unirte a mi *team* y, más que ayudar, por aportar color, chispa y alegría con tu personalidad tan chula.

Abuelito José: Por llegar bello y precioso, vestido de punta en blanco, con tu sonrisa de oreja a oreja, y lucirte como modelo. Por tu sinceridad al probar mis recetas, siempre empujándome a mejorar por tus altos estándares para la comida criolla—y no te culpo, cuando tienes a Abuela cocinándote todos los días. Por sembrar frutos y permitirme disfrutar de las cosechas.

Papa: Por llegar cargando con un candungo de jueyes vivos de no-sé-dónde (y tampoco voy a preguntar), por sujetarlos por mí para la foto porque me daban miedo, por salirte de la cocina y dejarme a mí. Por tu boqueta de apoyo, pero también por susurrarme discretamente "lo estás haciendo bien" cada vez que notabas mis párpados sosteniendo un río de lágrimas como una represa. Por cuidar a los viejitos. Por cuidarme.

Mama: Por estar siempre al alcance como "la niña de los siete traseros"—chofer, mensajera, *shopper*, vigilante de flanes. Por permanecer a mi lado en mis momentos lindos y en los no tan lindos—por nunca soltarme. Por creer en mí, incluso cuando yo no podía verme con claridad. Por inspirarme, apoyarme e impulsarme desde el comienzo—este logro es tuyo.

. . . y mi **Abuelita Sara:** Por tus cafecitos, tus asopaítos y tus pantuflas. Por tus manos santas. Por saber quererme. Por ser mi refugio. Por existir. Viviré eternamente agradecida de ti. Te amo con todo mi corazón.

INDEX

Note: Page numbers in *italics* indicate photographs.

C

D

E

O

P

Q

R

S

T

V

Y